THE RIGHT TO BELONG

FOR MARTIN DAUNTON
WELSHMAN

THE RIGHT TO BELONG
Citizenship and National Identity in Britain, 1930–1960

Edited by
Richard Weight and Abigail Beach

I.B.Tauris

London · New York

Published in 1998 by
I.B.Tauris & Co. Ltd
Victoria House
Bloomsbury Square
London WC1B 4DZ

In the United States of America and Canada distributed by
St Martin's Press
175 Fifth Avenue
New York
NY 10010

A full CIP record for this book is available from the British Library
A full CIP record for this book is available from the Library of Congress

ISBN 1–86064–311–6

Library of Congress Catalog card number available
Copy-edited and typeset by Oxford Publishing Services, Oxford
Printed and bound in Great Britain by WBC Ltd, Bridgend, Mid Glamorgan

Contents

Contributors

Maggie Andrews is Field Leader in Media Studies, Chichester Institute. She is the author of *The Acceptable Face of Feminism* (1996).

Abigail Beach is Research Fellow at the School of Health and Social Welfare, the Open University. She is writing a study of ideas of citizenship in the Labour Party between 1920 and 1960.

Nicholas Crowson is Lecturer in History, University of Birmingham and is currently writing a history of national service in Britain during the 1950s.

Toby Haggith is film archivist at the Imperial War Museum, London. He is currently completing a thesis on 'Films on the reconstruction of the built environment, 1939–1951' at the University of Warwick, Centre for Social History.

John Kent is Emeritus Professor of Theology, University of Bristol. Among his publications is *William Temple: Church, State and Society in Britain, 1880–1950* (1992).

David Matless is Lecturer in Geography, University of Nottingham. He is currently writing *Landscape and Englishness, 1918–1990*.

Siân Nicholas is Lecturer in History, University of Wales, Aberystwyth. She is the author of *The Echo of War: Home Front Propaganda and the Wartime BBC, 1939–45* (1996).

Kathleen Paul is Assistant Professor of History, University of South Florida, USA. She is the author of *Whitewashing Britain: Race and Citizenship in the Postwar Era* (1996).

Nick Tiratsoo is Senior Lecturer in History, University of Luton.

Among his publications are *Reconstruction, Affluence and Labour Politics: Coventry 1945–69* (1990) and, with Stephen Fielding and Peter Thompson, *'England Arise!' The Labour Party and Popular Politics in 1940s Britain* (1995).

Richard Weight is a former Fellow of the Institute of Historical Research, London, and is currently writing a history of British national identity since the Second World War, to be published by Macmillan in the year 2000.

Abbreviations and acronyms

ABCA	Army Bureau of Current Affairs
ACWW	Associated Country Women of the World
AGM	Annual General Meeting
ARP	air-raid precautions
BBC	British Broadcasting Corporation
BLPES	British Library of Political and Economic Science
CAB	Citizens' Advice Bureau
CEMA	Council for the Encouragement of Music and the Arts
CFL	Central Film Library
CPRE	Council for the Preservation of Rural England
CVE	Council for Visual Education
DP	displaced person
ENSA	Entertainments National Service Association
FA	Football Association
FLC	Foreign Labour Committee
GI	US serviceman
GPO	General Post Office
ICI	Imperial Chemical Industries
IWM	Imperial War Museum
LPA	Labour Party Archives
LSE	London School of Economics and Political Science
MOI	Ministry of Information
NALGO	National Association of Local Government Officers
NFWI	National Federation of Women's Institutes
PEP	Political and Economic Planning
POW	prisoner of war
PPS	Principal Private Secretary
PRO	Public Records Office
RAF	Royal Air Force

RIP	rest in peace
RKO	Radio-Keith-Orpheum
TCPA	Town and Country Planning Association
TUC	Trades Union Congress
USSR	Union of Soviet Socialist Republics
VE	victory in Europe
WASA	West African Students' Association
WI	Women's Institute

Introduction

Richard Weight and Abigail Beach

Since ancient times, but particularly since the French Revolution, the twin pillars of citizenship and national identity have met to form the central arch of Western political discourse. Together, they have given scholars and politicians a philosophical framework with which to explore the relationship between the individual and society.[1] In recent years, they have often been regarded as paradigms of opposing political philosophies. Generally, those on the left have looked to the promotion of citizenship as the most effective way of uniting conflicting classes, races, genders and creeds, while those on the right have looked to national identity. However, in the period of British history examined in this volume, the two concepts were regarded as complementary, if not virtually indivisible, by the many different groups using them as a guide to practical policy-making. It was generally accepted that the nation could not survive without its people adhering to certain codes of conduct and receiving in return certain rights. Equally, those codes of conduct were seen to be meaningless unless they pertained to a commonly agreed idea of what the nation was: its unique customs, traditions, mores and overall culture.

The concepts began to attract more widespread attention in the late nineteenth century. Among Britain's academic elite, for instance, a debate on the nature of citizenship was generated through a revival of interest in classical idealism, particularly in the works of Plato. This, combined with the study of the philosophies of Rousseau, Kant and Hegel, and an enduring interest in English 'organic' theories of the state, produced a discourse of citizenship that stressed the 'fundamental unity of state and society and the participation of the citizen in the larger social whole.'[2] For much of the nineteenth century, citizenship had been seen in terms of an individual's rights, whereby people were deemed to be autonomous, responsible, and ultimately sovereign agents, whose rights derived from 'natural law' and their humanity. Citizenship, in this sense, was a status that required only limited obligations — the discharge of basic civic responsibilities of voting, the paying of taxes and the defence of the nation when it was under threat of dissolution or invasion. It did not create or sustain social solidarity, or even a sense of common purpose. A number of thinkers, such as R. H. Tawney, A. D. Lindsay and Harold Laski reacted to what they saw as the atomistic philosophy of Victorian liberalism. To them, state and society were not simply mechanisms for material growth but were the embodiment of real moral and spiritual bonds. Viewed from this perspective, citizenship expressed a dynamic social relationship; it was an activity as much as a status that entailed the discharge of a wide range of duties.

Ultimately, shared responsibility for the continuity of the nation remained the most important of these duties. For this reason apart from any other, the British intellectual imagination was gripped by the question of national identity from the 1880s onwards. Academics — not to mention poets, composers and artists — scrutinized the human characteristics that lay behind Britishness. Montesquieu first elaborated the idea that different peoples possessed unique vices and (more often than not) virtues in the early eighteenth century. Known collectively as 'national character', these virtues were thought to be the product of a number of factors ranging from geography to divine intervention and, more commonly, history. In turn, national character was thought to have shaped the country's history, its present-day institutions and the daily life of its inhabitants.

The concept appealed to a wide range of commentators. Some retained confidence in the old certainties of Victorian liberalism, in the greatness of Britain, her empire and race. Troubled by class conflict at home and imperial competition abroad, the idea of an immutable national character offered a reassuring sense of what it meant to be British. The virtues most often cited were a 'common-sense' empiricism that eschewed continental systematic thought; tolerance; stoicism; eccentricity; inventiveness; and a gentlemanly individualism — manifested, among other things, in a love of privacy and a dislike both of excessive entrepreneurialism and excessive state intervention. Britons were also seen to be reticent about their virtues. In a paradoxical twist, this reticence was paraded as the ultimate virtue, one that had prevented the nationalistic excesses of other countries in Europe. All of this, it was thought, combined to produce the oldest and most successful democracy in the world.

Reinforcing this litany of Britishness, particularly after the First World War, was a growing belief that the countryside was the ultimate repository of the national character. The idea of a peaceful, picturesque landscape in which an organic society had survived, untrammelled by the modern world of the factory, the trench and, latterly, the aerial bomber, not only appealed to romantics of the left and right. It gripped the entire generation who had witnessed the worst war in human history. The Conservative prime minister, Stanley Baldwin; the dean of St Paul's, the Reverend W. R. Inge; the historian Arthur Bryant; and continental Anglophile writers like the Czech, Karel Capek, were among those who popularized this particular vision of Britishness during the interwar period. As Julia Stapleton has concluded, they all satisfied 'a deep yearning for national self-understanding and reassurance in rapidly changing and threatening times.'[3]

Others, however, embraced the fact that Britain was moving into a new age, and regarded national character as an essential part of the changes that were sweeping Britain. Just as seventeenth century parliamentarians had cited 'ancient' Anglo-Saxon laws to justify regicide or as 'patriots' between 1790 and 1850 had used the notion of the 'freeborn Englishman' to campaign for franchise and taxation reform, so in mid-twentieth century Britain commentators saw Britishness as the moderating factor in a radical social transformation based on universal principles. Specifically, political theorists sought to link the Whiggish belief in essential British virtues with the Idealist revival described above.

The most important of these thinkers was Ernest Barker. The first professor of political science at Cambridge, Barker had taught Laski and Attlee, who once described him as his favourite tutor. Barker summarized the British character as one of 'civility'. He argued that it was an inheritance from the Greeks and that, among the nations of the world, Britain had received the largest share. Civility had a dual function: it was the most dynamic social element within Britishness, one that made a moral community of Britain as it had the Greek city states of Plato's day. However, civility also tempered the potential excesses of idealism. With its inherent respect for the individual, it ensured that the moral community did not become a totalitarian one. This it threatened to do in the thought of Hegel and Rousseau, both of whom in different ways equated the *patria* too closely with the *polis*. Barker's vision was buttressed by the pluralism of F. W. Maitland, which emphasized the importance of voluntary association and local culture as vital complements to the activity of the state.

Barker's suspicion of the state frequently put him at odds with Tawney, Laski and other left-wing thinkers of the time. They accused him of not grasping the full extent of the inequality that frequently lay behind the veneer of 'civility' in Britain, nor the necessity of harnessing the power of the state to eradicate it. Nonetheless, as they all acknowledged, these thinkers had much in common. They shared an idealist belief that social problems should no longer be viewed in isolation but should be incorporated within 'a vision of reconstructing the whole of British society'.[4] They also shared an underlying faith in the efficacy of British culture and, in particular, the importance of pluralism. As such, their thought, although heavily influenced by a European intellectual heritage, stood apart from the more radical political philosophies of left and right that were emerging from the continent in the same period.

The influence of such writers was not confined to a small, self-referential elite. The establishment of social science and public administration as academic disciplines in the Edwardian era did much to amplify their work. But, whereas many of their literary counterparts reacted to the growth of mass democracy with an elitist disdain for the 'masses',[5] these political thinkers shared the optimistic belief of their Victorian forebears that the public were receptive to practical intellectual discourse. They regarded it as their duty to disseminate their knowledge and ideas to the public through adult education and popular journalism. Moreover, the movement did not lack its own populists.

The novelist J. B. Priestley was the most celebrated of those in the interwar period who attempted to construct a social-democratic patriotism with a wide appeal. As a result, the thought of Barker et al. spread outwards from scholars and administrators through an 'interlocking seamless web' into a middle-class culture of activism, expressed through a wide variety of civic societies, social reform associations and preservation societies.[6] Many on the left remained hostile to the notion of patriotism, as George Orwell so effectively pointed out in the 1940s. Nonetheless, the attempt to reconstruct Britishness was to have an enduring influence on the national polity, shaping discussions on democracy from the early years of the twentieth century to the period of postwar reconstruction. In part, this stemmed from what Jose Harris has identified as the widespread consciousness of living in 'a form of society totally different from what had ever occurred before'.[7] Rapid change swept over all aspects of life in Britain and appeared to strike at the heart of established views of what it meant to be a citizen-subject of the British nation.

During the first decades of the twentieth century, Britain became a more centralized and homogeneous society. As technological innovations in communications and transportation enlarged the scale of private businesses and public services alike, social relationships were extended beyond the locality to a far greater extent than had previously been possible. At the heart of this transformation lay the growth of the economic and cultural power of London. The gravitational pull of the City, for instance, had already made the capital the unrivalled centre of business and economic activity by 1914.

Local engines for economic growth, like provincial stock exchanges and country bankers, dwindled in importance as the prominence of international finance and trading relationships to the British and world economies escalated. By the interwar years, London's financial prominence was supplemented by the capital's embrace of modern manufacturing with new scientifically-managed 'Fordist' assembly lines producing consumer durables for the domestic market and motor vehicles for the empire. Indeed, during the Depression, as key sectors of northern manufacturing slumped to new production lows, the greater London region gained over 40 per cent of England and Wales's new factory developments.[8]

Centripetal forces were also felt within the sphere of culture. Monuments to an avowedly national culture such as the *Dictionary of*

National Biography or Wembley stadium, contributed to the development of a national memory and self-image. Meanwhile, the Newbolt
Report on the Teaching of English in 1921 called on English
literature and history to 'sustain a national ideal' and started the
ousting of the classics as the main subject of study in the schools of
England and Wales.[9] Above all, the revolutions in retailing, leisure
marketing and in communications and the media — in particular the
creation of the BBC in 1925 — cemented popular tastes and
interests. These and other developments undoubtedly signified the
emergence of a more unified Britain.

Nevertheless, there remained cultural differences between the four
nations of the British isles. The Welsh passion for rugby was stronger
than that for football shared by the British and Scots, and in Northern Ireland the supremacy of popular Protestantism began to create
an altogether hybrid culture within the Union. In Scotland, meanwhile, the separate educational and legal systems were augmented by
the creation of a national library in Edinburgh in 1925, and in the
same decade a literary renaissance began, led by the poet, Hugh
MacDiarmid, which gained some influence beyond intellectual circles
through the Scottish popular press. Some important elements of a
'variegated local and provincial culture' also remained intact
throughout Britain, as reflected in the municipal pride of town councillors and members of civic trusts, and in the fierce local patriotism
of the supporters of football and county cricket clubs.

However, despite the establishment of Plaid Cymru in 1925 and
the Scottish National Party in 1928 in the wake of the Irish war of
independence, the continuation of these identities was not, generally,
a fissiparous tendency. National, regional and local diversity was a
widely cherished heritage in mid-century Britain: the plurality of the
nation, its people and their customs was still held, by commentators
on both the left and the right, to be a quintessential part of what it
meant to be British.[10]

The changing structure of social relationships also aroused
concern during the first decades of the new century. As the face-to-
face community of the traditional British village receded through the
combined pressures of rural depopulation and ribbon development,
the crowded city and its suburbs grew ever more polarized as civic

elites moved out of city centres to suburban and country areas. This social stratum had been instrumental in the development of a strong civic culture in the mid-Victorian period, a movement which, it was felt, had stabilized urban life. But now, with their residential withdrawal from the city centres and their replacement by large and impersonal multi-plant businesses, the social cement that civic elites had provided was seen to be in danger of disintegration.

In 1937, a Royal Commission on the problems of local government in Tyneside, for example, heard that in Hebburn, out of a population of 24,000 only 50 'belonged to the employing class and there were no professional men, except the doctors or clergymen whose work more or less compelled them to reside in the town'.[11] Such an imbalance, many felt, had serious social and political implications, not least of which was the tendency towards an extravagant level of local government expenditure, as local councils responded, perhaps irresponsibly, to the needs of an overwhelmingly working-class electorate. Local identities in both urban and rural areas were perceived to be dissipating, and from the early years to the middle of the twentieth century, a range of commentators urged their reconstruction.

Similar concerns were voiced about the shifts occurring in the political arena. The widening of the franchise in 1918 and 1929, for instance, affirmed the nation's commitment to a comprehensive and pluralistic polity, but these political changes left the social dimensions of citizenship ill-defined. The 1918 Representation of the People Act removed the penalty of franchise exclusion from those receiving poor relief, but the social stigma of public assistance remained into the 1930s. As unemployment rose to new heights in the early years of the Depression, the extent of the nation's detachment from the mid-Victorian association of citizenship with independence from the state was tested, a process which continued into the period of the Second World War.

Similarly, those who wished to make Britain their home (or, indeed, those who wished to move from one country of the British Isles to another) faced conflicting signals about their right to belong. In the later years of the nineteenth century, a growing concern for the national and international implications of immigration had begun to shift the locus of the rights of entitlement from the local state's rules of 'settlement' to the national state's conception of citizenship.[12] Increasingly, it was the boundaries of the national state itself that determined the parameters of entitlement. In practice, though, the shift to a more inclusive conception of welfare entitlement was gradual. With local government retaining a considerable degree of control of social welfare into the 1920s and 1930s, the echoes of England's long history of parish 'settlement' remained. The allocation of social housing, for instance, was characterized by a 'points' system, which meant that in-migrants from other parts of the country would find themselves excluded from access. Unnaturalized immigrants, from the empire or elsewhere, were even less likely to receive support.

The middle decades of the twentieth century were a time of considerable change in British society: they saw the realization of mass democracy, a second world war within as many generations, unprecedented affluence, and the start of irreversible imperial decline. These developments presented the British with a complex mixture of opportunities and dangers. Mass democracy, augmented by affluence, offered citizens a greater chance than ever before to shape their own future and that of the nation as a whole. At the same time, it raised the prospect of widespread disillusionment and social conflict as many were unable to take advantage of these new freedoms. Similarly, Britain's altered relationship with the empire and the rest of the world placed in doubt traditional images of the nation, which had buttressed the national polity since the eighteenth century.[13]

The Second World War heightened national consciousness in Britain by creating the potentially inclusive, democratic sentiment of the 'people's war' and, in doing so, it prompted a thorough examination of what constituted British national identity. Change brought uncertainty among Britain's elites, which in turn encouraged them to reflect more acutely on the direction the country was taking. Questions were posed. What was the role of ordinary men and women in mid-twentieth-century Britain? What were their needs, their rights, and their responsibilities? How did they stand in relation to each other, to their regions, to their nations and to the state in general? How were these objects of loyalty or disloyalty defined? In short, what was the British nation and how did its people acquire their right to belong to it?

In recent years, historians of mid-twentieth-century Britain have been preoccupied with a debate on the origins, nature and extent of the social democratic consensus upon which the welfare state was built in the 1940s. The debate has been fuelled by a fierce argument about whether the reforms of the Labour governments of 1945–51 were economically and morally responsible for the relative decline of Britain in the postwar period. Did the cost of the welfare state prevent us from investing in new technologies to compete with the USA, Germany and Japan, and did it create a 'dependency culture' in which enterprise and individual responsibility were forfeited in the bid to redistribute wealth?[14]

Not surprisingly, most scholars have argued that this is a canard of the new right, which has merely used the welfare state as a whipping boy to explain a complex national malaise for which Conservative policies are partly responsible. A series of revisions of the 'consensus' thesis were set in motion. Scholars, for instance, have pointed to the ease with which the postwar consensus was destroyed in the 1980s, concluding that it was at best a fragile one, if indeed it ever existed at all.[15] This body of work has shone a penetrating light on Britain's political elites at a crucial point in the nation's history. And recently, historians — among them a contributor to this book — have directed some of that light on popular attitudes to reform, revealing that a significant number of ordinary British people remained unmoved by Labour's moral exhortations, even when the party was at the height of its authority.[16]

The limits to the postwar consensus, therefore, have been both more imaginatively and more precisely scrutinized. But, as with most revisionist movements, criticisms have sometimes been pushed too far. As Paul Addison recently pointed out, despite the fundamental differences that remained between the parties during and imme-diately after the war, their 'comparative moderation . . . lowered the ideological temperature and opened the door . . . to the politics of the centre'.[17] The historiography of 'consensus' naturally informs much of this book, for it would be difficult to assess 'the right to belong' in mid-century Britain without referring to the changing role of the state in that period.

However, the parameters of scholarship on twentieth-century

Britain need to be broadened. With respect to the distinguished historians engaged in its study, the desire of some scholars to peer into every corner of government activity in an attempt to unravel the 'myth of consensus' has sometimes produced an almost Namierite obsession with party politics. Angus Calder's monumental *People's War*, which brought the then new social history to the study of modern Britain in 1969, has remained a respected but rather forlorn classic. Though often cited, its heirs are only beginning to appear through the undergrowth of political studies of twentieth-century Britain. Yet this has been a century in which social developments have taken place that are as revolutionary as the Beveridge Report, or indeed the great moments of British history like the Act of Supremacy, the Act of Union and the Reform Bill, which provide the focus for historians of earlier periods. Consumerism (in particular the mass ownership of television sets), foreign travel and the growth of youth cultures are some of the areas crying out to be seriously studied by historians and woven into the vast material that already exists on twentieth-century politics.

A recent wave of scholarship by historians of earlier periods might point the way forward. It has examined state formation between the sixteenth and nineteenth centuries. This in itself is not new. The study of state formation was the mainstay of Whig historians who sought to explain the national past in terms of England's inexorable progress towards democracy, prosperity and imperial supremacy. But recent scholarship — dubbed 'Waggish' history by one of its detractors[18] — has ruthlessly deconstructed what schoolchildren once knew as 'Our Island Story'. And it has done so in an imaginative way, by showing how Britain's elites forged a group of disparate peoples into a single powerful nation, using not only economic activity and political legislation, but also art, sport, religion, architecture, philosophy, science and music.

Scholars have explored how these molten forms were hammered into shape for a growing population. Public ceremonial from official occasions like coronations and Armistice Day to popular events like Guy Fawkes night; the iconographic display of artefacts such as the Tyndale Bible and the piston engine in the great museums of the nineteenth century; the official patronage of composers like Elgar;

the growth of sporting events like the FA Cup Final; state festivals such as the Empire Exhibition of 1924 and the Festival of Britain of 1951 and the memorialization of national heroes on banknotes and on plinths in town squares across Britain — all this and much more combined to form the robust Britishness, which was ripe for amplification by the modern media of the twentieth century.

This kind of work has been greatly influenced by the social anthropologist Benedict Anderson. His theory that nations are 'imagined communities' of vernacular culture that were spawned by the 'print-capitalism' of the fifteenth century is certainly not the last word on the subject. But it has offered historians a more subtle mode of enquiry than those that were available a generation ago.[19] Like any intellectual development, this cultural approach has advocates who, in their hurry to legitimize the subject, have rejected traditional forms of enquiry. Those forms remain essential for a full understanding of the past, and it is not the purpose of this book to denigrate them. Sadly, many of those active in the field of 'cultural studies', or 'grievance studies' as Stefan Collini has called it, do reach for their revolvers if a Cabinet document is cited in a text and refuse to believe that in a postmodern world it is possible, or even desirable, to construct an historical narrative from such chaffs in the wind of time.[20] Others see a national narrative as the ultimate confidence trick ruling elites can play on the unsuspecting historian. However, as David Cannadine has written: 'Nations may indeed...be inventions. But like the wheel, or the internal combustion engine, they are endowed, once invented, with a real, palpable existence, which is not just to be found in the subjective perceptions of their citizens, but is embodied in laws, languages, customs, institutions — and history.'[21]

What are the achievements of the new British history? First, its empathy for the modern nation state has helped to overcome the hostility towards the notion of patriotism that for many years distorted the work of a substantial section of the historical profession. In their eagerness to create a 'people's history' from below, social historians of the 1960s too readily equated patriotism with conservatism. In eighteenth-century Britain, for example, citizenship was largely defined in terms of property. Yet, as Linda Colley has shown, when people protested about the limitations of their citizenship, their fury was 'expressed as much if not more in support for the nation-state, as it was in opposition to the men who governed it'. 'People's History' obscured a tradition of radical patriotism in Britain which stretches back to the Cromwellian era and, as a result, it was often a one-dimensional account of Britain in which class conflict was seen to be the basis of most human activity. The birth of gender history in the 1970s as a sister subject was an overdue historiographical development, but did little to help its sibling mature.

The second major achievement of recent scholarship is that it has widened the scope of British history by encouraging scholars to take a less Anglocentric view of these islands. It does not argue, as some have done in the past, that the Welsh, Scots and Irish were victims of 'internal colonialism' as ever stricter uniformity was imposed on the periphery by the core. Instead, it argues that Irishness, Welshness, Scottishness and Englishness all continued to flourish within the Union, sometimes in opposition to the new polity but more often in alliance with it, as the four nations became mutual beneficiaries of the powerful nation state to which they belonged. Scholars should beware of historiographical correctness: the unique aspects of English history may be obscured in the rush to apologize for past Anglocentric misdemeanours. Throughout this collection, indeed, there are occasions when contributors have chosen to refer to a distinct English culture. There are broader dangers. As David Cannadine has pointed out, 'an identificational teleology which merely and mindlessly claims that, at any given time, the British were actively engaged in the process of becoming more British than they ever had been before' may simply replace the 'political teleology of ordered constitutional development, and the sociological teleology of an ever-rising middle class', with which the historical profession previously saddled itself.[22]

Nonetheless, when the current interest in national identity subsides, one thing should remain. Recent scholarship has been more methodologically sophisticated than ever before. Fusing cultural, political and social analysis, it has produced, on occasions, *histoire totale* in a continental manner that is all too rare in this country.[23] That is the third major achievement of the new British history and it is the most important one. 'Waggish history' is, and no one should be ashamed of the fact, a modern version of 'Our Island Story'.

Tentatively placing ourselves within this historiography, in *The Right to Belong* we aim to provide a different angle on existing research by scrutinizing the individuals and organizations responsible for generating ideas about citizenship and national identity in mid-century Britain. Some, like the Women's Institute and the BBC are famous. Others, like the think-tank, Political and Economic Planning (PEP), and the Council for Visual Education (CVE) are less well known. Our authors explore the relationship between all these groups and the main political parties, in order to show the extent to which their ideas were absorbed by policy makers and subsequently translated into practical action by those with direct political power. Some focus on party politics itself. The contributors' main purpose, however, is to explore the delicate patterns of thought within Britain's various elites. By doing so, they aim to reveal the rich diversity of ideological channels through which the 'British way of life' was nurtured in this period.

The most neglected element in the study of twentieth-century Britain is religious history, and it is for this reason that an essay on William Temple begins the collection. The central tenet of Linda Colley's *Britons* is that 'Protestantism lay at the core of British national identity in the eighteenth and nineteenth centuries.' She rightly argues that it glued the otherwise fractious four nations of the Union together against a common Catholic enemy during the Napoleonic wars, and that long after Waterloo and Catholic emancipation, a Protestant world-view underwrote the economic benefits of imperial expansion. She concludes that one of the reasons for the present crisis within the Union is that 'Protestantism, that once vital element, now has a limited influence on British culture, as indeed has Christianity itself.'[24]

There is little doubt that, after a major decline in church attendance began in the early twentieth century, Protestantism was no longer the force it once was. Yet, we would argue that, at least until the 1960s, it did retain a significant influence on British culture, not least because of the continuing establishment of the Church of England. Anglican leaders of the period, like their Edwardian predecessors, were able to present their institution as a national church that was an essential part of English, if not British, identity. William Temple, who became known as the 'people's archbishop', was the most successful proponent of this strategy. John Kent shows how Temple linked the church to the postwar redefinition of the right to belong by arguing that the prime function of Christian morality was not to buttress traditional sexual mores, but actively to support social reform. The continuing existence of Christian social-ism within Labour's ethos ensured that he found a welcome among the major proponents of the New Jerusalem.

The BBC is another institution some people blame for promoting the New Jerusalem at the expense of economic recovery. Since Asa Briggs wrote his four-volume institutional history of the corporation, there has been a gradual attempt to place the history of broadcasting in a wider social context. Siân Nicholas does this by examining the BBC's promotion of citizenship and national identity during the Second World War, and shows how a backward looking emphasis on traditional stereotypes of national character, designed simply to boost morale, evolved into a more complex pattern of regional, class and gender identities. The new approach was a conscious attempt to redefine the listener as not simply the passive product of a proud but static heritage, but an active citizen, capable of making a direct contribution to the reconstruction of the nation. As a result, she argues, the BBC directly contributed to the British people's image of themselves as a people at war and as a people looking ahead to the peace. Toby Haggith follows suit by examining how documentary film makers working for the government's Crown Film Unit attempted to challenge conventional notions of citizenship by pro-moting peace aims in their films.

One of the major criticisms of the social reforms of the 1940s by both left and right-wing commentators is that, for all the democratiz-ation of Britain which wartime propaganda claimed they would create, in practice the reforms relied too heavily on centralized state control by a benevolent elite. Abigail Beach questions this assump-tion. She shows how planners in the influential think tank Political and Economic Planning urged the need to make citizens participants rather than spectators by encouraging activity in local government and voluntary organizations. Only through decentralization, they believed, could an animated sense of national purpose flourish.

The second half of the book explores how those principles were put into practice. Nick Tiratsoo shows that planners in town halls across Britain shared PEP's concerns and did their best to involve people in the planning process of reconstruction through exhibitions and public meetings. Maggie Andrews examines one of Britain's best known voluntary organizations, the Women's Institute (WI). She shows how it accepted a return to a predominantly domestic role for women after their wartime mobilization. Yet, she argues, this did not mean a return to subservience. As well as continuing to provide fellowship for large numbers of women, the WI saw reconstruction and affluence as opportunities for women to improve their material circumstances and to assert themselves as 'citizen-consumers'.

Richard Weight examines one of the strategies by which reformers attempted to create a more democratic national culture after the war. Spurred on by the successful wartime promotion of 'art for the people' by the embryonic Arts Council and the BBC, educationists hoped that the building of arts centres would make the arts a 'living element in the life of every community'. He argues that their failure to do so was not entirely the result of an elitist cultural policy or lack of sufficient state funding, as is often supposed. It was more the result of the changing priorities of ordinary Britons who, after the hardships of war, devoted energy to raising their living standards and consuming new forms of popular leisure. David Matless takes up the question of leisure with regard to the countryside. Because rural Britain — and particularly rural England — had been perceived as the spiritual core of British national identity since the 1880s, the postwar expansion of democracy depended on providing greater access to it through, for example, the creation of national parks. The essay shows how access rights for urban holidaymakers were seen to be dependent on behavioural obligations, and it charts how planners, environmentalists and leisure organizations attempted to promote 'recreational citizenship' through a variety of educational schemes.

Taken together, these essays provide further evidence that, however well-intentioned reformers of mid-century Britain were, they were not entirely successful in their attempts to transform the nation.

As critics have long pointed out, this was partly the result of the Christian socialist strain within the labour movement, which made some reformers prone to moralizing. The major reason for their failure, however, was not the spirit of William Temple but something far simpler: the inability of the Attlee government to satisfy the economic aspirations of ordinary Britons quickly enough after the war. The delivery of affluence by the Conservative governments in the 1950s did not put an end to the problem. Indeed, affluence complicated the attempt to forge a modern code of belonging with which Britons could locate themselves in the nation and the world at large.

Rising living standards brought more material choice and, by the mid-1950s, both major political parties were faced with popular demands for concomitant social freedoms, which neither fully understood because most of their leaders and members were so rooted in the ideological assumptions of the 1940s. They were also faced with the arrival of ethnic minorities who, despite colonial bonds, brought with them their own customs and mores, which undermined some of the cultural assumptions on which Britishness had previously been based.

With this in mind, the final section of the book examines two attempts to define the right to belong amid the rapidly changing society of the 1950s. Nicholas Crowson looks at the dilemma the Conservative Party faced in abolishing national service. The party's traditional ethos championed the rights of the individual against the interference of the state. Yet, at the same time, it was reluctant to scale down the armed forces too drastically in the face of imperial decline and domestic fears about the rise in juvenile delinquency and the consequent need to discipline the nation's youth. Kathleen Paul, meanwhile, examines the issue that was to haunt the party for many years: immigration. She shows how postwar immigration policy was based on the cultural identity of Britons promoted since the war, rather than on the legal framework of British citizenship that facilitated black immigration in the first place. This confusion, she concludes, exacerbated racial tensions and led to the first major race riots in 1958. As such, it is the most telling example of what occurs when notions of citizenship and national identity become separated from each other.

The editors of *The Right to Belong* do not present this book as an exemplar of how British history should be written. They do hope, however, that some of the historiographical ideas outlined above will be seen to be at work in its essays. In particular, the aim has been to show how closely linked the concepts of citizenship and national identity were in mid-century Britain. They remain amorphous concepts, the meanings of which vary between different groups of people and across different periods of time. Sensitivity to the historical context of their articulation is therefore fundamental to any study that seeks to understand their impact on society. However, where the twentieth century is concerned, the conflict that ensues when they become separated in the public consciousness surely demonstrates that a truly democratic polity cannot exist unless both are nurtured simultaneously. As Maurizio Viroli has argued, a modern language of patriotism has to connect a 'political love of the republic with the attachment to one's own cultural identity' or citizenship would become an arid, legalistic creed to which few give their allegiance. Similarly, 'without a political culture of liberty, ethnocultural unity generates love of one's cultural uniqueness (if not superiority) and a desire to keep it pure from external contamination and intrusion. We would have the nation, but it would not be a nation of citizens.'[25]

Notes

1. See Maurizio Viroli (1995) *For Love of Country: An Essay on Patriotism and Nationalism*, Oxford.
2. Jose Harris (1992) 'Political thought and the welfare state 1870–1949: an intellectual framework for British social policy', *Past and Present*, vol. 135, pp. 116-41.
3. Julia Stapleton (1994) *Englishness and the Study of Politics: The Social and Political Thought of Ernest Barker*, Cambridge.
4. Harris: 'Political thought and the welfare state', p. 123.
5. See John Carey (1992) *The Intellectuals and the Masses: Pride and Prejudice among the Literary Intelligentsia 1880–1939*, London.
6. Ibid. p. 122.
7. Jose Harris (1994) *Private Lives, Public Spirit: Britain 1870–1914*, Harmondsworth, Penguin, pp. 32–6.
8. Richard Dennis (forthcoming) 'London, 1840–1950', in Martin Daunton (ed.) *Cambridge Urban History of Britain*, Volume 3, Cambridge, Cambridge University Press

9. Brian Doyle (1989) *English and Englishness*, London, p. 27.

10. Harris, *Private Lives Public Spirit*, pp. 17–23.

11. *Report of the Royal Commission of Local Government in the Tyneside Area,* Cmd 5402 (London, HMSO, 1937), p. 88.

12. M. Rose (ed.) (1985) *The Poor and the City: The English Poor Law in its Urban Context, 1834–1914*, Leicester; and David Feldman (1994) *Englishmen and Jews: Social Relations and Political Culture, 1840–1914*, London.

13. See David Reynolds (1991) *Britannia Overruled: British Policy and World Power in the Twentieth Century*, London; and John Darwin (1988) *Britain and Decolonisation: The Retreat from Empire in the Post-War World*, London.

14. Corelli Barnett (1986) *The Audit of War*, London.

15. See Ben Pimlott (1988) 'The myth of consensus' in Smith, Lesley M. (ed.) *The Making of Britain: Echoes of Greatness*, London.

16. Stephen Fielding, Peter Thompson and Nick Tiratsoo (1995) *'England Arise!' The Labour Party and Popular Politics in 1940s Britain*, Manchester.

17. Paul Addison (1994) *The Road to 1945: British Politics and the Second World War*, 2nd edn, London, p. 290.

18. John Casey, 'Waggish not whiggish view', *Daily Telegraph*, 9 September 1996.

19. Benedict Anderson (1983) *Imagined Communities*, London.

20. Stefan Collini (1994) 'Escape from DWEMsville: is culture too important to be left to cultural studies?', *Times Literary Supplement*, 27 May.

21. David Cannadine (1993) 'Penguin Island Story: planning a new history of Britain', *Times Literary Supplement*, 12 March.

22. David Cannadine (1995) 'British history as a "new subject": politics, perspectives and prospects', in Alexander Grant and Keith J. Stringer (eds) *Uniting the Kingdom: The Making of British History*, London, pp. 25–6.

23. The most notable work on the subject is Linda Colley (1992) *Britons: Forging the Nation, 1707–1837*, Yale. For a comprehensive survey of the field by its leading exponents see Grant and Stringer (eds) *Uniting the Kingdom: The Making of British History*; Raphael Samuel's earlier three-volume collection, *Patriotism: The Making and Unmaking of British National Identity* (London, 1989) contains some extremely valuable essays but some of its contributors were rather tortured by their subject. For a cogent analysis of why, see Miles Taylor (1990) 'Patriotism, history and the left in twentieth-century Britain', *Historical Journal*, vol. 33, no. 4.

24. Colley, *Britons*, p. 374.

25. Viroli, *For Love of Country*, pp. 175–6.

1. William Temple, the Church of England and British national identity

John Kent

A distinction is sometimes made between a public realm monopolized by the state, and a 'private' sphere — often called 'civic society' — in which the individual is technically, and to some extent actually, free. In a society where this kind of distinction is effective, the individual is protected in certain areas of life against the demands of citizenship and national identity. This is because he or she can retreat from them into smaller and smaller subcultures, of which the family may be one and a local religious group another. These subcultures may deny that the state has significant legislative power over them.

In the 1930s and 1940s, in some modern states such as Germany, Italy, Portugal, Russia and Spain, there were powerful centralizing political movements that wanted to incorporate much of the private sphere, including the family, into an organic state system, often described as totalitarian. The Russian state set out to destroy organized Christianity; fascism and Nazism preferred to confine it in a much-reduced private sphere. In Britain, some Christian, especially Roman Catholic, opinion saw the global war of the 1940s as an ideological struggle against totalitarian systems in general, and was never entirely happy with the pragmatic alliance Britain and the USA were prepared to make with the USSR. Though he shared their hatred of totalitarian systems, the wartime leader of the Church of England had few qualms about the state and the churches working closely together.

William Temple, who was born in 1881, was essentially a late Victorian Anglican in background but Edwardian in sensibility. He was the younger son of the Bishop of Exeter, the bleak Frederick Temple, who was nearly sixty when William was born, and who became Archbishop of Canterbury in 1896. William was ordained in 1909, became Bishop of Manchester in 1921, Archbishop of York in 1929 and finally Archbishop of Canterbury in 1941, before dying prematurely in 1944. His family experience, training and cast of mind put him in the camp of those who believed that Christianity had been and should remain at the centre of Western culture, and who thought that national identity and citizenship had their true basis in the Christian Church.

As a young man, he had been educated as a classicist whose tendency to philosophical idealism was stimulated by the English Hegelianism that dominated Oxford in the late nineteenth century. He consequently rejected the view that, to prevent religious emotions complicating secular political conflicts, religious institutions should be confined to a safe area outside the political life of the state. He preferred an Aristotelian view of politics in which the identity of state and society — the oneness of the world within the city's walls — had been fundamental. The Greek *polis* could be thought of as both an end in itself and as a moral community. People could only fulfil themselves as human beings in and through a state that trained, equipped and sustained them to do so: the individual was not autonomous, could not contract out, could not properly invent a separate social existence and so escape the consequences of living in the *polis*. Temple habitually applied this political approach to British institutions. To the end of his life he defended the formal establishment of the Church of England on the grounds that Christian theology itself implied that national unity had to be grounded in a common, Christian set of religious and moral values. He argued that, in the twentieth century, Protestant Christianity in its sophisticated Anglican form was still the most appropriate religious expression of this ideal.

One should not exaggerate the importance of intellectual origins. In nineteenth-century Germany, for example, Greek political ideas of this kind were more pervasive than in Britain. They formed part of the intellectual background of an authoritarian, anti-bourgeois, anti-urban, anti-trade union and anti-communist politics that glorified national identity but demoralized and finally depersonalized the individual, who ceased effectively to be a responsible citizen. In the Nazi period, there was no permanent intention of making even a modified form of Christianity part of the state system. Temple, on the other hand, thought of the unity and identity of the 'British people' as fundamentally Christian, so that the state ought to accept the moral guidance of the Church of England when such guidance was clearly and responsibly offered.

Temple believed that Britain's leaders were in urgent need of some ecclesiastical advice. Like many other members of the Edwardian upper middle class, his social imagination was gripped by the persistence of large-scale unemployment, by the huge inequalities in the distribution of housing, health care, education and the possibilities for leisure. Already deeply divided in 1914, British society had not been united by the First World War, and after 1920 there was no real equivalent of the 'front experience', which drove so many Germans towards an hysterical cult of political violence.

The leaders of the British Churches for the most part shared the view of the dominant political centre-right. They believed that no more power should be conceded to the working classes, whose political representatives were no longer prepared to accept a role on the radical wing of the Liberal Party with the advent of the Labour Party. Most supported Stanley Baldwin, who, after his destruction of Lloyd George, had combined opposition to 'socialism' with a gentrified nationalism. Baldwin did not think that there was any need for the state to intervene in the social system before all citizens were able to gain their nationhood.

It is true that Temple, like Baldwin, offered citizens a part in a national consciousness that transcended social division, and if one uses the word 'religious' very loosely it is possible to argue that both men were offering a 'religious' vision. However, in Baldwin's case the emotional stimulant was not Anglicanism itself but an English countryside in which Anglicanism, through its buildings and rituals — was one of several aesthetic factors. As Stuart Ball has written: 'the evocation of an idealized past, the rejection of class politics and thus in part of industrialization itself, and the conviction that politics were concerned not with economic materialism but with the defence of church and constitution, were hardly novel features in the

Conservative Party.'[1] The soul of the nation, Baldwin implied, was safest with the Conservative Party.

Rather than a geographical space, Temple's 'imagined community' moralized national existence through a single religious culture. Ideally, he wanted this to include all forms of British Christianity and he worked hard, though unsuccessfully, to find a formula for the union of British Churches. Such a union, he hoped, might not only have more political clout, it might also give substance to a society in which the Christian Churches and the British people were already one in his mind. This aspect of Temple's vision closely resembled the Hanoverian Protestant British nationalism of the mid-eighteenth century. Then, the new German dynasty needed a strong state religion to bind the crown and the peoples of the British Isles together, while the Anglican Church needed the support of the monarchy in its long struggle with Roman Catholicism: both encouraged a popular nationalism grounded in loyalty to the Protestant faith. By the 1920s, it was questionable whether any of the centres of British power still needed the support of organized Christianity, or indeed whether there was a precise form of national unity with which Anglicanism could identify in order to justify its privileged status. Even so, the Cecil Report on Church and state, drawn up by a small committee on which Temple sat as Archbishop of York, asserted that the value of establishment was great: 'We are convinced that even in those parts of the Empire where the Church is not established, they value the Establishment in England as a recognition for the British peoples as a whole of the connection between Christianity and the Empire.'[2]

Despite the evident divisions within British society, Temple shared the refusal of his ecclesiastical contemporaries to accept that conflict was the necessary outcome of those divisions. He belonged to the centre-right in politics to the extent that he wanted Christian institutions to give expression to an organic national unity, which, he believed, underlay the artificial divisions created by the excesses of the capitalist system. There was, according to his theology, a divinely-given 'nation' to which the British had an innate right to belong. Conservative clerics, while they stressed the moral duties by which citizens were bound rather than the rights owed them by the state, also took an 'innate' view of nationhood.

Temple differed from them in that he thought Britishness should be expressed not only through a bonding religion but also through a moderate redistribution of opportunity, wealth and political power, without which national unity would be impossible. Furthermore, he believed the church had a duty to promote this more equitable society. Temple had a life-long friendship with the Anglican socialist historian and political thinker, R. H. Tawney. Tawney was sceptical about the possibility of turning the Church of England into a great reforming institution. Nonetheless, both men believed that the Church should not take its economic and social views from one class or party, as it had often done in the past, but should state its own conception of the rights and duties of the Christian citizen, and decide its attitude to political parties by that standard.

Temple's own position was clear. After becoming an early president of the Workers' Educational Association in 1908, he had joined the Labour Party in 1918: at that time he foresaw conflict between organized labour and the rest of society after the war, and he wanted to show that Anglicans were not automatically in the employers' camp. He left the party in 1921 when he became Bishop of Manchester, arguing that membership conflicted with the pastoral relationship of a bishop with his diocese. Temple was also suspicious of the atheistic tendency of many on the left of the labour movement as a whole. At the height of his fame during the war, in a letter to P. T. R. Kirk of the Industrial Christian Fellowship, Temple warned that 'we must be very careful that we do not give the impression that the church is an agency for supporting Left-Wing policies which are often based on presuppositions which are completely un-Christian.'[3] Yet, he remained convinced throughout his life that the values the Labour Party espoused came closest to fulfilling his idea of a Christian society. Furthermore, his formal distance from the party machine undoubtedly helped him to become the major social-democratic church leader of mid-century Britain, by reassuring many clergy that he was not turning the Church into the Labour Party at prayer.

Temple first came to prominence at the Birmingham Conference on Politics, Economics and Citizenship in 1924, where he was the dominant figure in the proceedings. The conference, whose member-ship was drawn from all the Protestant English churches, had produced 12 volumes of material, covering such subjects as the home, leisure, industry and property, international relations, and politics and citizenship. These reports contained a basic ambiguity. On the one hand, traditionalists held the view that 'social service' ought to emerge naturally from the religious subculture and make professionalized social work superfluous.

On the other hand, Temple took the view that the voluntary charity of individuals was not enough and that the whole community had to act together to reduce inequality. The report on industry, for example, originally suggested that industry should substitute the motive of service for the motive of gain, but the conference majority preferred to advocate simply that service should be a part of corporate culture. These were two radically different concepts of citizenship. Temple was prepared to say that the state was divinely ordained to bind men together in a justly ordered social life, but he could not carry the conference with him: there were many Nonconformists at Birmingham to whom suspicion of the state was second nature. Temple would have liked to have gone further and organized a Christian social movement with a clear programme of its own, specifically concerned with the physical, educational, moral and religious needs of the poor, but he was hampered by other church leaders who, he discovered at Birmingham, were largely on the centre-right.

Although significant, the Birmingham conference had little effect on interwar politics. This was why, shortly before being enthroned as Archbishop of Canterbury, Temple assembled the so-called Malvern Conference in January 1941. At this smaller and virtually Anglican meeting, Malvern considered exactly what social changes would be needed after the Second World War and how the economy should be run to effect those changes. The conclusions of its 400 clergy and 15 bishops were distinctly left of centre. Despite the attempts of Richard Acland, the conference pulled back from stating that private property and Christianity were incompatible. But it did conclude that the concentration of the nation's 'principal industrial resources' in private hands 'may be . . . a stumbling block . . . contrary to divine justice, making it harder for men to live Christian lives'.[4]

Temple was able to carry most of the Church with him on this occasion because the Conservative Party, as a result of the policies followed by Baldwin and Chamberlain, was by then firmly identified with the rejection — as expensive, profitless and socialistic — of major government intervention to deal with unemployment. As many historians have recounted, despite the preoccupation of most Britons with waging and surviving the war, and the full employment, which mobilization brought, the memory of mass unemployment in the 1930s remained strong. In this climate, Anglican opinion decided that it had to support economic aid for the deprived, if there was to be any chance of persuading the majority that the Churches were anything more than an institutionalized way of sanctifying inequality.

A year after the Malvern Conference, Temple wrote *Christianity and Social Order* — with some advice from John Maynard Keynes — as a way of advertising the discussions that had taken place. As a Penguin special, it sold 140,000 copies — an extraordinary figure for a book by a religious leader at that time. In it, he laid down the basic social terms for a common citizenship with which to sustain a wider sense of national identity and make it easier for the more deprived sections of society to choose to be British as well as having British-ness thrust upon them. He asserted that, to be designated a minimally Christian state, the state should guarantee decent housing and a reasonable family income to every family, whether employed or not. In addition, and this was not the least controversial of his views, he said that every individual should have some voice in the control of the business in which he worked. Also, because of the emphasis he placed theologically on the full development of human personality, he said that adequate leisure, including paid annual holidays, should be assured. Finally, Temple stated that universal free education — religiously slanted — should be available to maturity. In common with Tawney and other Edwardians, Temple believed that education was 'the supreme regenerative force' and that reform of the educational system was the key to preventing social conflict. In *Christianity and Social Order*, he concluded 'that what is generally thought to be the best form of education should be reserved to those whose parents are able to pay expensive fees, or expensive preparatory education with a view to winning scholarships, makes a cleavage in the educational and social life of the country as a whole, which is destructive of the best fellowship'.[5]

Thus, Temple conceived of national identity in terms of a specifically Christian religious tradition, which bound a people together, and of citizenship in terms of mutual responsibility and cooperation through which that identity would be maintained. For most of his contemporaries, Temple's ideas placed him firmly on the centre-left. He was not by nature a revolutionary man and responded to economic, social and cultural inequality more wholeheartedly than he did to political inequality.

Throughout his life, Temple argued against the view that the Christian Churches must never directly challenge the form of society in which they found themselves. Yet, he shared the inability of Britain's governing elites to accept the 1926 general strike as permissible political action. Temple did not believe, as the Roman Catholic Cardinal Bourne did, that the strike had been 'a sin against the obedience which we owe to God'. Nor did he endorse the enthusiasm with which his own bitterest Episcopal critic, Hensley Henson of Durham, described Baldwin as 'a Christian statesman' because he had defeated the strikers. Rather, he reacted against trade unionism because he felt the movement showed signs of asserting the sort of irresponsible political power wielded by Baldwin.

When it came to serious domestic or international conflicts, Temple usually found it difficult to support one side of an argument and wanted instead to act as a broker between the two sides. The problem was partly theological. If Christianity was defined as 'love', then conciliation, arbitration and compromise were its natural political expression. The moneylenders should not be whipped out of the temple, but asked into the vestry to discuss a possible compromise on times, sites and profit margins. Temple's position also had much to do with modern ecclesiastical history. Throughout the Christian world, as the real power of the Churches in society declined, Church leaders discovered in arbitration a way back into the structures of power from which they had been gradually evicted since the eighteenth century. This trend was even more pronounced in England, for since the Elizabethan *via media* moderation had been the declared ethos of the Church of England.

On the question of how far that arbitration should go, there was a significant difference between Anglicans and Roman Catholics in this period, which tested Temple's ecumenical outlook. As the Vatican saw its ability to influence the legislation of sovereign nations decline, it became more willing to countenance the formation of Catholic political parties, and where this was out of the question, to support nationalist parties. Such parties usually offered corporatist manifestos, through which the Vatican hoped to counter the spread of socialism. Anglican leaders, on the other hand, were virtually uninterested in the idea of a Christian, let alone an Anglican, political party. The remaining influence they had was based largely on the Establishment of the Church and the monarch's role as its governor. Were the Church to sponsor even a new political party, disestablishment would almost certainly follow in order to protect the constitutional propriety of the Crown.

As we have seen, disestablishment was anathema for Temple, for in his mind it tore apart the link between God and the nation. There were also differences outside the political arena. In Ireland and throughout Europe, the Catholic Church tried, with some success, to build a self-sufficient religious subculture within national communities, providing its own schools, universities, trade unions and entertainment clubs.

In England, although a school system was steadily created from the nineteenth century onwards, efforts to set up a Catholic university in Oxford or London failed. Official Vatican Catholicism was hostile to the modern secular nation-state and struggled to preserve the social authority of the hierarchy over the laity. Temple, on the other hand, proposed that rather than setting up their own alternative society, the Churches should encourage moderate changes in the structure of the secular society to which they ministered.

Nor were Temple's views in line with the Anglo-Catholic Christendom Group, the only other significant Anglican centre of thinking about socioeconomic policy at the time of Malvern. Its leader, V. A. Demant, shared much of the European Roman Catholic right's rejection of the eighteenth-century Enlightenment, the French Revolution, 'usury', modern industrialism and any kind of 'new morality'. Moreover, the Christendom Group held that a Christian society could only emerge from a pre-existent mass Christian belief. It supposed this had been the case in the Middle Ages and that, until such a time, direct political action was pointless. In short, it argued that in a democracy the power of the state existed to restrain evil but not to promote justice.

Ultimately, Temple accepted that English Catholics were patriotic citizens. The problem official Vatican policy set was not whether Catholics had a right to belong to the nation, but how far the Established Church was prepared to accept the existence of what we would now call the multicultural nation-state. It should be remembered that in Temple's lifetime, liberal Anglicans identified official Catholicism with the papal repression of 'modernism', that is of the kind of theological freedom Anglican theologians took for granted. Nor did they sympathize with ultramontane attitudes to pilgrimages, relics and contemporary miracles. The decision of the 1930 Lambeth Conference, with which Temple agreed, to abandon absolute opposition to contraception, suggested that Anglicanism was willing to accommodate itself to the introduction of moral ideas that were humanist in origin. At this point, it became obvious that Anglican and Roman Catholic criteria of what the right to belong meant were diverging; and that process has continued to the end of the century.

In the mid-century period, many Anglicans remained content with a sentimental image of English identity based on a description of Anglicanism as anti-dogmatic, anxious to compromise, and charged with a mission to civilize, which had aesthetic as much as religious overtones. Temple was not immune to this view. As we have seen, although he wanted the Church to create alternative patterns of community, he also saw its role as that of a 'reconciling power' offering an emotional bridge between conflicting social groups. Moreover, Temple's patriotism led him to assert that the Church of England, by its very nature was best placed to perform that task.

In July 1943, for example, he had to defend the 'Penguin Special' publishing programme and the Beveridge Plan against a right-wing Roman Catholic critic, Major Kindersley, who had asserted that they advocated socialist planning, which would inevitably lead to Hilaire Belloc's 'servile state' and communist totalitarianism — a theme that the cold war would later amplify. Temple conceded that 'all this planning, which I regard as quite inevitable but also, as an alternative to the condition which we have been in for the last thirty years, desirable, will result in servitude unless it is consciously what Karl Mannheim describes as "planning for freedom",' but he asserted that Britain had 'a peculiar genius for working out in practice the correlation of principles which seem to be logically opposed to each other', and might be able 'to show the world what is not so much a middle path between communism and individualism as a genuine expression of the sound principles lying behind each'. He thought that Anglicanism exemplified this 'peculiar genius' and that the twentieth-century Church of England was the result of 'planning for freedom'.[6] At its most romantic, Temple's patriotism could lead him to say that 'the Church of England, like other Churches, has often failed to be completely Christian . . . but it has never failed to be utterly, completely, provokingly, adorably English.'[7]

Whatever Temple's credentials as a Protestant patriot, any Christian social teaching that seemed to imply some degree of equality remained anathema to most of the political right. Churchill resisted his appointment as Archbishop of Canterbury in 1941 for as long as possible and was later, according to his private secretary, John Colville, 'ribald' about his death.[8] In *The Audit of War*, Corelli Barnett specifically attacked Temple as one of the main creators of the 'New Jerusalem' movement, which, he argued, had persuaded the postwar British to opt for utopian socialist politics at the very moment when the salvation of British power — and so of British 'identity' — required the people to face the pain of rebuilding its economy. Barnett described Malvern as 'one of the first and most effective gambits in launching the New Jerusalem movement'.[9]

The Malvern Conference certainly had a positive influence on the climate of opinion that supported the social legislation of the Labour government of 1945. Temple did much to publicize its conclusions — not only in the best-selling *Christianity and Social Order*, but also in the public meetings that followed the conference. In September 1942, for example, he shared the platform at a rally at the Albert Hall, which heard a speech in support by Stafford Cripps, the most devout and ascetic Anglican layman within the hierarchy of the Labour Party.

Temple had no close association with the party, except in his friendship with R. H. Tawney, and his appointment to Canterbury was a complete surprise to Clement Attlee. Ultimately, Barnett exaggerated the extent to which a united but naïve British 'people' had been led into the wilderness by a handful of Christian utopians; Temple offered some religious reinforcement to a predominantly secular mood, but that was all. Critics of 'New Jerusalem' ideology on both the left and the right also exaggerate the moralizing tone in its prescriptions, which, they argue, is redolent of the Victorian era. The basis of Temple's thought certainly was ethical, but his position had little in common with the mid-nineteenth-century Christian socialist tradition, which was more utopian in nature and local in intent.

The leading Christian socialist of his day, F. D. Maurice, could produce trenchant socialist aphorisms — 'they say that competition is the law of the universe: that is a lie,' for example. However, he did not want to translate his moral judgements into national economic and social programmes. Personal morality was paramount for Maurice and, he believed, one should think and act within the confines of the parish. Similarly, J. M. Ludlow longed for a utopian world of local producers' cooperatives and ended his days railing against the 'materialism' of trade unions. Temple's vision, on the other hand, was a resoundingly national one, both in his analysis of Britain's problems and in his readiness to use the state as a tool to solve those problems.

The question of how a Christian state ought to behave became still more acute for Temple when he transferred his attention to international politics. Even after the outbreak of the Second World War, he was still unable to free himself from the guilt induced by sustained propaganda about the unfairness to Germany of the so-called 'guilt clause' in the Treaty of Versailles in 1919.

This clause effectively made Germany and Austria wholly responsible for the outbreak of the First World War. Temple told the 1932 International Disarmament Conference in Geneva that the clause offended the Christian conscience and should be deleted. He added that 'no one can read [modern] history, with the Christian ideal of the community of nations in mind and not confess that here and there his own country contributed to the frustration of that hope. We have to ask not only who dropped the match but who strewed the ground with gunpowder.'[10]

The assertion, put forward on Christian grounds, that the British nation should accept some 'guilt' about the origins of the First World War, illustrates what Barnett had in mind when he accused Temple of helping to foster a national malaise based on guilt about British power in the world. The Archbishop no doubt felt guilty about the failure of the Edwardian elites, with which he identified, to prevent the conflict. He was also deeply disturbed by the war itself, by the magnitude of a tragedy that had shaken the rational basis of theism and whose repetition would be unendurable. If mutual forgiveness and reconciliation could overcome this legacy and create political harmony in Europe, then the rational order of the universe would be restored.

This faith led Temple to argue that Britain had to transcend the normal idea of a great power and base its foreign policy on its national religion. The Anglican gift for arbitration could, he believed be applied to the resolution of international as well as domestic disputes. Indeed, he seems to have toyed with the idea of a European federal union for a brief time in the 1940s. He acknowledged that it would involve the loss of some national sovereignty, but argued that 'it is a Christian solution, because it rests on the recognition that we are fellow members one of another in the family of God'.[11]

Temple did not, however, feel guilty about British power or about the British Empire. Nor was he applying one oversimplified Christian idea to international politics, as the growing pacifist movement did for much of the 1930s. Temple dismissed pacifism as theologically unsound. He wrote:

If you look at the New Testament, there can be no doubt that there is a theology of the state as well as of the Church, and that it is our duty to do as citizens in support of the state things which it would be inappropriate to do as Churchmen in support of the Church. ... The duty to fight is a civic duty which, if the cause is good, Christianity accepts and approves, but it is not a duty which has its origin in Christianity as such.[12]

Temple's sense of Britishness, after all, was still set in a living imperial context: one has to remember that the widespread British possessions in Africa only became independent African states after 1960. For all the agitation over India, in the mid-century period many senior politicians still thought of the state as the centre of a world empire and were preoccupied with organizing a global system of 'imperial defence'. Many of Britain's church leaders shared this view. This was a world in which many felt that the League of Nations ought to be modelled on the British Commonwealth and share the mission of the global Anglican community to bring international peace. At the very least, the idea that world peace was impossible without world Christianity was taken for granted in British and American Christianity up to the 1960s.

Moreover, the ethos of the British Churches was deeply influenced by the practical fact that their extra-European mission fields in Africa, China, India and the Pacific still operated through the Victorian imperial structure, cooperating closely with the state, especially in the field of education. Indeed, 'the needs of the mission fields' were much more likely to be pressed on the ordinary church-goer on a Sunday morning than the needs of local people who were suffering hardships of some kind. The misled late-Victorian dream of 'the conversion of the world' lingered into the 1940s partly because many missionary leaders still thought of the British Empire as a divine gift, which provided a new Roman imperial space in which they could build up dominant religious institutions. Moreover, Church leaders, like many of their political counterparts, had little sense of imperial decay, still less any foreboding of imperial collapse. They were therefore reluctant to imagine a different international structure for the church.

Nonetheless, Temple differed from many of Britain's elites in his approach to the empire. He was, more than most, a committed ecu-menicist. He became the undisputed leader of the world ecumenical movement, and the establishment of the World Council of Churches in 1948, four years after his death, was largely his achievement. In his brief time as Archbishop of Canterbury, Temple sought to ally the ecumenical movement with the International Missionary Council, in the hope of detaching missionary work from its imperial foundations and creating a world Church that would act as the Christian counterpart to what became the United Nations, taking on the role of the ultimate peacemaker as the Established Church would do in the British state.

The leaders of the British Free Churches, in Scotland and Wales as well as England, were sympathetic to ecumenical negotiations well into the 1960s. However, by then, the ecumenical campaign began to falter with the establishment of the second Vatican Council. The council released the energy British Catholicism had generated in the long period of separated existence and recovered the ecumenical initiative by concentrating the idea of a united world church once again on Rome.

The decision of the Church of England under Michael Ramsey to endorse many of the social reforms of the Labour governments of the 1960s with regard to divorce and abortion, and latterly its decision to ordain women as priests showed that Temple's struggle to give religious sanction to a new form of Britishness was not over. However, it was done at the expense of relations with the Vatican, particularly after the liberalizing energy of the second Vatican Council gave way to a more conservative papacy towards the end of the century. To some extent, therefore, the belief of Temple's generation, that Roman Catholicism was morally irrelevant and did not form part of the central stream of British identity was perpetuated. The growth of British religious pluralism as a result of post-colonial immigration in the 1960s meant that the possibility of a united nation grounded specifically in the Christian Church effectively disappeared altogether, and with it the case for a state-church that could claim to be a truly 'national' Church.

Throughout his life, Temple emphasized that the prime duty of the church was to create a more Christian society. In *Christianity and Social Order*, for example, he declared 'there is no hope of establishing a more Christian social order except through the labour and sacrifice of those in whom the Spirit of Christ is active, and that the first necessity for progress is more and better Christians taking full responsibility as citizens for the political, social and economic system under which they and their fellows live.' Despite such reassurances, the Labour Party and particularly the Conservative Party remained hostile to the principle that the Established Church should give independent ethical guidance whether it suited the government or not. Moreover, a report, dedicated to Temple in 1945 concluded that there remained a 'wide and deep gulf' between the Established Church and the people — a gulf which of course has continued to grow as a result of the increasing secularization of British society.

What then did Temple achieve? If nothing else, he established that if the modern Church of England chose to speak out on political matters, it was no longer necessarily the mouthpiece of government. Twice in the first half of the twentieth century, Britons had been expected to fight to defend their nation, but few had asked them seriously whether they thought that what they had was worth defending. In 1940 Winston Churchill romantically declared that he had nothing to offer but blood, sweat and tears and for many ordinary people, he was right. Temple, on the other hand, offered what religious support he could to a secular attempt to change, or perhaps even to discover, the true nature of 'British' identity by means of what came to be known as the 'welfare state'. His crisp assertion, as the head of a state Church, that in various fields of life ordinary people could not be expected to accept the obligations of citizenship, still less to feel that they 'belonged', unless they were given a fairer social deal than they had been given in the past, still carries weight today.

Notes

1. Stuart Ball (1988) *Baldwin and the Conservative Party: The Crisis of 1929-31*, London.
2. *Church Assembly, and State: Report of the Archbishops' Commission* (London, 1935), p. 50. Cited as Cecil.
3. John Kent (1992) *William Temple: Church, State and Society in Britain, 1886–1950*, Cambridge, p. 164.
4. Kent, *William Temple*, p. 158.
5. William Temple (1942) *Christianity and Social Order*, London, p. 68.
6. F S. Temple (ed.) (1963) *Some Lambeth Letters 1942–1944*, Oxford, pp. 91–2.
7. A. E. Baker (ed.) (1958) *Religious Experience*, London, pp. 88–90.
8. John Colville (1985) *The Fringe of Power: Downing Street Diaries 1939–55*, London, p. 526.
9. Corelli Barnett (1986) *The Audit of War*, London, p. 16.

10. F. A. Iremonger (1948) *William Temple Archbishop of Canterbury: His Life and Letters*, Oxford, p. 376.
11. Kent, *William Temple*, p. 107.
12. Iremonger, *William Temple*, p. 544.

2. From John Bull to John Citizen: images of national identity and citizenship on the wartime BBC

Siân Nicholas

One of the commonest refrains in the literature on the Second World War is that during the war the British people 'discovered' a new sense of national identity. Contemporaries identified the conflict as 'the People's War' long before reconstruction became the watchword, and the collective identity of a citizenry at war provided a comforting national self-image in the postwar years. This theme is central to most popular accounts of the war, and is explored in the principal historical works on the period. However, recent studies have sought to challenge the realities behind the myths, focusing on public attitudes to such issues as evacuation, housing and the welfare state, and questioning the extent of national consensus in wartime Britain.[1]

Several questions are thus raised. Were there changing perceptions of national identity, patriotism and citizenship during the war and, if so, whose perceptions changed? What did the terms 'patriotism' and 'citizenship' in fact mean in this period? How was citizenship defined? Or, since concrete definitions were and are rare, how were ideas of citizenship formulated and projected during the war?[2] One forum of national debate that offers an important perspective on this question is the British Broadcasting Corporation. Despite its role and status in national life both before and during the war, the BBC has rarely been cited in this context beyond reference to J. B. Priestley's celebrated series of *Postscripts to the News* of 1940–1.[3] Yet the way in which the wartime BBC constructed images of patriotism, national identity and national aspirations in this period vividly illustrates how a new vocabulary of citizenship developed in Britain through the war.

The BBC began the war with a crude emphasis on traditional stereotypes of national character. This emphasis evolved into a more complex pattern of regional, class and gender identities, in which the listener was represented not simply as a British subject (the product and representative of a proud but static heritage) but as a British citizen, actively engaged in the national struggle, looking to make a direct contribution to the future of his or her country. The BBC's own audience research during the war suggests that the listening public took an active interest in these questions. During the war, the British people had a choice between identifying themselves in old 'John Bull' stereotypes or casting themselves in the new role of 'John Citizen'. In this chapter, I examine this choice.

Concepts of national identity in interwar Britain were fraught with contradictions, with old imperial certainties persisting but overlaid by new more insular and domesticated images of the nation. Jingoism of the 'John Bull' and 'Britannia' kind had worked well enough for the home front for most of the First World War, but had been discredited in the years after the armistice. Although the conventional imperial imagery of late-Victorian and Edwardian Britain certainly survived, the aggressive, confident and overtly Anglocentric portrayal of the British nation was increasingly downplayed. A more popular interwar construction of the nation centred around a mythic rural vision of the 'traditional' English countryside. This construction was inherently contradictory. It was self-effacing yet self-absorbed, implicitly reactionary in its ideal-ization of the past yet radical in many of its preoccupations, notably the interwar campaigns for public access to the countryside itself. While progressive campaigners such as J. B. Priestley and C. E. M. Joad voiced the radical democratic strain of this idealized 'Englishness', its greatest proponent remained Conservative leader Stanley Baldwin, popularly identified as 'the most typical Englishman of his day'.[4]

One particular form of popular national self-portrayal, the political cartoon, demonstrates the changing self-image of the nation in this period. In the interwar years, John Bull, always a staple feature of patriotic cartooning, fell increasingly out of favour. Although Bernard Partridge of *Punch* maintained the John Bull tradition throughout the period (notably during the general strike, when a Union Jack-flourishing John Bull faced off the trade unionist and his red flag), the popular mass-circulation newspapers shifted to an increasingly informal and populist perspective on politics and introduced cartoon characters of a more 'Everyman' type to their editorial pages.

The most popular was probably Sydney Strube's 'Little Man', featured in the *Daily Express* from 1925: a small, bowler-hatted and besuited character with an untidy moustache and baffled expression, described by H. V. Morton (one of the chief architects of interwar ruralism) as 'the ordinary good-humoured well-mannered long-suffering person known as the Tax Payer . . . that splendid monument of fortitude and gallantry — the postwar Middle Classes of England'.[5] Although David Low had begun his career in England at the *Star* drawing John Bulls, at the *Evening Standard* he adopted his own autobiographical variant of the 'little man', identified by his heavy eyebrows and perpetual frown. Meanwhile, in 1928 he introduced to his cartoons the eternally bemused but plain-speaking 'flapper voter' Joan Bull, and in 1934 Colonel Blimp, the ultimate parody of John Bullery.[6] The archetype, however, to which the others all more or less referred, was 'John Citizen', created by 'Poy' (Percy Fearon) of the *Daily Mail* at the end of the First World War: again small, timid, bowler-hatted and, as Low himself described him, 'the representative of the Common Mass, the first variant of the obsolete figure of John Bull to win general acceptance'.[7]

Conceptions of 'citizenship' in the interwar years appear imprecise and defensive. In response to the perceived dangers of the spread of totalitarianism, an increasing interest was shown in some quarters in 'education for citizenship'. But difficulties in balancing an education in liberal democracy with more sinister visions of political indoctrination saw citizenship playing only a limited part in the school curriculum in the 1930s.[8] The BBC's role in the interwar years is similarly qualified. During the 1920s and especially the 1930s the BBC established a sense of national and regional identity throughout Britain, through its two services, the National and the Regional

Programmes, that each provided a 'mixed' fare of broadcasts for the growing radio audience.

Contemporary commentators praised its 'unifying and equalizing' role in ordinary life, its ability to draw the nation together during national events (such as Christmas, sporting occasions and royal ceremonies) and its role as a national cultural cement.[9] The BBC also articulated a more proactive conception of 'citizenship' in the 1930s, seeking to inform listeners about national affairs and periodically raising the issue of broadcasting from Parliament. Yet the BBC's director-general, Sir John Reith, increasingly saw broadcasting as an 'integrator of democracy', a policy intended not only to secure the nation's political health but also to persuade the authorities of the BBC's overriding sense of national responsibility.[10]

Citizenship was addressed in broadcasts as something understood and incontrovertible. Series such as *Men Talking* (1937), originally designed as a talks vehicle for the unemployed, were hamstrung by the prohibition on discussing issues of immediate political importance. Any potential for radicalism was stifled by the corporation's fragile status as a public institution. The BBC, characterized by its middle-class image and accent, continued to project a muted and uncontroversial conception of what it meant to be a citizen.[11]

Thus, the concept of the 'active citizen' appears little in evidence in interwar popular culture. The 'ordinary little man' of Poy and Strube's cartoons was an almost completely powerless figure, a class-specific and even exclusive portrayal of the 'oppressed' middle-class male. Depending on the occasion and context, his foes were variously politicians (particularly Chancellors of the Exchequer), bureaucrats (civil servants, tax inspectors), trade unionists and wives. This 'John Citizen' was hardly a conventionally patriotic image of the British citizen. He was not a triumphalist character, quite the reverse. His relationship to his government was resigned. It was his peace of mind rather than his civil liberties that were at risk. However, as H. V. Morton pointed out, he did have at least one positive trait. 'No matter how dire his peril, how deep his woe, he is always dignified, he is always brave, he is always keeping his end up.'

During the Second World War, a more positive model of patriotism and citizenship was articulated, particularly by the political left, with progressives such as J. B. Priestley, George Orwell, the 'Mass-Observers' and the 'people's Archbishop', William Temple projecting a more inclusive and participatory concept of citizenship. Patriotism was increasingly seen as a rational choice rather than an unthinking response.[12] Certainly, much of the propaganda (both official and unofficial) of the period centred on the importance of responsible citizenship, a theme deemed necessary both to project an optimistic vision of the future and to place limits on popular aspirations. Both propaganda for the war effort itself and competing ideas of postwar reconstruction focused on the social and political role of the British citizen.[13] However, this conceptual shift was by no means immediate.

Appeals to patriotism in the early weeks and months of the Second World War shifted uneasily between imperialistic triumphalism and interwar circumspection rather than assuming new characteristics. True, there were few outbursts of the 'mafficking' that had character-ized the outbreak of the First World War. David Low himself in a BBC talk in late October 1939 affirmed that 'The British lion and what-not are nothing but a lot of obsolete rot. ... RIP to all that Britannia stodge, I say. And that includes John Bull, that symbol of smug and narrow patriotism, too, who bears no resemblance, inside or out, to the modern educated fit Briton.'[14]

Early British wartime propaganda was characterized above all by simple patriotic nationalism. 'The Charing Cross Road', the British popular song industry, led this mood by producing a succession of rousing patriotic choruses in the first months of war (notably 'We're going to hang out the washing on the Siegfried Line' and 'There'll always be an England'). The Ministry of Information's (MOI) own guidelines were based on simple national stereotypes. The basic theme for home propaganda was to be 'national character' and the 'patriotic spirit'. Britain's military past would be used to suggest the nation's martial confidence and indomitable spirit. Britain's democratic traditions would contrast with Nazi tyranny, and celebrations of the British character would highlight the perfidy of the German soul.[15]

The BBC's wartime role was not in dispute. Although a wartime regional programme was considered both impractical and unneces-sary, the importance of a centralized wireless service in providing information, encouragement and a sense of national unity in time of war was recognized as early as 1935.[16] However, although in December 1939 the *Listener* proclaimed the BBC's duty to raise national morale 'without descending to the level of cheap jingoism',[17] in the first months of war BBC output was self-consciously nationalistic. From the first wartime *Radio Times* cover ('There'll always be an England') to such features as *For Ever England*, the BBC projected a conventional vision of England's green and pleasant land, its history and heritage.

The BBC steered well clear of an MOI proposal to hold a competition to find the best new patriotic song, but set out to encourage more 'highbrow' musical patriotism, commissioning Britain's leading composers (including Ralph Vaughan Williams and John Ireland), to compose patriotic 'lay hymns ... with a direct appeal to the emotions'.[18] Meanwhile, talks programmes such as Sir William Beveridge's discussion series *This Freedom* (January 1940) made constant reference to Britain's civic heritage and traditions of freedom and liberty. There was even a full day of celebration in June 1940 to mark the 725th anniversary of the signing of the Magna Carta. Rather than embodying a new sense of Britain, this was essentially an extension of interwar portrayals of British civic liberties and virtues, unquestioning, complacent and rooted in celebrations of the past rather than visions of the future ('what we should lose if the Nazis had their way').[19]

There were immediate problems with this vocabulary of national identity. It was quick to stale: in February 1940 *Listener* critic Grace Wyndham Goldie derided the whole genre ('the speeches of Queen Elizabeth ... linked by snatches of Elgar to the sonnets of Rupert Brooke. ... I have never heard one [such programme] which had a spark of broadcasting life in it').[20] These types of programme also implicitly celebrated 'England' rather than 'Britain'. The MOI warned the BBC as early as October 1939 to avoid using England as a synonym for Britain as it provoked 'irritation among the minorities'.[21] The easiest way to avoid such problems appeared to be to place particular emphasis in broadcasts on Britain's regional variety. Thus, in parallel with the tributes to 'England' appeared a strand of self-consciously 'British' productions. *Britain Now* (from November

1939) and *The Microphone at Large* (from April 1940) sought directly to represent the regions of Britain to each other. The North, the most successful and innovative of the BBC's prewar regional organizations, was particularly heavily featured, with *The North in Wartime*. The Welsh and Scottish contribution to the war was consistently underlined, and the BBC's commitment to broadcasts on the Home Service in Welsh and Gaelic was extended (including the news in Welsh daily at 5.00 p.m.). Such attempts often threatened to veer between tokenism on the one hand and parody on the other (a letter to the *Radio Times* enquired, 'are all soldiers Cockneys? Or are all Cockneys soldiers?').[22] Welsh and Scottish listeners continued to complain at the BBC's persistent Anglocentrism; listeners from all around England continued to object to its London bias.

With the end of the phoney war, a new tone entered discussions of patriotism and national identity. The BBC acknowledged its critics and modified the 'Rupert Brooke' element. Triumphalism seemed inappropriate after Dunkirk ('In these days of trial one has a new sense of England [*sic*]. One never today sees a flag — one never hears a patriotic song. Flag-waving and singing ... are unnecessary.')[23] On 4 July 1940, a *Listener* editorial put 'the true nature of English patriotism' under the microscope:

> Our patriotism is not of the kind that passionately protests its love. ... To some people there was something almost indecent, as well as platitudinous, about that lyrical affirmation, heard so much a few months ago, that 'there'll always be an England'. ... The BBC has no intention of ... setting up standards of self-conscious nobility that are foreign to our nature as a people.[24]

Low abandoned his cartoon alter ego in favour of bluff Tommies ('Very well, alone') and Churchill at the head of the British people ('All behind you, Winston'). Strube's 'little man' discovered reserves of stoic heroism under his new tin hat.

The BBC's depiction of the nation over the course of 1940–1 demonstrated both continuities and new emphases. Celebrations of the English rural tradition persisted (for example, *The Land We Defend*, July 1940), as did features built self-consciously around 'any speeches which contain suitable sentiments about democracy or free-dom or the greatness of Britain' (for example, *Great Parliamentarians*, May 1941).[25] However, the BBC also ventured into new areas of broadcasting in order to present a more comprehensive and realistic 'voice of the people'. The war effort, it was repeatedly emphasized, rested on the endurance and character of the British people. From the summer and autumn of 1940, a succession of new programmes (such as *My Day's Work*, *Everyman and the War*, and *We Speak for Ourselves*) sought to illustrate the resolve of the ordinary British worker by bringing on to the airwaves the people of Britain from all regions, occupations and backgrounds.

Talks, discussions, features and light entertainment programmes incorporated a cross-section of regional dialects and class accents. The intention was twofold: to demonstrate to listeners in every part of the country that they too were being heard, but also to foster a sense of communal identity by portraying a democratic and inclusive nation proud of its diversity. This stress on the 'ordinary voice' was noted among listeners, and was cited by several radio critics as evidence of a new national awareness on the part of the BBC. Prominent among these was W. E. Williams, the *Listener's* critic of the 'spoken word', who noted that the working classes were at last being given representation beyond 'gag-fodder for the Variety pro-grammes. ... They are the people of England — they have not spoken yet.'[26]

This 'democratization' of the airwaves continued throughout the war. In October 1941, with Parliament in recess, the Talks Depart-ment took the unprecedented step of featuring 'The Voice of the British Worker' (Leslie Merrion, a London bricklayer) in the *Week in Westminster*. Meanwhile, the theme of the brave but diffident 'ordinary' national character was consolidated in magazine pro-grammes like *Marching On*, where anonymous fighter pilots, fire-fighters or ordinary workers, taken from all walks of life and all regions of the country, recounted their own stories of heroism in suitably modest tones. Critics lauded the insights provided by the 'authentic Voice of the People'.[27]

The BBC not only disseminated this refined national self image, but appeared to embody it. BBC newsreaders, already cult figures in the interwar years owing to their tantalizing anonymity, became personalities in their own right during the war years. They came to represent the 'British character' itself: reserved, imperturbable, unimpeachable — and, on rare but treasured occasions, impetuously proud of the war effort. Bruce Belfrage's impromptu announcement in November 1942 before a midnight news bulletin that the latest communiqué from Cairo was a 'cracking good one' made headlines the next day. When two years earlier, on 15 October 1940, the newsreader (Belfrage again) had paused only for a moment in the middle of the *Nine O'clock News* as a bomb audibly fell nearby, the blitz spirit appeared to have been made manifest at Broadcasting House.[28] Most famously, Wilfred Pickles, to many people the voice of the North Country, started newsreading in November 1941, an experiment that received massive publicity, a mostly favourable reception by listeners, and which was followed up by the introduction of a Scottish-accented newsreader, James Urquart.[29]

Above all, J. B. Priestley in his celebrated two series of *Postscripts to the News* on Sunday nights between June 1940 and March 1941, secured a vision of the British people that persisted for the remainder of the war. Priestley's *Postscripts* are more generally remembered for their reconstruction message, which so upset the Conservative Party and (according to some accounts) Churchill himself.

What was perhaps most striking about these broadcasts was not their 'peace aims' message, which was largely unspecific beyond the refrain that 'it must be better than it was before', but their conjuring of a national identity based around vignettes of ordinary life in prewar and wartime Britain: a people prosaic yet romantic, ordinary but capable of extraordinary things.[30] Despite subsequent claims on their behalf, Priestley's *Postscripts* captured the public mood of these months because they appealed to the ambiguities as much as the certainties of the British outlook, looking back as well as forward for their message of hope and reassurance, and chiming a chord with 'a very large section of the population who look for a better world but have no party allegiances'.[31] They provided a groundwork on which future developments could take shape rather than a decisive break with the past in themselves.

However, Priestley's *Postscripts* illustrated the dilemma inherent in any emphasis on the British character. Calls for renewed national pride, for active participation in the war effort, inevitably led to a blurring and broadening of conventional conceptions of national identity. Increasingly, the call for effort and sacrifice was couched in terms of obligation and reward: the British public had an obligation to the war effort, and might expect, once victory was assured, rewards commensurate with the sacrifice. The debate about reconstruction implicitly represented a debate about citizenship: increasingly, the British character was being defined as the responsible active citizen with both duties to the state and rights deriving from those duties.

The BBC reflected this shift with a perceptible extension of their obligation to encourage and inform the responsible citizen, not only representing to the nation at large that everyone was participating, but also facilitating that participation. Programmes (many of which dated from early in the war) that came to embody this participatory ideal included the advice programme *Can I Help You?* (initially presented in association with the Citizens' Advice Bureaux) and the several BBC series produced in collaboration with government ministries, notably *The Kitchen Front* (in association with the Ministry of Food). Programmes such as *From Factory to Front Line* demonstrated the essential wartime role played by the humblest factory worker. *Music While You Work* (the first BBC programme designed to cater for an undiscriminating mass audience, a broadcasting breakthrough in itself), implicitly performed the same task.

Shirkers and black marketeers were singled out in talks, features and plays as undermining the communal national effort. While much of this accorded directly with propaganda policy, the importance of radio's role was crucial. Government spokesmen or MOI officials were often seen by the public as interfering or unsympathetic to the problems of home front life. The BBC's unique status halfway between officialdom and the general public meant that it was generally cast by listeners as a responsible and helpful presence, even when presenting essentially the same message as the MOI. This 'double standard' on the part of the listening public was vital to the BBC's wartime success. Meanwhile, the simmering public resentment at the government's persistent refusal to ration fuel underlined a widespread perception that everyone should be doing their bit, and that the government should be doing more to ensure this.[32]

This, then was John Citizen: but a John Citizen redefined. For a short time, in fact, the term 'John Citizen' seemed to be a shorthand for everything represented in the ordinary person's search for a better Britain. No longer was he the put-upon middle-class taxpayer of the interwar cartoonists. John Citizen was an active citizen, a fully fledged shaper of and participant in the future of his nation. He was also quite possibly a she. The change in tone in programmes for women in the second half of the war is striking. From *The Kitchen Front* and *The Housewife in Wartime*, women's programmes during the war years evolved via the forces' *Women and War* and the war-workers' *Women Can't Do That*, into serious topical and current affairs programmes such as *Mostly for Women* (explicitly devised 'to make women more aware of themselves as citizens') and *Woman's Page*. The latter deliberately steered clear of 'domestic' subjects to consider such topics as equal pay, postwar education, and career opportunities after demobilization. Although the audiences for these programmes were relatively small, they filled a niche not previously addressed. However, just as opportunities for women evaporated once the war was over, the BBC's more hard-hitting 'women's pro-grammes' disappeared and were superseded by the more 'traditional' *Woman's Hour* (complete with male compere) after the war.[33]

Ironically, the term 'John Citizen' seems to have been used only once by BBC programme makers. The 1942 series *I am John Citizen* was the flagship of the BBC's notorious (and unsuccessful) policy to provide the nation with 'virile dance music' to counterbalance the allegedly debilitating (and thus by implication un-British) influence of another of the Corporation's music programmes, *Sincerely Yours: Vera Lynn*, a series (and a star) too popular to axe. John Citizen's eponymous front man was an aircraft factory worker (real name Charles Durning) plucked from obscurity to represent the 'ordinary working man', singing and presenting favourite hearty tunes. The series was short-lived, though the policy continued to haunt the BBC's music and variety departments for the remainder of the war.[34]

In his catalogue of 'New Jerusalemists' who led the wartime reconstruction debate, Correlli Barnett accords a prominent position to the BBC.[35] Yet, it is clear that after the Priestley controversy of 1940–1, and while extending a generalized vision of citizenship in other respects, the BBC self-consciously did not take this new emphasis to its logical conclusion, neither leading nor indeed hardly even addressing the reconstruction debate until comparatively late in the war. The BBC's role during the war was a peculiar one. Initially a semi-official government voice, it increasingly acted during the war as a mediator between government opinion on the one hand and public opinion on the other. Thus, the BBC controllers remained reluctant to endorse the reconstruction debate even as individual production staff sought to keep the issue alive. The BBC's belated entry into the reconstruction debate in 1943 represented less a victory for the 'progressive establishment' as an acknowledgement of the need to follow public opinion.

As early as the spring of 1941, the BBC Talks Department discussed (with MOI approval) how to address the nation's postwar plans. Although director of talks, Sir Richard Maconachie, objected to a suggested series, *Where Are We Going?*, on the grounds that the answer would probably be 'still further towards socialism',[36] Patrick Ryan, MOI liaison with the BBC (later the BBC's controller (Home)), believed that such a series might serve as a useful conduit of public opinion, providing ministers with 'helpful clues to what is being thought about matters on which Government policy may still be in the making'. With no guarantee of full government support for such a controversial enterprise forthcoming, the programme was dropped.[37]

Only after Churchill and Roosevelt's signing of the Atlantic Charter did the BBC return to reconstruction. The series *Making Plans* from October 1941 ('rebuilding Britain as it affects the ordinary man and woman') was designed in part to test the public's response to postwar planning suggestions, both critical and audience reception was encouraging. ('Nothing could more truly fortify the morale of the average citizen than the conviction that good health, good schools and good homes are elements in that New Order for which we fight. ... Here was "England Arise" put to a rousing topical tune.') A *Listener* editorial at the end of the series made much of the nation's apparent endorsement of a future policy of 'rationalism strongly tempered by humanism'.[38] The *Working Man Looks at*

Reconstruction, Westminster and Beyond and a second series of *Making Plans* all continued the theme of 'politics and the ordinary man' [*sic*] into 1942.

During 1942, the Labour Party conference's call for a 'New World after the war', Tom Driberg's by-election victory at Maldon, and the formation and by-election successes of the Common Wealth Party kept 'peace aims' in the public mind. The MOI film division broke ranks from the rest of the ministry to produce explicitly pro-reconstruction documentaries. G. D. H. Cole's reconstruction survey noted how respondents consistently looked to 'the state' to improve national welfare provision after the war. Archbishop Temple's *Christianity and Social Order* sold more than 100,000 copies. The Army Bureau of Current Affairs (ABCA) instituted a wartime 'education for citizenship' among British servicemen, and its 'British Way and Purpose' series of pamphlets explicitly addressed the life and role of the British citizen. The progress of the 'Forces Parliaments' set up under ABCA's aegis (notably in Cairo in 1944) were followed with keen interest in Britain.[39] While an MOI investigation into public attitudes to reconstruction in November 1942 suggested a widespread distrust of government promises, BBC Listener Research's own contemporaneous study found 'lively interest' in reconstruction, especially among working-class listeners.[40]

Public response to the Beveridge Report underlined this interest in reconstruction. The BBC was dragged along in the wake of the wider publicity drive, with Maconachie warning that to publicize the report would imply an endorsement of its recommendations. On 1 December 1942, on the instruction of the Minister of Information, Brendan Bracken, a cautious *Six O'clock News* bulletin outlined the main provisions of the report — though it also reported the government's warning to beware of slogans about 'promised lands'.

Beveridge's own talk on the following night (again opposed by Maconachie) attracted a 'quite outstanding' audience of 38.4 per cent — more than 11.5 million listeners. From 7 December, in accordance with the '14-day rule' prohibiting discussion of issues before Parliament, the BBC withdrew from further coverage of the report.[41] Yet, in six by-elections in February 1943, the Beveridge Report was the principal issue. In April 1943, the BBC's reluctance to publicize issues so clearly in the public mind prompted a parliamentary vote on the question of whether the BBC was being directed by the government on totalitarian lines.[42]

The subsequent evolution of BBC policy indicates a corporation reluctantly but with increasing momentum coming to terms with the fact that reconstruction could no longer be ignored. The changing mood at the BBC can be seen in the decision to allow J. B. Priestley a new series from June 1943, *Make It Monday*, in which in far more overtly 'political' tones he warned against the public undermining of 'the reformer'.[43] A *Listener* editorial in September 1943 marks the decisive shift in the BBC's attitude to the reconstruction debate:

> Without widespread advance discussion many hopes may be shipwrecked after the peace. ... What [people] are waiting for is the education and the leadership which will bring great issues to a clearly graspable point ... [so] that some day they will know better where to put a cross in a polling booth. ... Broadcasting might in this field of popular 'enlightenment' do the maximum amount of good, just as under the Goebbels recipe it has unquestionably done the maximum amount of harm.[44]

The explicit reference to the ballot box is important. Listeners were envisaged as citizens playing their own part in the decision-making for the nation's future; but to play this part they had to be informed citizens. The BBC's departure from its interwar role could not have been more clearly expressed: it was no longer educating the nation to respect its institutions and heritage but was informing the nation about the choices facing it in its future.

Thereafter, the BBC became one of the principal voices framing the debate. With a season of experimental new discussion series, from the end of 1943 the BBC recast itself as the discussion forum for active citizenship. *The World We Want* (subtitled 'The Voices of the People') looked at such issues as employment, social security, housing and education, punctuating the discussion with 'man-on-the-street' interviews gathered by the Outside Broadcast department. The programme's cautious line was singled out by listeners for criticism, with the negative attitude of some of the people featured criticized as being 'more typical of 1918 than of 1943'.[45] The series *Homes for All*, 'a broadcasting experiment without precedent' (and a subject with particular resonance for veterans of the First World War) comprised nine talks crammed into a three-week period in March/April 1944, with expert witnesses testifying before a chairman and two 'assessors' about postwar building plans and policy. This programme received a generally positive listener response, and each edition attracted an audience higher than usual for that time slot. In this instance, however, producers were appalled at the apparent cynicism of respondents regarding future government action ('It is up to "Them" to provide homes for all but "They" are going to let "Us" down as they did last time.')[46]

The BBC's attempts to address this fatalism more directly took it down new avenues of 'controversial' broadcasting. *The Friday Discussions* (from October 1944) aimed to help the public 'make up its mind on the many questions which become more urgent the nearer we approach final victory', and received praise for its unusually combative tone (in particular a discussion between Quintin Hogg and Aneurin Bevan on whether party government should return after the war).[47] The most striking example of the BBC's reconstruction agenda was *Jobs for All* (December 1944), the most ambitious discussion series the BBC had ever broadcast. Comprising eight talks over a two-week period, it set out to address the widespread 'gloom and despair' about the future noted by *Home Intelligence*.[48] It was meticulously planned over a three-month period (with Maconachie warning about the 'great educational responsibility' with which the BBC had burdened itself), and its reception by listeners was minutely researched. Coming six months after the government's precedent-setting White Paper on Employment Policy, both the content of the series and its reception by listeners illustrate important features of the continuing debate.[49]

The 'editorial direction' of the programme clearly took as its lead the government White Paper. Full employment was possible, and was fully compatible with capitalism. The problems associated with achieving full employment did not really emerge in discussion until the fourth and fifth programmes. Much store was set on an unconventional approach to presentation — a mixture of expert debate, 'public' discussion and 'arguments' (scripted). The series concluded with a discussion that stressed public responsibility on the part of both employers and employees if full employment was to succeed, but which suggested that the will to succeed was there.

Although the White Paper on Employment had caused 'hardly a ripple of reaction',[50] the public interest generated by *Jobs for All* astonished its producers. Audiences for the series averaged over 26 per cent (more than eight million listeners), with little fluctuation over the fortnight. Closer enquiry revealed that a quarter of the listeners had been unemployed between the wars. The most popular programmes were those featuring outspoken experts in their particular fields. However, what clearly affected listeners most was the 'ordinary voice' again: personal testimonies from people who had suffered from unemployment between the wars. Most remarkably, and especially so for a series that rested so heavily on discussions of economic theory and practice, these talks beat in the ratings the entire rival schedule on the BBC General Forces Programme — including *Music Hall*, one of the most popular of all the BBC's programmes, whose audience figures plummeted to 14.7 per cent. Although a pervasive cynicism about the government's intentions persisted, listeners almost universally endorsed the role of radio in tackling such an issue at such a time.[51]

During the 1945 general election the BBC's mission to inform came into its own, as it cast itself as the conduit between politician and citizenry. With so much apparently at stake, many commentators remarked on the unexpected quietness of the campaign, in particular the low turnout at political meetings. Yet, public interest in the election broadcasts was unprecedented. The equivalent broadcasts during the previous general election in 1935 had attracted audiences estimated at about 25 per cent (though Baldwin had attracted about 40 per cent). The 26 election addresses broadcast between 4 and 30 June 1945 averaged almost 45 per cent (around 15 million listeners, comparable with the audience for a top Variety broadcast), with remarkably little variation between parties or speakers.[52]

As McCallum and Readman noted in the first Nuffield election survey, the evidence from the broadcasts both explained in part the apparent quietness of the campaign (electors chose to listen to the broadcasts rather than attend meetings) and also rebutted some people's suggestions that electors were, contrary to expectations, apathetic about the issues facing the country ('since much interest and concentration were required of the elector if he were to sit through, and listen intelligently to, twenty minutes of political argument from an unseen voice, often of dull delivery'). While no clear evidence exists for the effect of these broadcasts (Churchill's infamous 'Gestapo' broadcast that opened the radio campaign, for instance, appears to have confirmed rather than changed listeners' attitudes), the public's turning to radio during the election appeared to mark a new trend in British political culture: a more widespread engagement with the political debate and a more serious search for information on which to base voting intentions. What remained in question was the longer-term effect. Would it make for a clearer-sighted and more rational electorate, less distracted by demagoguery and emotional appeals, or a more passive electorate, willing to listen but not to get involved?[53]

From its overt early wartime patriotism through the changing focus on the British people during and after 1940 and then the increasing emphasis on reconstruction in the last years of war, the progressive shift in the character and vocabulary of national identity on the wartime BBC was considerable and wide-ranging. When, in September 1944, the new director of music Victor Hely-Hutchinson came across the BBC's forgotten 'patriotic hymns', he was appalled by both the tunes and the reasons for their commissioning.[54]

During the war, the BBC made a sincere effort to respond to new public demands and moods, and to break out of its London-centric middle-class tone and preoccupations. The success of the new approach was mixed. Such laboured programme titles as *Politics and the Ordinary Man* or the *Working Man Looks at Reconstruction* still smacked of paternalism, and listeners continued to complain about artificial and over-optimistic broadcasts.[55] However, the style and tone of wartime radio often owed more to wartime production constraints (such as the prohibition on live debate that made scripted discussions unavoidable) than to systemic 'middle-classness'. During the war, the BBC set out to address the concerns, fears and aspirations of the majority of the public in new and more inclusive ways.

They thus both reflected and perpetuated the contemporary idealization of 'the people's war'.

The response of listeners themselves to these developments demonstrated both a clear dislike of traditional stereotypes and an unwillingness to break completely away from them. Just as in other manifestations of the 'myth of the blitz', one finds a reciprocal construction of national identity: the BBC adapted its portrayals to circumstance and to public opinion, these portrayals then became part of the wider popular culture, to be modified again in turn. Such innovations as the introduction of a greater range of dialect voices to national audiences were mostly welcomed — yet the much derided 'BBC accent' had the virtue that it was one of the most generally understood across Britain, many listeners also continued to consider it 'more appropriate' for such broadcasts as the news. The introduction of Wilfred Pickles as newsreader caused more hostility in the North than the South.

In addressing the public not simply as an audience but as a citizenry, the BBC also reflected and represented the debate about 'the people's peace'. Much of the BBC's coverage of the problems facing the country after the war can be criticized for both partiality and shallowness. Yet, though listeners remained cynical about government plans, they clearly appreciated and responded to the broadcast debate on reconstruction. Audience response to *Jobs for All* and its precursors suggests that the undoubted anxiety and mistrust felt by a large proportion of the general public about Britain's postwar reconstruction plans by no means implied a lack of interest.[56] Indeed, the evidence of interest in the subject substantially surpasses the MOI's own identification in its 1942 survey of a 'thinking minority' of between 5 and 20 per cent of the population interested in reconstruction.

Public responses to these new conceptions of 'citizenship' were complex and even contradictory. The British public appears not to have undergone a revolutionary transformation in either self-perception or political outlook during the war. Responses to such wartime challenges as evacuation suggest a good deal of ambivalence about some of the implications of wartime community feeling, and all too frequently national unity appears to have been an aspiration rather than a statement of fact.[57] In the pages of the *Daily Express*, Strube's 'little man' remained the same put-upon victim of (wartime) bureaucracy and petty injustice as before, albeit with a new heroic streak. But, if the ideals of citizenship to which people looked in 1945 were not as wholehearted or interventionist as some historians have liked to think, they were certainly not as passive as others have maintained. The electorate of 1945 had a more clearly articulated choice in 1945 than in any previous election and appears to have approached that choice with 'great seriousness'.[58] It is in this context that one can identify the vote for Labour in 1945 as a vote for active citizenship. That voters appear not to have expected Labour to win suggests that some of the old interwar passivity still remained.

Interestingly, after 1945 the BBC failed to capitalize on many of the most important features of its wartime development. The postwar BBC again retreated from political controversy. By its restructuring in 1946, the 'mixed' scheduling of the Reithian era was abandoned in favour of stratification by 'taste', but it was the 'middlebrow' Home Service rather than the 'lowbrow' Light Programme or 'highbrow' Third Programme that became the postwar 'voice' of the BBC.

With much fanfare, Director-General William Haley reinstituted regional programming on the Home Service in 1946, specifically to foster 'those national and local cultures which are an enduring part of our heritage'; yet, the reintroduction of varying regional schedules prompted new disagreements over the definition of a 'region' for broadcasting purposes, controversy about the role and purpose of broadcasting to the regions, and a questioning of the internal 'competition' that regional broadcasting purported to encourage.[59] Ironically, the postwar BBC would be seen in many respects as more homogeneously 'home counties', middle-class and middle-brow than ever before.

Meanwhile, the wartime attempts by the BBC and others to reject simplistic stereotypes of national identity and provide practical, useful and realistic representations of the British citizen and his or her aspirations, seem to have achieved above all the substitution of one stereotype for another. In the postwar years, John Citizen's People's War would become a cliché of national identity as powerful as that of John Bull's Island.

Notes

1. See Angus Calder (1969) *The People's War: Britain 1939–1945*, London; Paul Addison (1975) *The Road to 1945: British Politics and the Second World War*, London. Recent challenges include Correlli Barnett (1986) *The Audit of War: The Illusion and Reality of Britain as a Great Nation*, London, Chapters 1–2; Harold L. Smith (ed.) (1986) *War and Social Change: British Society in the Second World War*, Manchester; Kevin Jefferys (1991) *The Churchill Coalition and Wartime Politics*, Manchester; Stephen Fielding (1992) 'What did "the people" want? The meaning of the 1945 General Election', *Historical Journal*, vol. 35, no. 3, pp. 623–9. See also Stephen Fielding, Peter Thompson and Nick Tiratsoo (1995) *'England Arise!' The Labour Party and Popular Politics in 1940s Britain*, Manchester, Chapter 2.

2. For the importance of investigating the 'changes of meaning of the vocabulary of patriotism and citizenship', see Miles Taylor (1990) 'Patriotism, history and the left in twentieth-century Britain', *Historical Journal*, vol. 33, no. 4, pp. 987 and *passim*.

3. See, for example, Addison, *Road to 1945*, pp. 118–19 and 144–5; and Fielding, Thompson and Tiratsoo, *'England Arise!'*, pp. 66–7. For studies of the BBC's wartime role, see Asa Briggs (1970) *The War of Words*, London; David Cardiff and Paddy Scannell (1981) 'Radio in World War II', U203 Popular Culture, Block 2, Unit 8, Milton Keynes, Open University Press; and Jean Seaton (1991) 'Broadcasting and the Blitz', in J. Curran and J. Seaton, *Power Without Responsibility: The Press and Broadcasting in Britain*, London.

4. Wickham Steed (1930) *The Real Stanley Baldwin*, London, quotation from dust jacket of first edition. For interwar national identity, see Martin Wiener (1981) *English Character and the Decline of the Industrial Spirit 1850-1980*, Cambridge; John M. MacKenzie (1984) *Propaganda and Empire: The Manipulation of British Public Opinion 1880–1960*, Manchester; Alan Howkins (1986) 'The discovery of rural England', in R. Colls and P. Dodd (eds) *Englishness: Politics and Culture 1880–1920*, London; Alex Potts (1989) '"Constable country" between the wars', in R. Samuel (ed.) *Patriotism*, vol. 3, National Fictions, London; Malcolm Chase (1989) 'This is no claptrap; this is our heritage', in C. Shaw and M. Chase (eds) *The Imagined Past: History and Nostalgia*, Manchester; Angus Calder (1991) *The Myth of the Blitz*, London, Chapter 9; Siân Nicholas (1996) 'The construction of a national identity: Stanley Baldwin, "Englishness" and the mass media in interwar Britain', in M. Francis and I. Zweiniger-Bargielowska (eds) *The Conservatives and British Society 1880–1990*, Cardiff.

5. H. V. Morton (1927) *Introduction to Strube: His Cartoons from the Daily Express*, London.

6.   See Colin Seymour-Ure and Jim Schoff (1985) *David Low*, London, pp. 28, 80–1, 129.

7.   David Low (1942) *British Cartoonists, Caricaturists and Comic Artists*, London, p. 45. See also Percy Fearon (1920) *One Hundred Poy Cartoons: From the London Evening News and Daily Mail*, London; the *Daily Express*' annual collections of Strube cartoons; and Roy Douglas (1992) *Between the Wars 1919–39: The Cartoonists' Vision*, London.

8.   Neil Grant (1984) 'Citizen soldiers: Army education in World War II', in [Formations collective] *Formations of Nation and People*, London, pp. 171–3.

9.   Hilda Jennings and Winifred Gill (1939) *Broadcasting and Everyday Life*, London, p. 40.

10. Paddy Scannell and David Cardiff (1987) 'Broadcasting and national unity', in J. Curran, A. Smith and P. Wingate (eds) *Impacts and Influences: Essays in Media Power in the Twentieth Century*, London, pp. 158–66.

11. See Asa Briggs (1965) *The Golden Age of Wireless*, London; and Paddy Scannell and David Cardiff (1991) *A Social History of British Broadcasting*, vol. 1: *Serving the Nation*, Oxford.

12. See Taylor, 'Patriotism', p. 982.

13. Grant, 'Citizen soldiers', p. 171.

14. *Listener*, 2 November 1939, p. 349.

15. Ian McLaine (1979) *Ministry of Morale: Home Front Morale and the Ministry of Information in World War II*, London, p. 21. See also Calder, *Myth of the Blitz*, p. 196.

16. See Briggs, *Golden Age*, pp. 625–50; and Siân Nicholas (1966) *Echo of War: Home Front Propaganda and the Wartime BBC, 1939–1945*, Manchester, pp. 15–22.

17. *Listener*, 14 December 1939, p. 1162.

18. 'The "Jerusalem" brand', Reith to Ogilvie, 21 February 1940, BBC Written Archive Centre, Caversham (hereafter BBC WAC) File R27/213/1. See also Note on Scheme for Commissioning Patriotic Songs, August 1940, and Boult to Vaughan Williams, 9 September 1940, BBC WAC R27/58. After a fraught production history they were finally broadcast on 14 December 1941. They were not considered a great success.

19. See the *Listener*, 4 January 1940, pp. 7–9.

20. *Listener*, 8 February 1940, p. 287.

21. Lee to Nicolls, 23 October 1939, BBC WAC R28/121/1.

22. *Radio Times*, 9 February 1940.

23. Dr J. J. Mallon, BBC talk reprinted in the *Listener*, 6 June 1940, p. 1084.

24. *Listener*, 4 July 1940, p. 10.

25. *Listener*, 8 May 1941, p. 680.

26. See *Listener*, 20 June 1940, p. 1176; 18 July 1940, p. 104; also Records of Propaganda Broadcasts October 1940, PRO INF1/172. W. E. Williams was also director of the Army Bureau of Current Affairs, 1941–5.

27. See the *Listener*, 2 April 1942, p. 444. One might also mention in this context Dorothy L. Sayers's dramatic serial, *The Man Born to be King*, first broadcast in December 1941. Sayers's adaptation of the life of Christ broke new ground by dramatizing the story in colloquial language ('as a piece of real life'). It prompted a heated public debate, but was very popular with audiences. See Briggs, *War of Words*, pp. 626–30; and Kenneth M. Wolfe (1984) *The Churches and the British Broadcasting Corporation 1922–1956: The Politics of Broadcast Religion*, London, pp. 218–38.

28. See Bruce Belfrage (1951) *One Man in his Time*, London, pp. 129, 111–12.

29. See *Manchester Guardian*, 17 and 18 November 1941; LR/533, 2 January 1942, BBC WAC R9/9/5.

30. See J. B. Priestley (1940) *Postscripts*, London. For extended discussion of Priestley's *Postscripts*, see Siân Nicholas (1995) ' "Sly demagogues" and wartime politics: J. B. Priestley and the BBC', *Twentieth Century British History*, vol. 6, no. 3, pp. 247–66.

31. *Listener* Research Department memorandum, 14 March 1941, BBC WAC Talks (Policy): J. B. Priestley, File 1. See also R. Crossman, quoted in Fielding, Thompson, Tiratsoo: "England Arise!" p. 67.

32. For examples of this 'doublethink', see Nicholas, *Echo of War*, Chapter 3.

33. See Nicholas, *Echo of War*, pp. 115–24, 139.

34. See Howard Thomas to assistant director of *Variety*, 24 March 1942, BBC WAC R19/683.

35. See Barnett, *Audit of War*, pp. 22–3.

36. This, he pointed out, might have an adverse response with both home opinion and the Americans. Maconachie to Nicolson, 16 March 1941, BBC WAC R51/383.

37. Ryan to Nicolson, 20 March 1941, BBC WAC R51/383.

38. *Listener*, 6 November 1941, p. 640; 29 January 1942. p. 136.

39. For ABCA, see Grant, 'Citizen soldiers', and cf. S. P. Mackenzie (1992) *Politics and Military Morale: Current Affairs and Citizenship Education in the British Army 1914–1950*, Oxford.

40. See Addison, *Road to 1945*, pp. 181–9; Jose Harris (1983) 'Did British workers want the Welfare State? G. D. H. Cole's Survey of 1942', in J. M. Winter (ed.) *The Working Class in British Politics*, Cambridge, pp. 213–14; Rodney Lowe (1990) 'The Second World War, consensus, and the welfare state', *Twentieth Century British History*, vol. 1, no. 2, p. 176; and LR/1330, 24 November 1942, BBC WAC R9/9/6.

41. See relevant internal BBC correspondence September 1942 to March 1943, BBC WAC R51/39; also Nicholas, *Echo of War*, pp. 250–1.

42. The motion was defeated 134–3.

43. *Listener*, 8 July 1943, p. 35.
44. *Listener*, 30 September 1943, p. 372.
45. LR/2117, 21 October 1943, BBC WAC R9/5/96.
46. LR/2553, 22 April 1944, BBC WAC R9/9/8.
47. LR/2959, 21 October 1944, BBC WAC R9/5/97.
48. Addison, *Road to 1945*, p. 248.
49. *Jobs for All* is only briefly mentioned in Briggs, *War of Words*, p. 701, and is not mentioned in any of the principal works on the period. However, see Cardiff and Scannell, 'Radio in World War II', pp. 56–9.
50. Addison, *Road to 1945*, p. 247.
51. LR/3164, January 1945, BBC WAC R9/9/9.
52. For 1935 listening figures, see Briggs, *Golden Age*, p. 141. For 1945 figures see R. B. McCallum and Alison Readman (1964) *The British General Election of 1945*, London, p.154. Labour and Liberal broadcasts averaged 44.5 per cent. Conservative broadcasts averaged 45.4 per cent, principally because Churchill's three broadcasts attracted the highest audiences (49 per cent).
53. McCallum and Readman, *British General Election of 1945*, pp. 153–5.
54. See file correspondence 19–29 September 1944, BBC WAC R27/58.
55. See Cardiff and Scannell, 'Radio in World War II', *passim*.
56. See Addison, *Road to 1945*, p. 248; and Fielding, 'What did "the people" want?', p. 632.
57. 'Whether or not people lived up to [their wartime ideals], they knew that they ought to' (Addison, *Road to 1945*, p. 18).
58. Ellen Wilkinson, quoted by McCallum and Readman, *The British General Election of 1945*, p. 155
59. Asa Briggs (1979) *Sound and Vision*, Oxford, pp. 84–117.

3. Citizenship, nationhood and empire in British official film propaganda, 1939–45

Toby Haggith

The Second World War forced the British state to confront established views of national identity and citizenship. A Nazi-controlled Europe and the protracted nature of the war, made it imperative to revise inappropriately conservative ideas of citizenship, class and empire as increasing demands were made on people at home, and as it became vital to win and maintain the support of international allies, particularly the USA.

Government propaganda and information films were one of the most important and obvious media through which to explore and display a revamped image of Britain. Some 26 such films that were released to the public, as well as a representative sample of films, mainly produced by the Ministry of Information (MOI), are used in this chapter to examine how new concepts of nation, citizenship and empire were presented.[1] There is evidence of a gradual democratization as the concepts underpinning the political and social status quo were reoriented from hierarchical and conservative definitions to more populist and dynamic versions. Other government films, however, adhered to a more traditional and conservative view of Britain and the empire.

Since the First World War, when the British government made widespread use of film for information and propaganda purposes, there had been a growing interest and belief in official circles in the value of film for promoting a positive image of the nation both at home and overseas.[2] That the government only made indirect use of films between the wars was more a reflection of Treasury constraints

than a lack of faith in the medium.[3] Indeed, the Ministry of Health
was so keen to use film propaganda that it pursued a policy of
cooperation with such commercial producers as the Gas Light &
Coke Company and Pearl Assurance.[4]

Moreover, with the advent of sound, the argument for film
propaganda became even stronger, for it facilitated the transmission
of more sophisticated messages. By the end of the 1930s, the
cinema's popularity as a form of entertainment meant that it was
potentially one of the best ways of communicating with the public.[5]
The prewar planners in the MOI were convinced of the value of film
during wartime and envisaged the government needing to distribute
information and propaganda films, largely obtained by commissioning independent companies, but also produced directly by its own
film unit, a role earmarked for the GPO Film Unit.

Much has been written about the wartime portrayal of Britain in
the cinema, but so far the majority of work has concentrated on
feature films, with little systematic study of official films. Historians
have made valuable observations about wartime films, but one of the
most relevant, and on which there is general agreement, is that
British films became more democratic during the war, that is they
portrayed the working classes more directly and more sympathetic-
ally. Feature films, such as *The Foreman Went to France* (1941),
Millions Like Us (1943) and *The Bells Go Down* (1943), stressed the
contribution of ordinary people to the war effort and argued in
favour of more social cohesion and a fairer distribution of rewards.
This is explained as a cinematic manifestation of the popular historical thesis that the conditions of the Second World War produced a
sea change in political attitudes resulting in the Labour victory of
1945 and the creation of the welfare state.[6] A more honest portrayal
of the life of ordinary British people, and of society in general, is also
seen as a result of the blending of realistic documentary film styles
with feature film methods. One of the purposes of this chapter is to
see whether this theory can be applied to official films.

Before analysing the films themselves, it is first necessary to
explain the process of their production and distribution. The degree
of state involvement in the production of film during the Second
World War was considerable. In organizational strength and film

output, it dwarfed the official film propaganda efforts of the First World War. It has been estimated that 1887 films were released for public viewing between 1939 and 1946, a statistic that does not include the millions of feet of film used by the military for reconnaissance work, operational assessment and for weaponry research and trials.[7]

As in the First World War, propaganda films of military campaigns, such as *Wavell's 30,000* (1942) and *Malta Convoy* (1944), were again produced. The major change from the previous war, however, lay in the scale and breadth of films released that related to matters on the home front. The exigencies of war resulted in the production of many films to instruct and inform people about how to tackle a variety of new procedures and situations. These ranged from explaining how to extinguish an incendiary bomb and fill in a new ration book to entreaties to save water when having a bath. Films also performed a number of direct domestic propaganda functions, such as countering communist subversion on Clydeside,[8] encouraging dockers to speed up turn-around,[9] and publicizing the efforts of farm workers to increase agricultural production.[10]

The bulk of film production for the public was overseen by the MOI (624 films), but other government departments, notably the British Council (72), the Colonial Film Unit (72) and the War Office also produced such films.[11] The role of the MOI's film division was to coordinate the production of all government film, organize distribution of these films and make foreign language versions for release overseas. In the early part of the war, senior MOI and film division staff conceived many of the ideas for films and there was little involvement from other ministries. But, as the war progressed, the use of film by the government in general grew rapidly. By 1943, it has been estimated, 50 per cent of the film division's 'budget was spent in close collaboration with other ministries'.[12]

MOI film commissions were shared out between its own production unit, the Crown Film Unit (formerly the GPO Unit) and a large number of independent film companies ranging from commercial companies such as Ealing, which usually produced feature films, to small documentary companies such as the Shell Film Unit, which specialized in technical films generally reaching small audiences. Documentary producers were given the majority of projects not awarded to Crown. In part, this can be explained by the close links that existed between some of the personnel of the film division and British documentary film making.[13]

However, the type and scale of government film work meant that there were sound practical reasons for enlisting the documentary film units for government production. First, documentary producers with their smaller staff and lower overheads were cheaper than commercial studios and more used to working with smaller budgets. Second, the particular film-making skills of documentary producers (using animation, diagrams and explaining technical processes) suited the informational and instructional style of many official films. Third, it was thought that documentary producers were more attuned to the notion of public information than commercial companies who aimed for 'box office appeal'.[14]

Despite these rational explanations, at least one historian has argued that documentary film makers were able to secure a disproportionate share of government film contracts by taking control of the MOI film division to peddle their own socialist propaganda.[15] As has been argued in depth elsewhere, this is a distortion.[16] Film makers working on government projects were highly constrained by the political and bureaucratic environment in which they worked; and this conclusion is borne out by looking at the range of government projects undertaken by politically radical film makers. For example, Strand Films, which was one of the most avowedly left-wing companies, produced both the controversial *Wales, Green Mountain, Black Mountain* (1942) and the conservative *The New Britain* (1940).

Distribution of MOI films was achieved in two ways. First, during a five-minute slot (later extended to fifteen) in every cinema programme and second, through the government's own non-theatrical network, whereby 16 mm prints were shown for free in factories, village halls and building sites. It is estimated that between 1942 and 1943, there were four million regular viewers on the non-theatrical circuit, although this was a fraction of commercial audiences.[17] Films for the non-theatrical circuit were held at the Central Film Library (CFL) and could be ordered directly from there, in addition to being regularly distributed around the country. The CFL catalogue mainly comprised films produced by the government, but it also included a number of films on topics of public information that had been sponsored by independent organizations and commercial organizations, such as *Housing Problems* (1935), financed by the British Commercial Gas Association, and *The Harvest Shall Come* (1943), which was funded by ICI.

The analysis presented in this chapter refers to approximately fifty official films released to the public during the war. Five of the films have been chosen for particularly close analysis. These are *If War Should Come* (1939), *The New Britain* (1940), *Dawn Guard* (1941), *Battle of the Books* (1941) and *Words and Actions* (1944).[18] These titles were chosen because all, with the exception of *Words and Actions*, received theatrical distribution and were, in consequence, viewed widely. Moreover, each clearly set out the key elements of democratization outlined above. Care has also been taken to select films that represent the work of a range of production companies (documentary and commercial) that had undertaken a substantial number of government commissions.

Not surprisingly, early propaganda shorts did not question or challenge a traditional view of the nation. British democracy was portrayed in an institutional and hierarchical fashion with images of the Houses of Parliament a recurring theme. The first official film to be released to the public, *If War Should Come* (1939), was designed to prepare the public for war and for air raids in particular.

The film opens with scenes of crowds in Downing Street and Parliament Square, apparently waiting for news and reassurance about the outbreak of war from their political leaders. Saloon cars draw up, delivering the nation's leaders to Westminster, presumably to hear and discuss the announcement of war. Brief sequences of British soldiers, the RAF and policeman follow, cutting back to scenes of Parliament Square to reinforce the message that our defence is rooted in this ancient British institution. Once hostilities had started, Parliament Square was shown as a fortified outpost of democracy, ringed defiantly with barbed wire, as in *Britain at Bay* (1940) and circled by armoured cars in *Words for Battle* (1941). This ordered and hierarchical imagery reflected the language of official propaganda guidelines, which spoke of 'the leaders and the led' and called upon 'you — the people'[19] to prepare for suffering and sacrifice.[20]

Images of the British countryside and pastoral life were another regular feature of propaganda films, often providing an emotional framing for other more political images. For example, *If War Should Come* ends with a timeless farmyard scene of men loading hay on to a horse-drawn cart, the emotion of the image reinforced with a swell of classical music. *Health in War* (1940), too, looked back to an idyllic Britain of village cricket, hay gathering in horse-drawn carts and carefree citizens running on wide beaches to introduce its survey of Britain's wartime health-care arrangements. These kinds of images had been specifically suggested for a 'reassurance' film, planned as early as June 1939.[21] Such scenes aimed to calm urban populations expecting massive devastation and loss of life from enemy bombers, but they also suggested or reinforced an idealized vision of nation; in fact, rural images remained common in official propaganda films, long after the threat from bombing had begun to subside.

In the summer of 1940, the MOI film division's planning committee instructed Jack Beddington, head of production, to prepare a 'short film on "What Britain means", with pictures of the countryside accompanied by music or spoken verse'.[22] The product of these instructions, *Words for Battle* (1941), presents an essentially conservative view of the nation. Although quotes from Lincoln's Gettysburg Address and Blake's *Jerusalem* infer a 'people's democracy', the imperial and militaristic tones of the quotations from Kipling, Churchill, and Browning are what endure. The imagery of rural Britain, its old towns and fine churches, present an uncomplicated and timeless nation, divorced from the political and social problems associated with cities and industry.

Britain at Bay (1940) opened with a defiant scene of a soldier on guard by the seashore, followed by romantic rural scenes of Britain's undulating countryside and the honest labour of the men who work its farms. The sense of reassurance is reinforced by the commentary's theme, delivered by J. B. Priestley, that Britain's historical development was organic and peaceful; a nation without a civil war for 200 years, which had tackled its problems alone and in a peaceful fashion. By contrast, *Peace and Plenty* (1939), a film made for the Communist Party and distributed independently, deployed images of rural England in a sarcastic and ironic fashion. Opening with scenes of the white cliffs of Dover and British countryside, the film bitterly attacked the government's appeasement of fascism and the widespread poverty of the British people.[23]

Behind the scenes, politicians responsible for guiding propaganda were becoming more acutely aware of the particular ideological challenges presented by the Second World War. As early as December 1939, a cabinet paper on propaganda produced by the minister of information, Lord Macmillan, discussed the problems presented by the fact that both Nazi and communist regimes had achieved massive social change through revolution. Macmillan suggested that, to avoid the criticism that British war aims were merely to defend the old order, some declaration of peace aims might be necessary. In his view, however, a considerable degree of caution was required; while the war could, and should, be seen as an opportunity for the nation to move forward from the old order, modernization would not involve the destruction of an age-old civilization.[24] Thus, he suggested, the themes for propaganda should be: '(a) the sanctity of absolute values; (b) the sanctity of the individual and the family; (c) the community of nations'.[25] At the heart of the document, as in the minds of many of Britain's policy-makers, lay a sense of ambivalence. While they were aware that some break with the old image of Britain would be needed in order to maintain credibility, the actual substance of this new world was unformed and frequently seemed little different from the old.

A related concern, held by those responsible for propaganda, was that the people were unresponsive and apathetic about the war effort. A recurrent theme of the MOI planning committee's meetings during the summer of 1940 was the need to counteract feelings of defeatism by making people think more closely about what life would be like under a dictatorship: 'Don't think you'll be as well off under Hitler,' was a suggested slogan.[26] MOI officials based in New York suggested that British propaganda should show that the war was in the people's interest, and that a German victory would have dire consequences for British life, effecting a 'radical change in the education of children, and the destruction of everything achieved by the working class "both through it's own struggles and through the cooperation of the Conservative Party"; a deterioration in the standard of living, and the destruction of Christianity'.[27]

Films such as *The New Britain*, *Health in War* and *Welfare of the Workers* (1940) reflected these new guidelines. Significantly *The New Britain* (1940) opens with archive footage of British troops on the Western Front, and the words that after the war 'Britain turned to build a new world. Over one million dead we raised this colossal monument. A new architecture for our people.'[28] The next section catalogues British achievements since 1918: footage of modern bridges, hydroelectric plants, new roads, factories and other techno-logical advances is paraded before us, the laudatory commentary punctuated with the warning, 'But we forgot Germany'. Turning to Britain's social achievements, the film outlines advances in health care, maternity treatment, nursery schools and public housing. As a man is seen striding confidently up the path of his suburban semi-detached, the commentary informs us that four million houses were built and 'a million people exchanged slums for sun'. A new kind of society has been created where the state undertakes to provide a number of protections and benefits for the people, irrespective of class. But this has been a move towards greater equality without recourse to revolution: 'We had our revolution quietly, no Brown shirts here.' There is a clear inference of an ongoing contract between the state and the people, by which the state's demands on it's citizens during war are to be rewarded in peacetime by improvements in general living conditions.

Dawn Guard, *Post 23* and *Five and Under* struck a different note in official propaganda films. Not only were they critical of interwar Britain, the unemployment, slum housing, poverty and empty government promises of the post-1918 period, but they asserted that the people would not allow a repeat of this situation, at the end of the second war in as many generations.

In *Dawn Guard*, two rustics of the Home Guard chew over the meaning and implications of the war while on watch by a windmill. The Nazis are likened to a sewer draining all over Europe threatening to destroy a 'liberty we had and never thought about'. These 'savages' are presented as a threat to a timeless tradition of Englishness, but a new note is struck. The younger of the two men points out how the war, by forcing the people to contemplate the meaning of their nationhood, has led to the realization that all has not been rosy. Mention is made of the unemployment and housing problems of the interwar years, illustrated with library footage of slum children. The two men determine that in the postwar period the new-found togetherness and purpose of the war will be channelled into 'a fine peace effort', which will bring jobs for all and eradicate the slums. By contrast with films such as *Health in War* and *The New Britain*, these films are surprisingly vehement in their attack on the broken promises of 1918. Particularly striking is the repeated inclusion of some famous sequences illustrating the poverty of the Depression: unemployed veterans busking, unemployed miners scouring for coal on the side of a slag heap and children playing in the gutters of slum-lined streets. The power of these images is frequently reinforced with biting commentary, as in the films scripted by Dylan Thomas:

> *Remember the procession of the old-young men*
> *From dole to corner and back again,*
> *From the pinched, packed streets to the peak of slag*
> *In the bite of the winters with shovel and bag,*
> *With a drooping fag and a turned up collar, . . .*
> (*Wales, Green Mountain, Black Mountain*, 1943)

The release of *Dawn Guard* was particularly welcomed by the *Documentary Newsletter*, the mouthpiece of those film makers who had, since the beginning of the war, argued vociferously that the discussion of a better postwar world was not only vital for maintaining public support, but a moral requirement of the government.[29] However, this does not mean that films like *Wales, Green Mountain, Black Mountain*, *Coalminer*, or *New Towns for Old* were made simply because of the existence of left-wing film makers. A conspiracy theory can only be sustained if one ignores the voices of those within government who were keen to discuss peace aims. From as early as December 1939, as we have seen, members of the government and various civil servants argued that the discussion of reconstruction would be a major boost to propaganda. But until the signing of the Atlantic Charter and the release of the Beveridge Report, the BBC and MOI were cautious about encouraging public discussion of peace aims for fear of raising objections from Churchill and others on the right wing of the Conservative Party. After the charter was signed, however, the atmosphere changed, with one MOI official suggesting that parts of the document, such as Article Six on freedom from fear and want, be used as the basis for propaganda.[30]

There was also a realization within Whitehall that the problems of the past could not be ignored if propaganda was to be authentic. Such realism was not limited to the MOI, where many of the most progressive public relations experts worked. Even at the Foreign Office (which funded the British Council) concern with the image of Britain abroad encouraged officials to take a positive and pragmatic attitude to film propaganda. When asked to comment on the treatment for the British Council's film on the history of town planning, they were enthusiastic, even approving some of the more critical aspects of the narrative: 'It is just as well to make a clean breast of our slum problems since the foreigner knows that these exist and the enemy makes capital out of them by reminding the world of their existence. As the public will in the film be shown the proposed remedies, the film can do nothing but good.'[31]

As this episode indicates, criticism of the past could be sanctioned in films where there was a resolution in the form of hopes and plans for peace. It also underlines the importance of foreign relations in the consideration of propaganda. During the war, British politicians and officials were very concerned about the power of German film propaganda distributed in neutral countries. German newsreels, in particular, were envied for the vivid nature of their campaign film, and the fast and wide distribution achieved.[32] German propaganda aimed to present Britain as an imperialist and class-bound nation in which the working class was downtrodden and in poor health.[33] MOI officials were anxious to counteract the impact of these messages, especially in the USA, where there was already evidence of a good deal of anti-British feeling.[34] Indeed, the MOI was so concerned about German propaganda film that it secretly destroyed film copies bound for the USA that had been impounded by British customs.[35]

Allied to the promises of a fresh start after the war was the discussion of a new kind of democracy. Films such as *Battle of the Books* (1941), *Ask CAB* (1942), *ABCA* (1943), *Words and Actions* (1944) and *Public Opinion* (1945), indeed, directly addressed the question of democracy and citizenship in wartime Britain. Unlike *Britain at Bay* or *The New Britain*, these films deliberately shifted the focus of democracy away from Parliament and towards informal and localized forums, such as trade unions, local councils and civil defence groups, advocating a new kind of citizenship that was direct, local and responsive. As the commentary in *Words and Actions* puts it, 'most of us confuse democracy with the machinery that's set up to conduct it. Parliament, councils, courts of justice etc. But the reality of democracy is made up of the everyday actions of its citizens in their homes and the everyday places where they work.'

Battle of the Books (1941) compared the attitudes to intellectual freedom in Germany and Britain. The film starts with scenes of Nazis burning books considered dangerous and immoral. By contrast, in the Britain we are shown, the war has led to a greater access to books of all types and an expansion in reading. The government's efforts to encourage wide and fulfilling reading, such as a system of travelling libraries and a scheme to supply free books to troops wherever they are posted, are examined. The development of cheap publishing, particularly on subjects of contemporary interest, is also lauded: 'The war has brought a flood of little pamphlets and books: on politics, scientific, controversial. ... Argument sharpens our wits and each new book and pamphlet is one more truth and freedom to speak our minds.'

Battle of the Books heralded the expansion of serious reading as an indication of the increased participation of ordinary people in political debate and, by implication, suggested that British democracy was being broadened and given greater vitality through its informed constituency. Similar claims were also made for wartime art. *Out of Chaos* (1944) cited the flocks of ordinary people taking up artistic activities, visiting exhibitions and attending concerts of classical music, as an indication of a popular interest in high art. *Breathing Space* (1943) argued that interest in British culture in general was experiencing a revival: 'all the arts are more accessible now, it's art for everybody.' But 'Art', like reading, was not just a leisure pursuit, it had a serious purpose: it was 'part of what we're fighting for, part of what we're fighting with'.

Words and Actions (1944) presented four examples of popular democratic action: the setting up of a street fire-watching group; a woman going to court to fight a hire purchase company; a harassed mother with money problems applying for a special allowance, and a woman cooking communal meals for a group of war workers. Although the film served as propaganda for the government's responses to a number of war-related problems, its main message was to encourage people to seize the initiative and become active in the public sphere. Interestingly, the state is shown to adopt a distinctly anti-capitalist line, taking the side of the vulnerable citizen in the courts when facing rapacious landlords and hire purchase companies.

Moving on to a discussion of the broader applications of people's democracy, the commentary of *Words and Actions* argues that it is 'rule by the people instead of industrial exploitation' that has ensured many of the most crucial improvements in people's lives, such as the end of child employment in the mines and the abolition of slavery. Moreover, accepted elements of British democratic life, such as trade unions, universal suffrage, and women MPs, have only been achieved because ordinary people have shown the commitment to fight for their rights. Returning to the opening theme of the film, the commentary stresses the significance of popular politics for the future of Britain:

Democracy means people taking the lead and backing their opinion with actions. The future of Britain will depend on the active involvement of these new citizens, introduced to politics by the conditions of war. The future will be decided by people who think things out for themselves, who know what they want and go all out to get it. These are the people who will make victory and make it a stepping stone to a worthy peace.

Words and Actions could be regarded as a special case because it was produced independently of the MOI and funded by the gas industry.

However, official approval of the sentiments expressed in the film must have been forthcoming, for it was added to the Central Film Library and screened through the MOI non-theatrical network. Moreover, similar themes were taken up in official films produced by the MOI and the Army Bureau of Current Affairs (ABCA) section of the War Office. For example, the MOI films *The Cotswold Club* (1944) and *Good Neighbours* (1945) also encouraged local initiative and cooperative effort, such as the establishment of a Village Produce Association and the building of a community centre.

The ABCA film *Public Opinion* (1945) presented British political tradition in a dynamic and populist fashion with pressure groups and trade unions credited with many civilizing reforms and political advances. Parliamentary legislation was described as 'simply the effect of public opinion getting what it wants done, things we want done like freedom from poverty, freedom from squalor, freedom from disease'.

Films that depicted Britain in more traditional and conservative terms, such as *The New Britain* and *Britain at Bay*, tended to adopt a formal documentary approach. Footage was assembled together in a structure dictated by the unseen commentator's script, a form not dissimilar to a leisurely paced newsreel. By contrast, as films about a new citizenship were aiming to stimulate mass participation in politics, it was necessary to adopt more populist styles. For example, in *Dawn Guard* the characters face the camera as they discuss the state of Britain, involving us in their musings and considerations. The viewer is in effect invited to take part in the film and comment on the scenes of unemployment, slum housing and poverty portrayed. Alternatively, a debate was staged between characters. In *New Towns for Old*, a blunt northerner, an advocate of urban planning, guides a highly sceptical southerner around 'Smokedale', initiating a polemical discussion about the merits of town planning. At the end of the film the two men look straight into the camera and address the audience directly, encouraging their participation in the political process:

Southerner: 'Yes you've got your plans for your town all right, but who's going to see that they don't just stay plans, who's going to make your dreams come true?'

(Both men turn to the camera and the northerner points his pipe into the camera)

Northerner: 'They are. You're the only folk that can make this plan come true. Not only plans for this town but for every town. For *your* town!' (The camera closes in on the man's face.) 'Remember it's your town!'

The director of *Builders* (1942), Pat Jackson, experimented with a technique later known as the 'subjective camera' so that the audience would be more engaged with the construction workers depicted in the film.[36]

> In planning this film an effort has been made to avoid the use of an impersonal commentator speaking in the familiar persuasive way about his subject and coldly introducing various characters to the audience. The aim here is to be the voice in conjunction with the camera so that together they react as a human being to what they see and the people they meet on the site. Therefore every member in the audience, will feel as though he is a frequent visitor to factory sites and will be agreeably surprised to be hailed by old acquaintances and to join in an informal discussion with them by means of his spokesman — the camera commentator.[37]

The documentary practice of featuring real people and situations, pioneered in prewar films like *Housing Problems* (1935) and *Workers and Jobs* (1935), was fully in tune with the wartime portrayal of populist democracy. Real people engaged in their usual activity were used in many films, notably the construction gang featured in *Builders* (1942). Increasingly, 'workers' or regional accents replaced the usual BBC or Oxbridge accent for film commentary.

Before the war, the portrayal of the working class in commercial films was generally patronizing and bound in cliché. This was compounded by the efforts of the British Board of Film Censors to prevent the release or production of any films that attempted to portray strikes or the realities of life for the unemployed. At the beginning of the war there was some continuation of this trend, with the release of the MOI film *Dangerous Comment* (1940), in which a gang of cockney villains pass military secrets, carelessly discussed by officers and society ladies, to the Germans. But with the suffering of working-class districts during the blitz and the increasing demands made on industrial workers as a result of war production, such derogatory portrayals became grossly inappropriate and were never repeated.

Instead, there was a growing preoccupation with the lives of industrial workers and what were perceived as their concerns. During the war, at least 129 films were produced that looked at the area of work. In a number of films such as *Welfare of the Workers* (1940), *Coalminer* (1943) and *Tyneside Story* (1944) there was a marked appreciation of the role of the trade union movement and a frank airing of sensitive issues of recent industrial relations. For example, in *Coalminer* reference was made to the poor management practices of the coal industry, the mass redundancies of the Depression and even the dreaded industrial disease, pneumoconiosis. Official films did not concentrate on heavy industry or political issues. *Essential Jobs* (1942) tried to raise the morale of those workers involved in seemingly meaningless tasks, which were nonetheless vital to overall production.

Aspects of the worker's life outside the workplace were also covered, particularly those schemes introduced by the government such as factory crèches or communal feeding centres designed to lessen the strain experienced by war workers. Two special factory newsreels were produced, covering a wide range of war industries and with many up-beat items.[38] To give some meaning to often laborious war work, *Warwork News* regularly included an item demonstrating how a particular manufactured product was used in the field, occasionally reinforced by the testimony of a soldier who had operated the radio, Bren gun, or mine detector, in combat. Many people considered that propaganda for war workers should include a discussion of the prospects of a better world. A welfare officer with the Factory Welfare Board, responsible for the Southern Division, urged that all media, including film, should be exploited 'to convince war workers that the nation is concerned not merely with the prosecution of the war but with the creation of a new industrial order'.[39] *Clydebuilt* (1944), which looked at shipbuilding in Scotland, suggested that worker's democracy through the yard committee and the adoption of modern techniques such as prefabrication would continue after the war.

Worker's newsreels and other films were shown during shows for workers organized by the Ministry of Labour and the MOI and held around the country in factories and construction sites. By the middle of the war, the number of workers reached by mobile cinemas was quite impressive. In December 1942 alone, there were 478 film shows in 149 factories or construction sites.[40] For many workers, commercial cinemas were not accessible: they worked long hours or were based far from towns, so these film shows were very important.

The need to promote a positive image of Britain abroad led to a democratization of propaganda films produced by the British Council.[41] Perhaps not surprisingly for an organization funded by the Foreign Office, British Council films had generally presented a deeply traditional and conservative view of Britain. However, during the war the Film Department tried to change this policy and produce films that addressed issues in a more contemporary way. In part, this move stemmed from external pressure, particularly from the MOI, which was concerned that the British Council's films were creating a bad impression abroad and tending to reinforce enemy propaganda. Indeed, after viewing four of them (*Clyde*, *English Inns*, *Western Isles* and *Kew Gardens*), Brendan Bracken, the minister of information, complained to the Council's chairman, Malcolm Robertson:

> To audiences in neutral countries they will seem to be living proof of Goebbels's statement that the British are frivolous, or that they are fighting the war to perpetuate a way of living long since outmoded or that they have lost the intellectual, moral and industrial lead which they once held. In allied countries and the US they can only have a bewildering effect since they are in sharp contrast to our statements that we are putting every ounce into the war effort. An accumulation of films such as these could go far towards bringing neutral countries in on

the German side and allied countries and the Empire to cynicism.[42]

These pressures, plus a genuine interest in the department to present more contemporary issues, led to a change in direction. Committee discussions about new film productions, for instance, stated that a key principle should be the creation of a good impression of Britain to foreigners: 'really important films' needed to be made 'which can show the world something better than they have'. Specifically, films were to show that Britain was improving the conditions of the poor by providing services and amenities and tackling problems of housing and unemployment. It was also suggested that a film on town planning should be made.[43] As a result, a number of films were made 'on public utilities and services'.[44] They included *National Health* on improvements in public health achieved through building sewers and supplying fresh water; *Second Freedom* on state social welfare provisions such as public housing, education and those elements introduced since 1939 like vitamin C supplements for children; and *The Development of the English Town* (1943) on the nation's history of town planning. *Second Freedom* ended with a particularly explicit statement of the role of the state indicative of the new image of Britain the British Council was willing to promote.

> Today the Jack's and Mary's of all ages are cared for by the state, and in the future, when baby Jack, who has only just come into this world, grows up, conditions will be better still, there'll be even less anxiety in his manhood years, he will live in an age of increasing security. The whole art of living has advanced in our time and will move on.

During both world wars, British propaganda films had tried to boost morale at home by displaying the ideological solidarity of the empire and showing the contribution of its member nations in manpower and material. In the First World War these ties were assumed to be uncontroversial, as illustrated in the government propaganda cartoon *Britain's Effort* (1918). In the opening tableau, Britannia blows on her horn to call the nations of the empire to her side. As if by instinct, the people respond. So natural are the ties to the motherland that even the indigenous animals (such as an emu in New Zealand, an elephant in India and a moose in Canada) are seen rousing the colonial soldier to action.

Paradoxically, one of the effects of the First World War was to encourage nationalist movement's throughout the empire. The white dominions felt they had earned the right to independence as a result of their military contribution on the battlefields of Gallipoli and elsewhere, while for India and other colonies the principal of self-determination, as enshrined in the Treaty of Versailles, was regarded as an indicator of the need for change. The emerging nationalist movements threatened to undermine Britain's international status and questioned cherished ideas of the empire as a family of nations and of the superiority of British rule and systems of government. Perhaps conscious of the fragility of the empire, films of the Second World War displayed a change in attitude. For example, although the film *Empire Marches* (1941) began with the familiar statement of the empire's solidarity: 'the alarm sounded and the many people of the empire sprang to answer the call to service in the cause of liberty and justice', the film's producers did not assume the same level of blind loyalty to the mother country: 'Is it not significant that from all parts of the world, men of every race, creed and colour are marching and fighting to the common end.' In the film *Arms from India* (1941), on the subcontinent's material contribution to the allied war effort, the commentary stressed that India's future lay with the British Empire and that it had nothing to gain from any alliance with the Axis powers.

This change may also have been motivated by a fear that the idea of empire was becoming unpopular in Britain. In Gilbert Highet's paper on ways to improve British propaganda, it was stated that: 'a united home front was vital — first the public must be made to understand that the war is not an "imperialist war" — since a fairly large body of opinion in Britain cares little for the continued existence of the empire.'[45]

The British Empire was also a popular subject for Axis propaganda. Films such as *Ohm Kruger* (1941) about the Boer War, were highly critical of British colonial history. A favourite angle was to portray Commonwealth troops as the victims of British colonialism.

In an issue of the German newsreel *Die Deutsche Wochenschau* released in January 1944, a film about Sikh POWs was accompanied by the statement that while Indians shed their blood, England waged a starvation policy against the inhabitants of the subcontinent.[46] As the creation of the Indian National Army from disaffected Indian POWs had proved, there was an audience for this kind of propaganda.[47]

As the war progressed, the concept of empire underwent further changes, challenged by more egalitarian and democratic ideas of interdependence and cooperation. This was particularly notable in films produced by Paul Rotha. In *West Indies Calling* (1944), the war was seen as an opportunity for an intermixing of races, resulting in greater mutual understanding — a development that augured well for international reconstruction. In a veiled reference to independence, it was noted that West Indians serving in Britain were learning skills they could take back home after the war to improve and rebuild their own countries. In more radical films, it was argued that traditional economic and political relations between nations should be replaced by planned systems of distribution and exchange, where 'use values' would replace capitalist profit motives. *World of Plenty* (1943) and, to a lesser extent, *The Harvest Shall Come* (1942) made practically no reference to the Commonwealth or imperial preference. Instead of carving the world up into trade areas or spheres of interest, each country was simply treated as a supplier and consumer, goods being distributed on the ability to supply and the particular human consumption needs of each country. The whole principle behind this system of exchange was to eradicate world hunger, thus removing conflict and the reason for war.

There was thus a powerful trend in British official films towards a more populist and egalitarian definition of the 'British idea'. However, one should be cautious about suggesting that these developments were witnessed in all official films or reflected an underlying commitment in government to alter Britain radically. For example, films made about British colonialism in Africa showed that old fashioned attitudes and racist stereotypes were hard to shift. *Men of Africa* (1940), a film about colonial development programmes in Uganda, Kenya, and Tanganyika, was very derogatory about native

life. Africa was described as 'the home of more primitive people' and
its villages portrayed as squalid and disease-ridden communities.
There was also little respect shown for native political culture.

In *Life in a Mamprusi Village* (1944), the partnership of colonial
and indigenous government in the northern territories of the Gold
Coast was seen as enabling the removal of the worst inequalities and
corruption of the tribal state. Moreover, the commentary warned
that, despite these first tentative steps, full self-government would
not happen for a long time because of the people's primitive background. A film script about colonial administration in West Africa,
Men of Two Worlds (1946) upset some African students so much that
they not only rejected an MOI invitation to appear as extras, but
urged that the film be scrapped. A central theme of the film was the
rational role of British administration in comparison with the
mysticism and 'mumbo jumbo' of African tradition, particularly the
'witch doctor'. Members of the West African Students' Association
(WASA) felt the film's stereotypical view was a total misrepresen-
tation of the 'witch doctor' and cast a slur on the 'prestige of African
people as a whole, and prejudiced further relations between the
African peoples and the British Empire.' They argued that, instead,
the film should include some discussion of the development of self-
government in Africa and the end of British rule. Significantly, the
MOI fobbed off WASA, ignoring its complaints and producing the
film as planned.[48]

A similarly colonial attitude can be discerned in the portrayal of
Scotland, Wales and Northern Ireland. In most propaganda films
designed to instil a sense of patriotism, such as *Britain at Bay*, *Words
for Battle*, and *Heart of Britain*, Britain meant England, with images of
the English countryside and people used throughout. A comparatively small number of films concentrated on the involvement of
Northern Ireland, Scotland and Wales. The only film about Wales,
Wales, Green Mountain, Black Mountain (1943), did little to express
Welsh cultural identity, except in a clichéd fashion, the film's power
being in its depiction of economic issues.

When there was a proposal at the MOI for a film on Northern
Ireland's war effort, most members of the planning committee were
against the idea. John Betjeman was concerned that the republic

would resent such a film. Ironically, the idea was passed over to the dominions officer.[49] In the end, only three films directly about the province were produced: the British Council film, *Ulster* (1940),[50] *A Letter from Ulster* (1943),[51] and a newsreel item in an issue of *Warwork News* (1944).[52] *Ulster at Arms* described the province's material contribution to the war in agricultural and industrial goods, but did not examine the impact of war on the country or any of the people's difficulties. The commentary's tone, describing the province as a 'loyal member of the British Commonwealth', and superficial treatment, made this film similar to those produced on India, Canada or other distant commonwealth nations.

Not surprisingly, in these films and those that covered the other home nations, the issue of nationalism was ignored or dismissed. *Scotland Speaks* (1941) laid particular stress on the country's long tradition of independence and freedom. A Scottish soldier is shown striding home on leave to greet his 'free family' living in a 'free land.' There is a recognition that the Scottish value this freedom particularly highly as it has been won in many fierce battles against great odds. The inference is that the Union respects this tradition and in return, during times of war, Scotland freely offers its men to fight: 'Scotland is as solid behind them [the Scottish soldiers] as the castle and the rock itself.' In common with the films about Ulster, *Scotland Speaks* ignored those aspects of Scottish life that were unrelated to the war effort.

While many official film makers espoused a populism and made a laudable effort to present the 'people' and workers at the centre of the war, not all films authentically articulated the voice of the people or presented an accurate picture of class relations. In films that depicted the wartime experiences and attitudes of the people, such as *Living with Strangers* (1941) about evacuees, one is often struck by the inappropriate speech patterns and accents scripted for supposedly working-class characters. Similarly, although reviewers remarked on the 'convincing' power of the 'Hertfordshire accent' used by the actors in *Dawn Guard*,[53] the film did not ring true with an audience of Scottish miners who saw it as a piece of 'very insincere' government propaganda in which 'someone was trying to put something over on them.'[54]

As Brian Winston has recently argued, some of the documentary
film makers who produced these films had a voyeuristic, elitist view
of working-class life and tended to manipulate working-class figures
into roles of hero or victim.[55] In the dramatized short *Post 23* (1941),
which celebrated the community spirit developed in an ARP (air-raid
precautions) post, the working-class figures are depicted as brave
and cheery, but politically passive. During a discussion about building a better postwar world, it is the middle-class architect who
articulates the social benefits brought by the war and fantasizes about
the homes he will build on behalf of the deprived.

In the much acclaimed feature-length documentary about the
auxiliary fire service, *I was a Fireman* (1941), the portrayal of
working-class firemen at a south London station absolutely glows
with warmth and approval, but again the characters are fairly simplistic, even stereotypical. The film's director, Humphrey Jennings,
appears most excited by the comradeship and conviviality of the
team and, most important of all, the ease with which they welcome
into their ranks the rather shy, middle-class advertising copy writer;
perhaps a character with whom Jennings could identify? This
interpretation is supported by an observation made about Jennings
by the film editor, Sidney Cole. Cole recalled the excitement of the
rather upper-class Jennings when he described talking to men on the
lower deck of a ship he had been filming. At this point Cole realized
that Jennings was effectively describing his discovery of the working
class.[56] While this is an indication of the possibilities of social
mobility in the war, it nonetheless reveals a potential gulf between
the perceptions of film makers and their subjects.

As has been demonstrated, films such as *Words and Actions* and
Public Opinion encouraged people to become more involved in
politics and public affairs and offered a less hierarchical definition of
British democracy. As radical as these themes may appear, they do
not amount to a criticism of the basis of British government and its
democratic process; the system merely needs to be revitalized by
popular participation in order to make it more responsive to the
needs of society. These themes were popular with many documentary film makers, but they had full official sanction. Towards the
end of the war, though, there was concern over the extent of public

ignorance of, and apathy about, the democratic process. This, it was anticipated, would surely have a detrimental effect on the whole effort of reconstruction, particularly as local government had been denuded of good officials by the war. The Consultative Committee for Local Government Information Services recommended that local public relations needed a complete modernization, making much greater use of modern media such as films.[57] At the MOI, plans for 'Education in Civics' involved the production of a number of films, including one called *The Vote*, and a further six just to explain how local government worked.[58]

Many government officials, however, were not so keen on films that advocated an increased role for the state. After reading the treatment for the British Council film *National Health*, one civil servant commented that it had 'a dictatorial tone and leaves the impression of too much state control on the Nazi lines'.[59] A later treatment by Technique Films again prompted grumbles about the depiction of state intervention, even though the film concentrated on relatively uncontroversial and long-standing provisions, such as refuse collection, water supply, sewage disposal and antenatal care.[60]

At the MOI, Paul Rotha's film *World of Plenty* met with considerable opposition, particularly at the Ministry of Agriculture, because of its socialist proposals for international food distribution.[61] Similarly, Reg Groves's script for *The Strategy of Manpower* was unacceptable to the MOI, partly because it argued for increased government planning and intervention in the economy and productive sector.[62]

Many of the films that offered the most progressive view of Britain received only limited distribution. The radical left-wing film maker Paul Rotha believed that films made by him and other left-wing documentary producers were relegated to the non-theatrical circuit (with its smaller audiences).[63] One survey, indeed, has shown support for his claim, although other factors such as the entertainment value of a film also influenced these distribution decisions.[64] Surviving film production files reveal that government officials took a very cautious and occasionally cynical approach to distribution. For example, *Children of the City* (1944), a film about the state's measures to tackle juvenile delinquency in Scotland, could not

qualify for overseas distribution until four scenes of 'great poverty
and physical degradation' were deleted.[65] In the case of *Five and
Under* (1941) though, it was British distribution that was regarded as
the greater danger. The film showed the workings of a local government day nursery, set up to provide care for the children of mothers
in full-time work. Typically for a film from Paul Rotha Productions,
there was also a lengthy discussion about the links between poverty,
bad environment and delinquent behaviour in English children. The
film ended with a commitment to provide nursery school places for
all children after the war. The Ministry of Health, the film's sponsor,
intervened to prevent British distribution because it was concerned
that it would create a demand that could not be satisfied without
central government support; something it had no intention of providing either during the war or after.[66] Yet, this did not prevent the
MOI fully exploiting the film's propaganda value abroad,[67] as an
example of 'British democracy at work.'[68]

At the British Council, civil servants readily admitted that the film
National Health was a distortion; one civil servant, Mr Simonds,
regarded it as 'good propaganda of the better kind of state socialism,
but hardly an accurate picture of Britain today'.[69] Gurney went
further:

> We are relatively backward in our health and social services
> (absence of sanitation, prenatal clinics, lack of cheap hospital
> treatment). To the initiated such a film must be largely eye-
> wash. But there has been an advance since the middle ages, and
> a film like this will be useful in Turkey and the rest of the
> Middle East, since although civilized countries regard us as
> medieval, uncivilized natives think we are in the van of
> progress.[70]

As we have seen, there was a striking evolution in official films of
the portrayal of the British nation and its relations with its citizens in
the war. From concentrating on a rather monolithic and conservative
view, in which parliamentary institutions took a central position and
where British history was characterized as a peaceful and evolution-
ary progression, the films moved towards the promotion of a much

more dynamic and populist version of democracy. This evolution can be explained by a number of factors: the recruitment of progressive film makers and public relations experts to government film production; the need to counter enemy propaganda; the importance of maintaining good relations with colonial allies; the need to bolster the morale of the British working population, and so on. However, the most surprising factor, and one that unites all these motivations, is the existence of a high degree of insecurity within sectors of the state about the idea of the British nation. Simply put, the prewar idea of what Britain meant, no longer seemed relevant.

Yet, there is also evidence of a countervailing trend of films that presented a more traditional, even reactionary view of the 'idea of the nation'. Evidence in the films themselves is supported by documentary accounts of official attitudes held by those who guided British propaganda. A significant number of Whitehall's propagandists clearly did not ascribe to the more populist and progressive vision of Britain and the empire. In some cases even, a duplicitous position was taken to government propaganda, with civil servants passing off films that totally misrepresented Britain. Although this reactionary trend may not have been large, it leads to some interesting conclusions. Normally, propaganda is seen as something monolithic and uniform. However, in the case of films about British nationhood and citizenship, the ideas presented were much more fluid. There was a struggle over what themes should be promulgated among the various groups vying for control of government propaganda — film makers, government officials, different and competing government departments, commercial film distributors and the military — as well as battles over policy formation in other areas of government and society.

Finally, while observations about wartime British feature films have some relevance to official films, they do not tell the whole story. Although there was a democratization of images of Britain, these were not the only versions promoted by the state. Moreover, the images of a new Britain themselves often suggested only a partial overhaul of traditional institutions.[71]

Acknowledgements

My thanks for advice and assistance with this chapter go to Roger Smither, keeper of the Imperial War Museum's Film and Video Archive, Kate Johnson of the IWM Sound Archive and Mark Harding of Yale University.

Notes

1. Most of the films referred to in this study are held at the Imperial War Museum's Film and Video Archive, and can be viewed by appointment. The following are held at the National Film Archive: *Housing Problems, Peace and Plenty, Welfare of the Workers, New Towns for Old, The World of Plenty*, and *Children of the City*. These were all produced by the British Council. *Five and Under* is held in the Library of Congress film archive.

2. In 1932, Sir Stephen Tallents, head of public relations at the GPO, wrote the influential *The Projection of England* (reprinted in London, 1955), which urged the production of films which, like the best Soviet examples, could present positive images of Britain abroad. *The Film in National Life* (London, 1932) was the report of an influential independent enquiry into the role of film and education. It expressed much admiration for the film propaganda policies of other nations, such as the Germans and Italians, and recommended the adoption of similar programmes to promote the national idea (p. 141).

3. The state was willing to finance film production, albeit indirectly, that had a commercial concern. At the Empire Marketing Board (1926–33), a style of film-making known as the 'documentary' was used to promote the sale of goods from the empire. When the board was closed, its film unit was transferred to the GPO (1933–40) where, under the guidance of the public relations pioneer, Sir Stephen Tallents, and the British documentary film theorist, John Grierson, documentaries were produced to train post office personnel and to advertise its services.

4. Pearl Assurance sponsored *The Health of the Nation* (1937) and *One Hundred Years* (1937). After a long period of discussion, the Gas Light & Coke Company's project fell through.

5. Estimated weekly cinema attendance in Britain had risen from 10 million in 1934 to 25 million in 1939. The wartime average was 31 million. Figures taken from British Film Academy (1950) *The Film Industry in Great Britain: Some Facts and Figures*, London.

6. Anthony Aldgate and Jeffrey Richards (1994) *Britain Can Take It: The British Cinema in the Second World War*, Edinburgh, p. 13. Similar

arguments are developed more fully by the contributors to Graham Dawson and Bob West (1984) *National Fictions*, London.

7. Frances Thorpe and Nicholas Pronay (1980) *British Official Films in the Second World War: A Descriptive Catalogue*, Oxford.

8. PRO INF 1/673, November-March 1942.

9. PRO BK 1/108, document dated 15 January 1942. An item in the November 1942 issue of *Worker and Warfront* addressed this issue.

10. *The Great Harvest* (1942).

11. Calculated from the entries in Thorpe and Pronay, *British Official Films*.

12. Imperial War Museum, Film and Video Archives, letter from Helen Foreman to Nicholas Pronay, 18 January 1981.

13. For example Jack Beddington, the head of the division from April 1940, had run the public relations section of Shell where he had built up personal contacts with many documentary film makers.

14. Paul Swann (1983) *The British Documentary Film Movement*, Cambridge, p. 151.

15. Nicholas Pronay (1983) 'Land of Promise: The Projection of Peace Aims in Britain', in K. R. M. Short (ed.) *Film and Propaganda in World War Two*, London.

16. Toby Haggith (1992) 'Post-war reconstruction as depicted in official British films of the Second World War', *The Imperial War Museum Review*, London, vol. 7.

17. Swann, *British Documentary Film Movement*, p. 169.

18. *Do it Now/If War Should Come*, release T September 1939, sp MOI, pc GPO, 11 mins; *The New Britain*, release T & Non-T October 1940, sp MOI, pc Strand, p. Alexander Shaw, d Ralph Keene, comm w Graham Greene, sc Reg Groves, music William Alwyn, ph Charles Marlborough, 10 mins; *Dawn Guard*, release T January 1941, Non-T March 1941, sp MOI pc Charter Films, p John Boulting, d Roy Boulting, original idea Anna Reiner, cast Bernhard Miles and Percy Walsh, 7 mins; *Battle of the Books*, release T 13 October 1941, sp MOI pc Rotha Productions, p Paul Rotha, d Jack Chambers, ph Peter Hennessey, comm w Henry Ainley, music Charles Ball, 7 mins; *Word and Actions*, release Non-T 1944, sp British Commercial Gas Association, pc Realist, p John Taylor, d Max Anderson, ph A. E. Jeakins, sc Frank Sainsbury, John Taylor, 15 mins.

19. Echoing the famous poster issued by the MOI in 1939, 'Your Courage . . . Your Cheerfulness . . . Your Resolution . . . Will Bring Us Victory'.

20. Imperial War Museum, Film and Video Archive, in papers of E. J. Embleton, 'Call to Arms, To Effort, To Self Sacrifice', in 'Principles and Objectives of British Wartime Propaganda', attached to a confidential circular to Mr E. J. Embleton, MOI General Division, 26 February 1940.

21. Clive Coultass (1989) 'The Ministry of Information and documentary film, 1939–45', *The Imperial War Museum Review*, vol. 4, p. 104.

22. PRO INF 1/249, MOI Planning Committee Meeting, 24 July 1940.

23. *Peace and Plenty* was produced by the Progressive Film Institute and distributed by KINO.

24. PRO PREM 1/441, Principles Underlying British Wartime Propaganda, 22 December 1939.

25. PRO PREM 1/441.

26. PRO INF 1/249, MOI Planning Committee Meeting, 24 July 1940.

27. PRO INF 1/848, Policy Committee Paper No. 23, Memorandum on British Counter-Propaganda, by Professor and Mrs A. G. Highet, 26 March 1940.

28. *The New Britain* was distributed commercially by Columbia Pictures for three years from 1 October 1940 to Great Britain, Northern Ireland, Eire, and the Isle of Man. The MOI retained the rights to distribute it non-theatrically.

29. Review of *Dawn Guard* in New Documentary Films, *Documentary News Letter*, February 1941.

30. PRO INF 1/864. Note by Mrs Hamilton, 'Policy for Reconstruction', to Home Planning Committee, 18 September 1941.

31. PRO BW4/45 K. T. Gurney, Foreign Office to Primrose, secretary of BBC Film Department, 8 April 1942.

32. PRO BW4/64 1941–42.

33. PRO LAB 6/123. Memo, Lindsey (MOI) to S. R. Chaloner (MOL), 15 December 1939. German broadcasts that say: 'British masses are being forced to fight for the sole interests of Jews, capitalists, profiteers, interested financiers, landlords and the upper classes generally, by whom they are exploited and down-trodden both in peace and war.'

34. PRO CO 875/18/11.

35. PRO INF 1/622.

36. Pat Jackson, draft autobiography, p. 82.

37. PRO INF 5/84, Notes on the synopsis for *Builders*, written by the director Pat Jackson, in October 1941.

38. *Warwork News* was issued fortnightly and ran for 81 issues between the spring of 1941 and 1945. It was produced by Paramount and sponsored by the Ministry of Supply. *Worker and Warfront* ran for 18 issues, from May 1942 to January 1946. It was produced by Paul Rotha Productions and Films of Fact, and sponsored by the MOI.

39. PRO LAB 14/425. Factory Welfare Board Committee Minutes, 12 December 1941.

40. PRO LAB.

41. During the war about 30 of its films were also distributed in Britain.

42. PRO BW4/64, letter from Brendan Bracken (Minister of MOI) to the BBC chairman, Malcolm Robertson, 21 December 1941.

43. PRO BW 4/17, memo to Primrose, Film Department secretary, 10 November 1941.

44. *War-Time Trading Bulletin*, p. 1910.
45. PRO INF 1/848, Policy Committee Paper No. 23, 26 March 1940.
46. Imperial War Museum, no. GWY 197.
47. The Indian National Army was formed in 1941 in Singapore from POWs serving with the British army. The 40,000 or so men were equipped by and fought with the Japanese, under the leadership of the nationalist leader Subra Chandra Bose.
48. INF PRO 1/218, 'Men of Two Worlds'.
49. PRO INF 1/249, MOI Planning Committee, Films Division, 12 August 1940.
50. The treatment of Northern Ireland in the British Council film was almost identical to that taken by the *Warwork News* item. The 12-minute film from Strand was a survey of the agricultural and industrial resources of the province.
51. *A Letter from Ulster* made by the Crown Film Unit was about US servicemen in Northern Ireland and provided only indirect impressions of the province.
52. *Warwork News*, No. 39, IWM Film no. S15 39.
53. Anonymous review of *Dawn Guard*, 'New Documentary Films', *Documentary Newsletter*, February 1941, p. 21.
54. Anonymous, MOI Films in Scotland, 'Report from a Mining Village', *Documentary Newsletter*, July 1941, p. 129.
55. Brian Winston (1995) *Claiming the Real*, London, pp. 44–5.
56. Imperial War Museum, Sound Archives, recording no. 15618, reel 8.
57. PRO HLG 52/1396, Consultative Committee for Local Government Publicity.
58. Helen de Mouilpied Papers, Films Division Production Plan, Production Conference, 5 October 1944.
59. BW4/42, 29 April 1942.
60. BW 4/42.
61. PRO INF 1/214.
62. PRO INF 1/215.
63. Aldgate and Richards, *Britain Can Take It*, p. 5.
64. Out of 38 'Peace Aims films' (MOI), only four were distributed theatrically. See Toby Haggith (1991) 'Post-War Reconstruction as Depicted in Official British Films of the Second World War', Birkbeck College, University of London, unpublished M.Sc. dissertation, p. 18.
65. INF 6/1247.
66. INF 1/249. Home Planning Committee, 10 April 1941.
67. *Five and Under* was distributed in Guatamala, Honduras, Canada, the USA and Egypt.
68. Imperial War Museum, Sound Archives, interview with film's director Donald Alexander, by Bert Hogenkamp, 14 February 1986, p. 10.
69. PRO BW 4/42, Simonds, 11 July 1942.

70. PRO BW 4/42. K. T. Gurney, Foreign Office, 28 July 1942.

71. Andrew Higson comes to similar conclusions in his recent book on British cinema. In his examination of the film, *Millions Like Us* (1943), he shows that overtures to democratization and radicalism, such as the disruption of traditional gender stereotypes or the dissolving of class barriers in human relationships, take place in a highly defined time period (the war only) and are contained within more conservative and patriarchal structures. Andrew Higson (1995) *Waving the Flag: Constructing a National Cinema in Britain*, Oxford, p. 243.

4. Forging a 'nation of participants': Political and Economic Planning in Labour's Britain

Abigail Beach

During the 1940s, the research organization Political and Economic Planning (PEP) set about reinventing itself. It had been established in 1931 in the context of what its first director, Max Nicholson, described as 'a world apparently on the point of falling apart'.[1] It was a 'private research society', created to inspire a dynamic response to the severe economic crisis of 1931 and the 'protracted slump which followed', and reflected a growing perception, felt right across the political spectrum, of the benefits to be achieved through reorganizing the economy, industry and social services along systematic and planned lines.[2] PEP's members — nearly all men in their thirties or forties, in or approaching positions of responsibility — could see what enormous damage a breakdown in the economy and society would bring.[3] Many of these people, Nicholson has argued, would have been Liberals in an earlier decade and, though left 'high and dry' by the Liberal Party's split and diminution in the 1920s retained, 'amid growing frustration', a large amount of hope in the New Liberal tradition of extra-parliamentary political studies.[4] The group's dominant message and its initial agenda was the promotion of 'conscious economic control' as an alternative to the 'discredited ethic of *laissez-faire*'.[5] But, in the early 1940s, with the world again in turmoil, PEP members felt themselves, and the concept of planning, to be in need of a re-evaluation.[6]

PEP's wartime reconsideration of its role and aims had a touch of irony about it. The war, horrendous as it was, was also an immediate opportunity for the group. PEP had long been calling for greater state intervention in the economy and, indeed, 'for a sense of national purpose' and now, under the unfortunate conditions of war, it had got what it wanted.[7] During the Battle of Britain, government interest in PEP's ideas escalated. In November 1940, for example, Lord Halifax of the Cabinet Sub-Committee on Reconstruction requested the submission by PEP of a series of reports on reconstruction problems and, in June 1941, PEP's official brief was extended when the Labour minister, Arthur Greenwood, asked for evidence to be submitted to the Beveridge Committee on social insurance.[8]

Yet, by the end of the war, many of PEP's members were beginning to inject a note of caution into their advocacy for planning, and attention was increasingly placed upon the apparent deficiencies of economic planning as it had developed during the period of national emergency. As François Lafitte, a left-leaning sociologist who participated in PEP's discussions, put it: 'It seems really that we have come to the end of a phase in PEP's work. ... We came together to preach planning,' but 'planning has been taken out of our hands — planners are doing too much.'[9] Vital decisions, he asserted, were now being taken at an unhealthy 'remoteness from the citizen'.[10]

PEP's wartime re-evaluation and self-assessment, in essence, reflected the group's desire to move on from 'material problems of structure and organization to the more intangible problems of human relations and attitudes'.[11] This, in turn, reflected a wider debate, that is, 'the place of planning in democracy'.[12] As the group stated in 1945:

> It is urgent that as much attention should be given to the frontline of British democracy as to the future of the British economy. It is time that there was talk of planning for democracy as well as planning for jobs and a high standard of life. It is time because if there is any country which can give a new meaning to democracy it is Britain.[13]

The development of a new programme to address these issues became a PEP priority. The main arena for these discussions was the 'active democracy' group, which had been formed towards the end of the war, largely at the instigation of Michael Young. Young was a graduate of the London School of Economics and had joined PEP as a research assistant in August 1939 at the age of 24. In 1942, after a period working in a munitions factory, Young returned to PEP as secretary, a post he held until joining the Labour Party's research department in early 1945. He remained a member of the PEP executive until 1958, and became a vice-president of it (by then renamed the Policy Studies Institute) in 1966.[14] Michael Young's chief interest during the war and immediate postwar years was the discovery of ways to aid the development of a participatory democracy. His work at PEP and also within the Labour Party, continually refers back to this premise.

The Second World War, as already suggested, provided an important context for the discussions of PEP, and the 'active democracy' group in particular. While the war had imposed certain restrictions on democracy, PEP argued, it had also increased the range of opportunities for citizens to take an active part in the affairs of the nation. If the formal processes of democracy had been compromised in the pursuit of national security, informal expressions of citizenship had increased in compensation. 'Opportunities for citizenship', PEP reflected, had accumulated in the areas of war and domestic production, civil defence, citizen information and advice, and in many other kinds of voluntary service.[15] In addition, and despite wartime restrictions, PEP detected a great 'increase of interest and participation in the British system of government at both ends of the scale', at the parliamentary and also the local level.[16]

War, in essence, had generated an animated sense of 'national purpose' within the country: a valuable and potent asset, the maintenance of which was vital for the success of reconstruction. Yet, doubt remained as to whether a nation like Britain, which was not characteristically or obviously 'fired by some overt and overwhelming national purpose', could preserve this sense of vitality during the different challenges of the peace.[17] There was apprehension among and beyond PEP circles that this 'glad confident morning' of rejuvenated democratic activity might quickly 'be followed by disillusion and reaction'.[18]

Participants in PEP's 'active democracy' discussions felt that a possible solution to these concerns lay in deepening the efficacy of the mechanics of democracy: 'if the awareness of political responsibility is to be maintained' among citizens, the group argued, 'greater knowledge is required of the means of its expression'.[19] A central theme of the group's discussions on this issue was the complementarity of a national sense of purpose and a decentralized and pluralistic participatory democracy. However, for these two facets to blend more perfectly into a constructive sense of citizenship, especially one that would remain vigorous during the peace, an improvement in the methods of democracy was required: citizens had to 'feel that it was worthwhile and exciting to take part in democratic activities'.[20] A sense of national purpose would then flow from an amalgam of individual and group participation and the pluralism of British political and social life would itself nourish a sense of national identity.[21]

The task of the 'active democracy' group, therefore, was to examine the working of democracy in postwar Britain and to press for improvements. The aim was to raise awareness of the potential contradictions between individual freedom and planning in a democracy in the hope that, in its translation into practice, democratic planning would 'choose a form which is least likely to allow relapse; which is least likely to allow power to slip into private hands where it can be abused; which is least likely to turn the citizens of a nation into spectators rather than participants'.[22] This goal, however, presented Britain with 'some fundamental difficulties which only hard thinking . . . [would] surmount'. At the heart of the issue lay the changing nature of modern society itself: 'The scale and complexity of modern civilization demands large scale planning, large forms of organization, expensive technical and administrative resources. How are these to be combined with continued free participation of the individual in social life and government?'[23]

The hope was that an answer could be found by devising 'machinery' for democratic planning that would 'to the greatest possible extent push responsibility and initiative downwards from the seat of power to regional organizations, to county organizations, to the parish and most of all to the individual citizen'.[24] With this goal in mind, it would be 'the business of PEP in its own field to exercise an eternal vigilance on the aims, the processes and the forms of planning'.[25]

The 'active democracy' group was set in motion around May 1945, and was accorded priority by PEP's Executive Committee. Its studies were generally divided along two parallel lines of inquiry: the interaction between local authorities and the public, and the role of voluntary associations in the process of active democracy.[26] Early deliberations of the group focused on the need to contextualize the 'active democracy' studies and to root the field work in a framework of common 'British democratic ideas'.[27] The decision to focus attention on local government and voluntary groups, therefore, stemmed from the perceived centrality of pluralism in British social and political organization: both elements, PEP argued, had been 'major influence[s] in bringing the British people to their present level of political consciousness.'[28] The significance PEP and many other commentators accorded to these two areas reflected the continued resonance of these strands, in the 1930s and 1940s, as fundamental elements in Britain's democratic heritage.[29] Free association for mutual aid and benefit, for instance, was regarded as a core component of Britain's heritage of liberalism and toleration and, as such, was praised by those on the left and centre-left of British politics who viewed it as part of a radical continuum for social justice and communality, as well as by those on the conservative right who cherished it as an affirmation of independence from the state.[30]

Democracy, as it had come to be understood in Britain, the PEP group argued, was not reducible to a 'single formula' and could not be enhanced by the application of a 'set theory'. Instead, 'democratic practices and ideals, the practice of open and free discussion, the equality of the members of the group', were to be sought 'in the development of associations, societies, groups of the Church, and many similar activities of private citizens, voluntarily joining in a common interest; in the varied life of the community rather than in the state'.[31] To illustrate this point, PEP prefaced its field studies of 'active democracy' with historical introductions explaining the development of local government and voluntary societies and their role in shaping the British democratic tradition. The independent association was described as having 'a very honourable' and lengthy history in drawing out a 'ferment of activity which had all the marks of democracy' from the British people.[32] But, according to PEP, and several other key social and political commentators located across the political spectrum, this heritage was in urgent need of attention.

The centripetal pressures of modern social and economic organization, PEP members noted, were now posing enormous challenges to traditional pluralistic democracy. As communication and other technological innovations enlarged the scale of public services and private business, so the *loci* and nature of social relationships changed: 'large organization — in industry, in leisure and, above all, in Government — is increasingly dominating the operations of our society; . . . the individual feels that centralized authorities which control his life are increasingly remote.'[33] As a counter to this pressure, PEP advocated the adoption of 'decentralization within the framework of the large organization', be it a statutory organ or a private company: 'Even in a massive organization like ICI or in a nationalized coal industry, or in a national health service, the citizen can be associated at every stage with the running of the show. There can be Production Committees in works and pits, there can be citizens' groups attached to every clinic, health centre and hospital.'[34]

The 'underlying proposal' of the 'active democracy' researchers, therefore, was to build pluralism and openness into government structures and social and economic organization at all levels: 'the way of reviving democracy is to associate the citizen with all the processes of government and to establish active and creative participation as the main feature of every social grouping.'[35] Even policies for the arts and leisure needed to be rethought with this aim in mind to counteract the 'danger' that 'more and more people in leisure as in work, will become passive spectators instead of active participants.' The recent growth and rising popularity of 'large-scale' entertainments such as cinema and radio had 'competed ruthlessly with the amateur activity of the ordinary citizen'. Although still a feature of 'out of the way villages remote from the nearest cinema' and in communities that retained strong local traditions of performance, typified for example by the Welsh commitment to the Eisteddfod, the North of England's support for brass bands, and Huddersfield's enduring tradition of choral singing, there was little doubt in PEP's mind, 'about the gradual decline in amateur activity, which is the essence of democratic participation as regards leisure'.[36] Along with many other commentators, PEP's members looked with interest at the possibilities for social and cultural regeneration offered by neighbourhood amenities, such as arts, health and community centres.[37]

The local, self-propelled responsibility for healthy living and fitness, which the Pioneer Health Centre at Peckham typified, for instance, had won many commendations since its establishment in 1926. In 1933, it was praised by Ernest Barker, chairman of the New Estates Community Committee of the National Council of Social Service, as an expression of a democratic and vital form of citizenship.[38] PEP, too, welcomed the idea of a locally-rooted and run health centre, seeing it as a socially integrative force. People, they argued, could meet their doctors outside the surgery and the sickroom 'in the centre's lecture-hall or in the community centre' where, it was hoped, 'social and educational activities' would act as a 'powerful instrument for breaking down the barriers of ignorance, misunderstanding and prejudice — on both sides': patients would lose their 'bottle of medicine' view of health care and doctors would 'learn to treat their patients, not as irresponsible children but as adult fellow citizens'.[39]

The importance PEP researchers attributed to pluralism and measured decentralization was also reflected in the subject matter and methodology of the 'active democracy' studies. An early broadsheet by the group noted that the aim was 'to arrive at an understanding of the vitality of our democratic institutions by finding out what they mean to the ordinary citizen and how far he is able to take part in running them'.[40] The broadsheets, therefore, tended to concentrate on the working of a particular service or activity in a particular community. The first study published by the group, 'A Local Election', which examined the quality and extent of political interest in Bristol and in several of the smaller communities of Gloucestershire, offers a good example of this approach.[41] The particular characteristics of each locality were examined in an attempt to chart the correlation between the size and type of community and the contours of public interest and participation in local government.[42] The group's findings, for instance, revealed that 'there tended in Bristol, more than in smaller places to be a separation of political from civic leadership', which 'inclined the ordinary citizen to feel that the Council was run by a set of people with interests different from his own, living in a remote world'.[43] Participation, as a result, was noticeably weak.

The position of local government, indeed, seems to have been the initial spur to the 'active democracy' group's activities, prompting exploratory discussions back in 1943 and 1944.[44] The examination of the role of local government in fostering and safeguarding an active democracy was approached in two main ways. The first, evident in early discussions, considered the potential problems for participatory citizenship attendant on the increased reliance on centralized planning and delivery of social services. The chief voice within PEP on this aspect was François Lafitte, whose main field of expertise was the administration of social welfare. While the battle for a national minimum of social service provision was virtually won, Lafitte argued, the victory was in danger of becoming a pyrrhic one since it was accompanied by a potentially alarming concomitant: 'The stress on efficiency and equality has been carried to the point where variety and richness of life are being neglected. One consequence of this pursuit is that it has completed in one field what has been the growing trend of the past half century — that is the complete disruption of representative local government.'[45]

A 'partnership' of central and local administrators was replacing the 'old style independent local government'.[46] Moreover, aside from the nationalization of some services, the period had seen 'the rise of new *ad hoc* bodies which are neither government departments [n]or local authorities, appointed from above and not in any sense responsible to any local community'.[47] Taken as a whole, Lafitte argued, 'the social services are being divorced from the ordinary citizen,' leading to the disruption of 'our traditional attitudes to representative local government'.[48] Lafitte's opinions on this matter were by no means unique or odd. Similar sentiments were expressed at this time by a number of social commentators, many of whom had the ear, if not always the full attention, of the Labour Party and government. G. D. H. Cole, for example, explored this theme in a number of wartime and immediate postwar writings, and the local government expert and Labour supporter, W. A. Robson, expressed similar sentiments, particularly in the pages of the *Political Quarterly*.[49]

The second strand of the 'active democracy' group's local government work stemmed from this rather generalized expression of concern. In an attempt to develop a more detailed analysis of the democratic role of local government in the postwar period, PEP researchers examined the impact of social policy changes in the areas of housing and town planning, health care and education. One of the chief concerns of the group was the stifling effect of bureaucracy on participatory citizenship.[50] This issue was addressed most directly in PEP's broadsheets on housing. In May 1948, for example, the group explored the management of housing estates owned by local authorities, taking as its starting point the growing contemporary concern that housing provision and management had become caught in 'a massive framework of bureaucracy'.[51] 'The council', it asserted:

is sometimes resented as an omnipresence controlling almost every aspect of the tenants' lives. They feel that it is impossible for them to escape its tentacles; it controls not only the routine services which local authorities were originally established to provide, but also the schools to which the children go, the clinics and health centres, the community centre in which the tenants amuse themselves, and finally the houses in which they live.[52]

Consequently, or so it was frequently alleged, there was an acute lack of personal responsibility and pride in the estates and a cumulative process of detachment from the community. Such difficulties, PEP pointed out, were often attributed to the 'lack of individual ownership'. How true were these claims? Was the lack of individual ownership of property chiefly to blame for this type of social indifference? Was a 'simple connection between ownership and responsibility . . . necessary' and a fundamental prerequisite of responsible social living in postwar Britain, or could 'tenants grow to have the same feeling [of responsibility, even] if they do not own their homes directly but share in communal ownership?'[53]

This was an important question to address; indeed, it was of national importance for a society pledged to a socialist government. After all, PEP argued, the question of how 'to develop respect for communal property and appreciation of communal responsibilities' was not 'a problem peculiar to housing management'. Housing policy simply illustrated a much more general theme, that is 'Can people feel the same way about things that they own in common as they do about things they own individually?'[54] Could incentives to social responsibility other than financial benefit be uncovered?

As part of its analysis of this matter, the broadsheet on housing management highlighted the potential benefits of a reduction of bureaucracy. The authors of the housing study, for instance, believed that, at the very least, small-scale and decentralized units of management improved the likelihood of tenant interest and participation in the running of estates. The most fruitful approach to public housing, in their view, was the continuation of local government-based planning and construction, but with a wider use of 'small self-governing units working under their aegis' for the day-to-day management of the estates.[55]

However, if an active and responsible citizenship was to flourish, policies and programmes in housing and in other areas had to extend beyond administrative decentralization: the people themselves needed to be actively involved. It was no good, for example, simply decentralizing housing management from the local authority housing committee to individual estate managers: while such a policy might 'bring management in closer touch with the tenant' it would neither by itself 'increase effective democratic control nor extend the participation of tenants in the control of their local community'.[56] So, how could the public truly become involved?

In 1950 the 'active democracy' group examined the issue of widespread public participation in community affairs in the context of town planning. The main focus of its study was the system established under the 1947 Town and Country Planning Act. In particular, the group wished to explore how the new town planning regulations and provisions affected the ordinary citizen and fitted into what the authors called 'our kind of democracy'.[57] Town planners in postwar Britain did not have a good image: indeed, to many, they seemed to be little more than the purveyors of arbitrary interference.[58] How could this negative interpretation be reformed? The key, PEP argued, was to involve the public in planning decisions at as many levels and as much as possible:

> to get people to see their own interests in relation to those of the community, local interests in relation to national or regional interests, and their immediate advantage or disadvantage in the light of future common benefits. They must be able to recognize that in the plan is expressed as far as is humanly possible all that they most want themselves, for their families and for the community. To do so they must be able to acclaim the plan as an idea which they have helped to form and in whose execution they have an interest and incentive. They must also be able to know, at least in broad terms, what the public interest is.[59]

PEP's evaluation of the relationship between planners and the planned raised a number of issues that were pertinent to the notions of citizenship and democracy and that illustrated the group's appreciation of the importance of pluralism to British society and national identity. In general terms, the group's analysis clearly linked local, or even personal, interest with the national interest: the two aspects, in PEP's view, drew sustenance from each other and made sense only in relation to each other. It was the planners' task, therefore, to encourage this recognition of the congruence of local and national interest.

This was not to be a process of one-way instruction, but was to include genuine opportunities for public involvement in the framing of the plan. However, for this engagement between planners and the planned to be productive, a certain level of awareness of what constituted the public interest was required. But, as PEP acknowledged in its broadsheet 'The Plan and the Public', reality did not fully correspond to this ideal: 'The nation as a whole is at present nowhere near possessing . . . a sufficiently wide and general understanding of social and economic affairs'.[60] Indifference to the wider needs of the community, be it the neighbourhood or the nation, continued to characterize the public's response to the physical reconstruction of

Britain. The further Britain moved from the difficult days of the blitz, the harder it was to raise the public's interest in the benefits of good town and country planning. Instead of feeding a national enthusiasm for the building of a 'New Jerusalem', the public's aspirations were beginning to settle upon the homely and the mundane: whereas public interest in housing remained strong, that in community-based town planning did not. People's interest focused on the home and the family, on returning to a life of domestic privacy.[61]

As PEP noted in 1947, 'even the most friendly observer would have had to search hard to find in the Britain of the first year of peace evidence of a keen sense of participation in "a great adventure in social planning".'[62] The fuel crisis of the winter of 1946/7, PEP acknowledged, had begun to rouse the nation:

> to some sort of bewildered realization that they were being called upon, in circumstances of great difficulty, in a country impoverished by war and in a world bedevilled by shortages of the most essential food and goods, to conduct a major experiment in social engineering which would call for a quite exceptional degree of understanding and devotion on the part of every man and woman in the country,

but a stronger awareness of the public interest was, in PEP's opinion, required if these difficult conditions were to be met.[63] Citing the views of Sir Oliver Franks, PEP analysed Britain's worrying production deficit in this context. Industry and commerce, Franks had argued, could not be expected to 'join in a national purpose that has not been explained or commended to them'. Intelligent participation and 'unity of purpose' required an understanding of and an interest in the aims of the nation.[64] Flexible and open channels of communication had to be encouraged. Yet, although this was clearly a matter of national importance, it was not simply a problem for the national government. Local statutory bodies, for instance, were failing to provide a vigorous forum for discussion: 'For a long time those who have been in touch with local government have been uneasily aware that [all] was not well. Although within the charmed circle its activities have been hailed as a linchpin of democratic government, the people in general have appeared to be indifferent to its existence.'[65] A continuous process of 'civic education' was needed.[66]

Increasingly, the group stressed the importance of a fluid circulation of information for the development of an active and participatory democracy. Drawing on the example of the Citizens' Advice Bureaux, which were established under the auspices of the National Council of Social Service at the beginning of the war, on rudimentary schemes already in place in some local authorities, and on recommendations from the National Association of Local Government Officers (NALGO), PEP urged the development of public relations services, especially within the local authorities, to encourage the growth of a 'civic interest', which in turn would foster a national sense of purpose.[67] This growing interest in the role of publicity and information in the fostering of a participatory citizenship was not confined to PEP's researchers. Advocates could be found closer to the Labour Party and government. For example, Stephen Taylor, PPS to Herbert Morrison at the Lord President's Office, explored the issue in a collection of essays entitled, *Socialism: The British Way*, published in 1948.[68] 'Socialism', he asserted, 'is a doctrine of participation and social justice'; its achievement required informed and activated citizens.

> Socialism demands mass education in all aspects of good citizenship as an essential for its success. Yet knowledge by itself is not enough. It must be followed by action, by effort and striving. So the emotions as well as reason must be awakened. Only if we feel the urgency and worthwhileness of our task shall we participate in it as we should.[69]

Civic education, therefore, involved much more than central or local government circulars. Indeed, according to Taylor, 'the more personal the approach, the stronger and more sustained . . . the result.' The gap between the citizen and the government had to be bridged with an effort made 'at every point where the citizen and the machinery of government make contact — over the counter of the post office, labour exchange, or national insurance office'.[70]

However, the enhancement of participation was not thought to be the task of government or the local authorities alone. Semi-official bodies and voluntary groups, the 'active democracy' researchers at PEP argued, had an equally important role in the fostering of a widely disseminated public knowledge. The radio, the press and film, trade unions and 'with them the whole multiplicity of independent associations which traditionally form the life-blood of active democracy in Britain', all had a part to play in fostering the 'growing public awareness of planning'.[71] Indeed, such groups as the National Council of Social Service, the National Trust and the Council for the Preservation of Rural England, the Royal Institute of British Architects and the Town and Country Planning Association, the Ramblers and the Youth Hostels Association could usefully work in conjunction with the local authorities, for example in the production of planning surveys, and begin to forge a stronger bond of common interest between the official and the citizen.[72]

This belief reflected a broader assumption that active citizenship was to be achieved through a combination of formal and informal participation. Indeed, in Britain the two were deemed to be complementary. The group's interest in voluntary associations and clubs, for example, lay not only in how far they acted as 'vehicles of participation' in their own right, but also whether they acted 'as training grounds for formal political democracy', that is, how far 'people receive[d] from them an understanding of the value of cooperative effort and a schooling in democratic technique which led them to take part in the activities of public bodies'.[73] Though not an issue addressed directly by the 'active democracy' group of PEP, interest was also expressed in the extent to which party political bodies could, and should, exercise a similar role in the education and motivation of individuals in their civic capacity.

During the 1940s, many in the Labour Party asserted the importance of party membership and activity in fostering social cohesiveness and civic participation. After the election victory in 1945, for instance, Transport House encouraged the formation of discussion groups (on the model of the wartime ABCA initiatives) in ward and constituency parties. Buttressed by the flow of pamphlets and other material from the party's research department, these would, in Michael Young's words, 'give democratic leadership to the people in Councils, in the factories, in the fields, in every activity of national life, so that there is wholehearted collaboration between people and Government — between "us" and "them"'.[74] For the party of government, though, the thin line between civic education and propaganda raised complicated issues of propriety: many members of the Labour leadership consequently tended to sidestep the question of the party's role as civic educator in fear of being branded propagandists.

PEP's understanding of citizenship was multifaceted; it explored both duties and rights, and formal and informal modes of expression. The subject matter of the 'active democracy' group's field studies undertaken in the late 1940s and early 1950s clearly indicated a definition of citizenship that extended beyond the elective principle to include spontaneous and informal forms of involvement in community life.[75] The concept of citizenship, similarly, was not limited in a spatial sense in PEP's analyses, restricted either to an inherently local bond or to a synonym for nationality. To the 'active democracy' researchers, the notions of citizenship and community could be, and were, narrowly defined in terms of the local neighbourhood, yet they could, and did, constitute a much broader constituency, that of the nation as a whole. Indeed, when taken together the discussions and writing of the 'active democracy' group indicate a belief that the ties and bonds of neighbourhood and nation made sense only as opposite ends of the same scale: the one giving substance and context to the other.

As stated above, the 'active democracy' group's activities can be seen as a reflection of a more broadly felt concern for the deployment of planning in a democratic society and should, therefore, be set within a wider context. Ostensibly, the group's discussions and field work might seem academic and insular, yet the ideas of the group were part of a more widely felt concern for the development of a participatory democracy in Britain — a concern exhibited not least from within the Labour Party and the Attlee government. While some examples of this wider interest have already been given, it is appropriate to conclude with a more general contextualization.

Political and Economic Planning's observations reflected, in microcosm, broader shifts of opinion on the issue of planning in a

democratic society during this period. The Second World War itself
had imparted an ambiguous attitude to state planning. If, in general
terms, the Second World War advanced the idea of planning through
fostering a favourable ideological environment and even, perhaps, by
vindicating the mechanics of state centralization, it also saw the
development of counter arguments.[76] The period saw an increase in
libertarian critiques of planning, most notably from Friedrich Hayek,
in his book of 1944, *The Road to Serfdom*. Set within the context of
war against totalitarianism, Hayek's rigorous critique received an
immediate and penetrating response and helped to fuel a reconsideration of the problem of freedom under planning, not least from
within the Labour Party and among its sympathizers in academia.[77]

In the middle and later years of the war, the publication of
pamphlets and articles outlining the compatibility of personal freedom and a planned socialist system, became increasingly widespread.[78] A central theme of this wartime reconsideration was the
assertion that planning and democracy need not be mutually
exclusive. In 1943, for example, Harold Laski declared, 'What we
seek to plan for is democracy and freedom.'[79] For democracy to be
truly participatory, Laski argued, freedom had to extend beyond the
political to the social and economic field. Planning, if sensitively
implemented, was the means to achieve this more genuine form of
citizenship: the greater economic security achieved through the
planned distribution of the nation's resources would reinforce, not
deny, self-expression and personal freedom. Yet, the reality of this
defence still had to be demonstrated in practice. In particular, it
remained to be seen if Britain could successfully fuse the social and
economic benefits of planning with its libertarian and pluralist
heritage. This was what PEP, and Michael Young in particular,
regarded as the social and political sciences' most urgent task.

If PEP did not evolve its opinions in a vacuum, neither did it pro-
claim them into a void. The main architect of the 'active democracy'
debate, Michael Young, took his interest in participatory citizenship
and many of his practical proposals into the heart of the Labour
Party's policy-making machinery during the important early years of
reconstruction. On announcing his acceptance of the job of research
secretary to the Labour Party to his PEP colleagues, Young asserted

that he 'felt it would be possible . . . to set up a new outpost for PEP's ideas, some of which were certainly needed by the Labour Party'.[80] One of Young's first tasks at his new post, the drafting of *Let Us Face the Future*, Labour's manifesto for the 1945 general election, reflected the fruits of this aim. As Young later remembered, the programme 'had as many ideas from PEP as I could decently get past Herbert Morrison, the manager of the campaign'.[81] This should not be taken to suggest that Morrison was against, or even ambivalent about, Young's 'active democracy' themes; in fact, Morrison, proved to be a significant ally of Young and other younger intellectuals who were coming into prominence within the party, advancing a number of their ideas for policy initiatives while Lord President of the Council.

Labour Party research department memoranda and papers of the later 1940s and early 1950s, clearly show that Young, and a number of other Labour figures who shared his opinions, such as Stephen Taylor, had some success at using the Labour Party's policy committees as an arena for the 'active democracy' debate. In 1949, for example, Young wrote a discussion pamphlet for the party entitled *Small Man, Big World*, which explored many of the ideas raised within the 'active democracy' discussions at PEP and, in April 1950, a memorandum by Young to the policy committee urged the party to redirect its attention to the development of institutions on a more 'human scale' to counter the 'bigness' of contemporary life and the distance between citizens and administrators.[82]

Though much of what Young advocated was novel, particularly his call on Labour to inform its policy discussions with sociological and psychological research into human behaviour, he was not marginalized or isolated at Transport House. Many of his ideas about citizenship and democracy meshed with those of other Labour and Fabian intellectuals, such as Anthony Crosland, Evan Durbin, Richard Crossman and Roy Jenkins, who tended to explore socialism and Labour's policy in a qualitative as well as quantitative sense. As noted above, support was also forthcoming from the upper levels of the Labour Party. In speeches to the party conference in 1946, and especially in 1948 and 1949, Morrison strongly emphasized democratic socialism's need for a participatory citizenship: 'Legislation', he argued was only one element in the achievement of democratic socialism, 'Parliament having done its part the ball is now passed back to the citizen. It is now the citizen's task to match the new legislation with a new spirit and a new effort.' The next stage was to make 'social democracy less of a mere platform word and more of a living reality':

> Ballot box democracy, where people go and vote — if they can be bothered and persuaded and shoved around to go and vote — every few years and do nothing much in between, is out of date. We must have an active and living democracy in our country and we must whip up our citizens to their responsibilities just as we canvass them in elections or just as the air-raid wardens did in the war. The individual today counts not less, the individual counts more and more as our Socialist programme goes forward.[83]

In a narrow sense, this participatory citizenship was a necessary palliative for Britain's postwar economic hangover. Participatory citizens were, as Morrison said, more than voters, they were consumers and, above all, they were active producers, contributing to the economic recovery of the nation. Yet, the search for freedom within a planned socialist system carried much more than this material benefit: it indicated the continued vitality of Britain, and British traditions, within a rapidly changing world. 'If in this we succeed', Morrison asserted, 'the British people will again have taught the world much of lasting value'.[84]

Socialism, in a democratic and free society, Young argued in his Labour Party pamphlet, *Small Man, Big World*, needed to fuse a Fabian's emphasis on efficiency and social justice with the humanitarian idealism of Robert Owen and William Morris. The pursuit of material equality had to occur alongside respect for the 'dignity of man and of labour'.[85] Only through such a synthesis could the 'small man' truly flourish in a modern and complex world. Britain, under the guidance of a Labour government, he believed, was well placed to deliver this combination, having both natural and historical characteristics conducive to its achievement. 'Great Britain', Young argued:

has the advantage of size over the two great United States of East and West. It is not so big that it will be impossible to form an integrated society within the ken of the individual. Moreover, our country is already the most mature democracy in the world, in its traditions as well as in its constitution. Tolerance, the very sinew of democracy, is part of our character. ... These assets must not be left in store. They must be used to the utmost extent so that we pioneer again, not in the world of power and wealth, but in the new frontiers of the human spirit.[86]

The orthodox interpretation of the British left, and of the Labour Party in the period from *c.*1931 to 1951 in particular, emphasizes its centralizing tendencies and collectivist nature.[87] Historical analyses stress the party's commitment, from the 1930s, to achieving the transition to socialism through a strategy of planning — planning of industrial development, production, investment and so on. The policies of the Attlee governments of 1945 to 1951, particularly the nationalization programmes, are seen as Labour's attempt to implement this strategy. Moreover, it has often been argued that the Labour Party's postwar programme was based on, to use the words of Stephen Fielding, 'popular passivity', and that 'except as a general and vague principle, the party leadership had no wish to encourage the public to take a more active role.'[88]

A common conclusion of studies on the Labour government during the 1940s has been that the party, motivated primarily by the search for efficiency, based its programme for reconstruction on a centralized, expert-driven state, with control removed from the grasp of the ordinary people. A series of rights, entitlements and benefits is deemed to have been adopted in preference to a citizenship of active participation. In part, this analysis reflects the methodological preferences of historians of the Labour government: the majority of studies focus on the policies of the Labour government, rather than on the ideological debates that informed and shaped the process of policy making. Approaches and analyses vary, but have included both charges of the party's irresolute and flimsy commitment to ideological socialism as well as assertions that, as a party of government, Labour gave priority to 'the administration of corporate socialism'.[89]

The reconstruction period, indeed, has tended to be regarded as ideologically sterile with Labour's postwar programme dictated by 'conceptions and ideas formed over the previous forty years'.[90] This concentration on the fruits of legislation, however, is beginning to be balanced by a closer reading of the intentions that informed and shaped policy discussions in the 1940s. Historians such as Stephen Brooke, Stephen Fielding and Martin Francis are challenging the view that Labour's first postwar government was essentially 'pragmatic and opportunist': the ideological debates that occurred in and around the party are, as a consequence, becoming clearer.[91] This study of the PEP research group has adopted a similar methodological commitment and, by focusing on the group's discussions of how an 'active democracy' could be built under the new Labour government, has explored some of the newer ideas that were influencing the party's policy discussions in the late 1940s. Not least of these was the concern to see the development of a 'nation of participants' in postwar Britain: a lesson in democracy which, it was hoped, could persuade 'the whole world to change its course'.[92]

As Britain began its extensive and costly process of postwar reconstruction, a significant amount of time and intellectual effort was given to the place of the 'small man' in a society 'dominated by hugeness'. Britain, like the rest of the developed world, was experiencing, in Young's words, 'the democratic dilemma': efficiency in a modern society required 'bigness', yet democracy thrived on 'smallness'.[93] The problem confronting the nation, therefore, was 'how to create an integrated but free society giving to every person that sense of belonging which a mechanical large-scale age has undermined.'[94]

It proved a difficult issue to resolve. While awareness of the potential contradictions between freedom and planning in a democracy was undoubtedly raised through PEP and Fabian Society publications and Labour Party memoranda, consistent and tangible success seemed illusive, hampered by interest group pressures, the lack of adequate resources for specific projects, the presence of differing opinions within the party itself, and by a generalized public apathy in response to the government's call for a responsible and participant society. These hurdles were recognized within the party and beyond. The need to modify structural deficiencies and to stimulate behavioural patterns towards a more overt community and civic consciousness was positively addressed by the Labour research department. However, this candidness was ultimately insufficient in the presence of other, more material priorities and given the strength of the public's preference for consumption, affluence and, crucially, privacy, rather than for an active and communally orientated citizenship.

Michael Young and certain of his colleagues tried to develop a notion of active citizenship, which could combine these apparently contradictory desires, for example, by focusing on the family as the chief building block of an actively democratic society and by urging the greater prominence of consumer issues in Labour's programme. But, deflected by Labour's successive election defeats in the 1950s and 1960s, and by disorientation in the face of the growing affluence of the working classes under a Conservative government, the necessary mixture of idealism and realism failed to fuse into practical policy: left-leaning intellectuals were ultimately unable to move beyond the mere depiction of a democratic socialism or social democracy based on the active and informed participation of citizens in civic affairs.

Notes

1. Max Nicholson (1981) 'Prologue', in John Pinder (ed.) *Fifty Years of Political and Economic Planning: Looking Forward, 1931–1981*, London, p. 5.
2. For the broad, cross-party interest in economic and social planning see, Arthur Marwick (1964) 'Middle opinion in the 1930s: planning, progress and political agreement', *English Historical Review*, vol. 79, pp. 285–98; Michael Freeden (1986) *Liberalism Divided: A Study in British Political Thought, 1914–1939*, Oxford; and Daniel Ritschel (1991) 'A corporatist economy in Britain? Capitalist planning for industrial self-government in the 1930s', *English Historical Review*, vol. 106, pp. 41–65. Cross-party interest in planning in the early 1930s, however, did not readily translate into consensus. As Ritschel notes, PEP itself experienced a bitter internal argument over the precise nature of the planned economy and the distribution of power within a new corporatist environment during the first year of its work: a controversy that undoubtedly reflected the presence of tension and variations in the interpretation of the meaning 'planning' far beyond the PEP circle.

3. The only women who were active working members of the group at this time seem to have been Elizabeth Denby, housing consultant; Eva Hubback, feminist social reformer; and Innes Pearce, doctor and co-director of the Pioneer Health Centre in Peckham, London.

4. Nicholson, 'Prologue', p. 5. See Susan Pedersen and Peter Mandler (eds) (1994) *After the Victorians: Private Conscience and Public Duty in Modern Britain*, London, pp. 8–12, for a discussion of the position of the liberal intelligentsia in the interwar years. For the New Liberal tradition of political study groups, particularly the Liberal Summer Schools, see Freeden, *Liberalism Divided*; Michael Freeden (ed.) (1989) *Minutes of the Rainbow Circle, 1894–1924*, Camden Fourth Series, Vol. 38, London. PEP was not the only research group to emerge at this time. The Next Five Years Group, a group of conservatives and liberals interested in notions of planning and led by Harold Macmillan, for instance, published their manifesto for change, *The Next Five Years: An Essay in Political Agreement*, in 1935. It was signed by inter alia Ernest Barker, Normal Angell, G. P. Gooch, J. A. Hobson and A. D. Lindsay.

5. Ritschel, 'A corporatist economy', p. 41. In the early years of its existence, PEP concentrated its efforts on developing a model for a planned economy based upon the principle of 'industrial self-government'. This agenda was outlined in its broadsheet, *Planning*. See, for example, *Planning*, vol. 16, 19 December 1933; vol. 26, 8 May 1934; vol. 35, 9 October 1934; vol. 37, 6 November 1934; and vol. 40, 18 December 1934.

6. British Library of Political and Economic Science (BLPES), London: Political and Economic Planning archive, PEP/PSI 12/13, 26, Executive and Council Minutes and Papers, 29 January 1940; PEP/PSI 12/16, 80, 'Some reflections on a PEP Philosophy'; 12/17, 27; 'PEP after the War: some points of discussion', 17 February 1944; PEP/PSI 12/18, 2, 'What is PEP's Future', Secretary's comments on the Annual Progress Report, 4 January 1945.

7. Michael Young (1981) 'The Second World War', in John Pinder (ed.) *Fifty Years of Political and Economic Planning: Looking Forward, 1931–1981*, London, p. 82.

8. Ibid., p. 89. Broadsheets written under these invitations included 'America and Britain', *Planning*, no. 171, 17 June, 1941; 'The New Pattern', *Planning*, no. 178, 30 September 1941; 'Britain and Europe', *Planning*, no. 182, 9 December 1941; and 'Planning for Social Security', *Planning*, no. 190, 14 July 1942. PEP also gave evidence to Beveridge for his report on full employment, published as 'Employment for All', *Planning*, no. 206, 11 May 1943.

9. PEP/PSI 12/42, François Lafitte, 'Social problems and social change', Executive Weekend Conference, 24 October 1948, p. 38.

10. Ibid., p. 28.
11. Report of the director to the Executive Weekend, 1947, quoted in Raymond Goodman (1981) 'The first post-war decade', in John Pinder (ed.) *Fifty Years of Political and Economic Planning: Looking Forward, 1931–1981*, London, pp. 108–9.
12. PEP/PSI 12/13, 26, Executive minutes, 29 January 1940.
13. PEP/PSI 12/196/E36, 61/45/Citizenship, 'Is Britain a democracy?', 9 April 1945.
14. Michael Young had both read economics at the LSE and trained as a barrister at Gray's Inn before joining with Max Nicholson and PEP. See Paul Barker (1968) 'Michael Young', *New Society*, 8 August, pp. 188–90; and Geoffrey Dench, Tony Flower and Kate Gavron (eds) (1995) *Young at Eighty: The Prolific Public Life of Michael Young*, Manchester.
15. PEP/PSI, 12/196/E36, 61/45/Citizenship, 'Is Britain a democracy?', pp. 4–12.
16. PEP, 'Active democracy – a local election', *Planning*, no. 261, 24 January 1947, p. 2.
17. PEP/PSI 12/20, Executive Committee Minutes and Papers, draft for broadsheet, 'A programme and a purpose', 22 February 1946, p. 8.
18. PEP, 'Active democracy – a local election', p. 2.
19. Ibid.
20. PEP/PSI 12/20 14–15, Executive Committee minutes, Michael Young, 15 January 1946.
21. PEP/PSI 12/196/E36, 61/45/Citizenship, 'Is Britain a democracy?', pp. 26–8.
22. PEP, 'A programme and a purpose', *Planning*, no. 246, 15 March 1946, p. 16.
23. PEP/PSI 12/20, 'Draft synopsis and notes for an introduction for group on "Active Democracy"', 11 January 1946, p. 10.
24. Ibid.
25. Ibid.
26. Goodman, 'The first post-war decade', p. 105.
27. PEP/PSI 12/41, Executive weekend, October 1946, Director's Report, p. 8.
28. PEP, 'Clubs, societies and democracy', *Planning*, no. 263, 21 March 1947, p. 1.
29. PEP, 'Active democracy – a local election', p. 5. Jose Harris (1992) explores elements of this issue in 'Political thought and the welfare state, 1870–1940: an intellectual framework for British social policy', *Past and Present*, vol. 135, pp. 116–41; see also the writings and ideas of Ernest Barker, first professor of political science at the University of Cambridge as examined by Julia Stapleton (1991) *Englishness and the Study of Politics: The Social and Political Thought of Ernest Barker*, Cambridge. Also note the influence of idealist thought on many key figures in the Labour Party, for example Clement Attlee, and R. H.

Tawney, and the persistence of a strong pluralist dimension, as in the political thought of G. D. H. Cole.

30. The idea that the Labour Party was the inheritor of the English Radical tradition, for example, is discussed in Stephen Fielding (1992) 'Labourism in the 1940s', *Twentieth Century British History*, vol. 3, p. 143. See also Richard Crossman (1950) *Socialist Values in a Changing Civilization*, Fabian Tract 286, London, pp. 6–7; and G. Cole (1947) *D. H.: Guide to the Elements of Socialism*, London, p. 26.

31. PEP/PSI 12/196/E36, 65/46/Citizenship, 'Active Democracy – draft report', 21 April 1946.

32. PEP, 'Clubs, societies and democracy', p. 3.

33. PEP, 'Review of a programme', *Planning*, no. 289, 18 October 1948, p. 131.

34. PEP/PSI 12/196/E36, 61/45/Citizenship, 'Is Britain a democracy?', p. 26.

35. PEP, 'Review of a programme', p. 131.

36. PEP 61/45/Citizenship, 9 April 1945, 'Is Britain a democracy?'

37. The New Estates Community Committee of the National Council of Social Service, which was chaired by Ernest Barker, was extremely influential in this area. See Margaret Brasnett (1969) *Voluntary Social Action: A History of the National Council of Social Service, 1919–69*, London; and R. Clarke (ed.) (1990) *Enterprising Neighbours: The Development of the Community Association Movement in Britain*, London.

38. Ernest Barker (1933) 'Community Centres and Circles', *The Fortnightly*, March, p. 266.

39. PEP (1944) 'Medical care for citizens', *Planning*, no. 222, June, p. 33.

40. Ibid.

41. PEP, 'Active democracy – a local election'.

42. PEP, 'A programme and a purpose', p. 132.

43. Ibid.

44. PEP/PSI 12/16, 91, Executive Committee minutes, 11 November 1943; PEP/PSI 12/17, Executive Committee minutes, 13 January 1944.

45. PEP/PSI, 12/42, Lafitte, 'Social problems and social change', p. 29.

46. Ibid.

47. Ibid.

48. Ibid.

49. See, for example, G. D. H. Cole (1947) *Local and Regional Government*, London; W. A. Robson (1931) *The Development of Local Government*, London; W. A. Robson (1953) 'Labour and local government', *Political Quarterly*, vol. 24, pp. 39–55. See also Abigail Beach (1996) 'The Labour Party and the idea of citizenship', unpublished Ph.D. thesis, University of London, pp. 130–68.

50. PEP, 'Review of a programme', p. 132.

51. PEP (1948) 'Councils and their tenants', *Planning*, no. 282, 21 May, pp. 325–40.

52. Ibid., p. 328.
53. Ibid.
54. Ibid.
55. Ibid., p. 335.
56. Ibid., p. 339.
57. PEP (1950) 'Town planning and the public', *Planning*, no. 316, 8 August, p. 2.
58. See, for example, Frederic Osborn Archive, Welwyn Garden City Library, B.117, correspondence, G. R. Pepler to F. J. Osborn, Secretary of the Town and Country Planning Association, 6 November 1942. Sections of the popular press, picking up the anti-planning rhetoric of the Conservative Party, continued to build a negative, indeed, ridiculous image of the planner into the postwar period.
59. PEP, 'Town planning and the public', p. 8.
60. PEP (1947) 'The plan and the public', *Planning*, no. 269, p. 53.
61. See Chapter 6 by Nick Tiratsoo below and also Nick Tiratsoo (1990) *Reconstruction, Affluence and Labour Politics: Coventry 1945–60*, London.
62. PEP, A11/2, Executive Committee Papers, 1947, 'Economic Planning and Active Democracy', 1 May 1947.
63. Ibid., p. 39.
64. Oliver Franks (1947) *Sir: Central Planning and Control in War and Peace*, London, cited in PEP, 'The plan and the public', pp. 52–3.
65. PEP (1947) 'Public relations and the town hall', *Planning*, no. 265, 2 May, p. 3. See also PEP's broadsheet on local government elections, 'Active democracy – a local election'.
66. PEP, 'Active democracy – a local election'.
67. Ibid. pp. 4–5.
68. Donald Munro (ed.) (1948) *Socialism, the British Way: An Assessment of the Nature and Significance of the Socialist Experiment carried out in Great Britain by the Labour Government of 1945*, London. Also see Beach, 'The Labour party and the idea of citizenship', pp. 245–77, for a discussion of the contemporary interest in public relations as a tool for the development of an active and participatory citizenship.
69. Stephen Taylor (1948) 'Socialism and public opinion', in Donald Munro (ed.) *Socialism, the British Way: An Assessment of the Nature and Significance of the Socialist Experiment carried out in Great Britain by the Labour Government of 1945*, London, pp. 225–6.
70. Ibid., pp. 241–2.
71. PEP, 'The plan and the public', p. 54; PEP, 'Town planning and the public', pp. 10–11.
72. PEP, 'Town planning and the public', pp. 13–14.
73. PEP, 'Review of a programme', p. 132.
74. Michael Young, in *Tribune*, 1 November 1946.

75. See, for example, PEP, 'Clubs, societies and democracy'; PEP, 'Councils and their tenants', p. 325; PEP (1948) 'The service of youth today', *Planning*, no. 280, 9 April, pp. 285–303; PEP (1948) 'Councils and their Schools: I and II', *Planning*, no. 287, 6 September, pp. 77–97 and 288, 27 September 1948, pp. 101–24 respectively; PEP (1949) 'Can communities be planned?', *Planning*, no. 296, 28 March, pp. 259–78; PEP (1949) 'The hospital service: I. System of management', *Planning*, no. 303, 26 September, pp. 96–100.

76. Stephen Brooke (1992) *Labour's War: The Labour Party during the Second World War*, Oxford, pp. 275–80.

77. See, for example, Jim Tomlinson (1992) 'Planning: debate and policy in the 1940s', *Twentieth Century British History*, vol. 3, no. 2, pp. 154–74, for the impact of Hayek on, for example, James Meade and Douglas Jay; Stephen Brooke (1991) 'Problems of "socialist planning": Evan Durbin and the Labour government of 1945', *Historical Journal*, vol. 34, pp. 687–702; see also Martin Daunton (1996) 'Payment and participation: welfare and state formation in Britain, 1900–1951', *Past and Present*, vol. 150, pp. 169–216, which makes the important point that the rising interest in the question of freedom under planning was not merely a *post hoc* reaction to Conservative criticisms of the bureaucracy accompanying Labour government policy: the debate within Labour circles had already begun during the 1930s.

78. Brooke, *Labour's War*, pp. 280–1. Evan Durbin, Harold Laski, Barbara Wootton, James Meade and R. H. Tawney, for example, all rose to meet this challenge.

79. Harold Laski (1943) *Reflections on the Revolution of Our Time*, London, p. 181. Cited in Brooke, *Labour's War*, p. 282.

80. PEP/PSI 12/18, 19, Executive Committee Minutes, 31 January 1945. PEP's first director, Max Nicholson also had access to Labour ministers through his position of under-secretary at the Lord President's office. See Martin Francis (1995) 'Economics and ethics: the nature of Labour's socialism, 1945–51', *Twentieth Century British History*, vol. 6, no. 2, pp. 220–43.

81. Young, 'The Second World War', p. 96.

82. See Labour Party Archives, (hereafter LPA) Memoranda to Policy Committee, RD 353, Michael Young, 'A plea for restatement of socialism', April 1950; RD 356, Stephen Taylor, 'The policy of democratic socialism. A restatement for 1950', May 1950. See also Michael Young (1949) *Small Man, Big World: A Discussion of Socialist Democracy*, London. In April 1950, and largely in the context of the inconclusive result of the 1950 general election, Young announced his intention to resign as research secretary to the Labour Party in order to pursue 'research on certain long-term problems of socialist policy'. The main question he sought to examine was 'how to secure full

participation by the people in a socialist democracy and so complete the achievements of the Labour government'. He proposed to act, instead, as research advisor to the party, which in turn agreed to help fund Young's research project. See LPA, RD 354, April 1950. I am indebted to Martin Francis for this last reference. See Martin Francis (1992) 'Labour policies and socialist ideas: the example of the Attlee government, 1945–1951', University of Oxford, unpublished D.Phil. thesis.

83. Labour Party (1948) *Reports of the Forty-Eighth Annual Conference*, Herbert Morrison, 'Production: the bridge to socialism', London, pp. 129–31. See also, for example, Labour Party (1946) *Reports of the Forty-Sixth Annual Conference*, London, Labour Party, p. 178; and Labour Party (1949) *Reports of the Forty-Ninth Annual Conference*, London, Labour Party, p. 156.

84. Herbert Morrison, in the foreword to Munro (ed.) *Socialism, the British Way*.

85. Young, *Small Man, Big World*, p. 13.

86. Ibid., p. 14.

87. See, for example, the recent book by J. Fyrth (ed.) (1995) *Labour's Promised Land? Culture and Society in Labour Britain, 1945–51*, London.

88. Stephen Fielding (1991) ' "Don't know and don't care": popular attitudes in Labour's Britain, 1945–51', in Nick Tiratsoo (ed.) *The Attlee Years*, London, p. 107. Fielding's view has shifted somewhat away from this analysis in more recent work. See, for example, his 'Labourism in the 1940s'; and Stephen Fielding, Peter Thompson and Nick Tiratsoo (1995) *'England Arise!' The Labour Party and Popular Politics in 1940s Britain*, Manchester.

89. For examples of the first, see Robert Miliband (1961) *Parliamentary Socialism*, London; James Hinton (1983) *Labour and Socialism*, Brighton; for the latter see Geoffrey Foote (1985) *The Labour Party's Political Thought: A History*, London, p. 191.

90. Foote, *The Labour Party's Political Thought*, p. 192.

91. Brooke, *Labour's War*; Fielding, 'Labourism in the 1940s'; and Francis, 'Economics and Ethics'.

92. Michael Young, 'Problems Ahead', in Munro, *Socialism: The British Way*, p. 345.

93. Young, *Small Man, Big World*, p. 3.

94. Young, 'A plea for restatement of socialism', p. 3.

5. 'For home and country': feminism and Englishness in the Women's Institute movement, 1930–60

Maggie Andrews

In the late nineteenth and early twentieth centuries, thinkers of both right and left from Rider Haggard to William Morris looked to rural life as a solution to the problems of urban degeneration caused by the industrial revolution. To Haggard, rural life offered a 'natural' hierarchical community held together by mutual obligations. Morris, on the other hand, saw 'England's green and pleasant land' as an arena for cooperative endeavour, and, though more utopian than practical, his thinking led to a number of cooperative settlements for the unemployed being set up in areas like Sidlesham, West Sussex in the 1930s. What the right, the left and the centre had in common was a belief that the countryside was the soul of the nation. Rural women played an essential part in this construction of Englishness, and the organization that for most of the twentieth century articulated their concerns was the Women's Institute (WI).

The movement originated in Canada at the turn of the century. In 1915, it was established in England under the auspices of the Agricultural Organization Society and it reached complete independence in 1918. By 1925, it had a quarter of a million members, a figure it has never since dropped below. From its early days, the Sandringham WI had royal members, notably the Duchess of York, who as Queen and then as Queen Mother took a close interest in the WI's affairs throughout her active life. But the WI never sought royal patronage and its royal members were accepted upon payment of the same membership fee as all its others. This was a symbolic attempt by the Institute and also by the royal family to demonstrate that their shared gender overrode class differences.

The WI's national leadership came primarily from the governing classes. Megan Lloyd George and Neville Chamberlain's sister were among those who sat on its executive, while the chairwoman of the National Federation of Women's Institutes (NFWI), Lady Denman, was the daughter of Lord Cowdrey, a wealthy industrialist and new Liberal peer. Active in birth control campaigns before the Second World War, she was typical of the philanthropic women who led the WI in the 1940s. At a local level, its chairwomen were mostly the wives of middle-class professionals, with a sprinkling of modest land-owning gentry. However, it would be wrong to perceive its membership during this period as either predominantly middle class or middle aged. Women of all social classes from their teens to their nineties joined and there is little evidence of any serious tension between the different groups.

Women's Institutes, then as now, were village-based. They were run by a committee, with their activities centred on a monthly meeting, held either in the afternoon or evening and lasting two to three hours. The meeting began with the business of the local institute, county and national WI issues and any campaigns they were involved in. Then followed one, possibly two, talks or demonstrations. The topics were wide ranging. For example, North Leigh in Oxfordshire in the 1920s covered the use of paper patterns, cooperative buying, local history, sightseeing in Italy, local government and a lecture on the empire among other matters.[1] After tea, known as 'the cement of the movement', there was a social half hour involving dancing, singing and playing games. Almost every meeting had some sort of competition, such as the best buttonhole or the best inexpensive Christmas gift. Most institutes had a sales table where members could sell produce. They also held classes in activities such as basket-weaving, country dancing and upholstery. Many had drama groups and choirs which often performed in their communities. These performances helped to raise funds, as did a variety of other events such as flower shows, whist drives and yearly outings, to name a few.

The WI's rural base enabled the organization to tap into a notion of Englishness that saw the village and the rural home as the heart of England. Within that notion of Englishness, the perception of rural womanhood, which had gained cultural currency since the Victorian era, was domestic, maternal and passive. The WI's members saw themselves primarily as rural housewives and their many campaigns focused on that role. From 1918 onwards, the WI promoted a particular concern with housing. It supported the government's 'homes fit for heroes' campaign, and campaigned for the building of rural council houses throughout the interwar years. The importance of the rural home was seen not just in terms of bricks and mortar. It was also seen as the typification of all that was English; a foundation of the empire and, symbolically, what wars were fought to protect.

In 1925, the Minister for Agriculture and Fisheries, E. F. L. Wood, speaking to the WI annual conference, explained the importance of 'a British character built up in and on rural life'. Wood concluded that the WI's practical and ideological work was vital in perpetuating this national character. 'The single aim and goal' of the institute, he said, was to 'lay firm the foundations on which the British citizenship of succeeding centuries is to be erected and sustained.'[2]

A part of the WI's mission was to ensure that traditional rural crafts such as basket-weaving were maintained. Not surprisingly, however, motherhood was seen to be the most important part of their work as keepers of the nation's hearth. During the interwar years, the WI, in common with other women's groups, actively supported attempts by the eugenics movement to improve the racial stock of England. In addition, members were encouraged to attend lectures on birth control given at monthly meetings, as well as those on 'mothercraft', designed to improve domestic hygiene and impart a range of child-rearing techniques.

Meanwhile, government ministers praised the mothers of rural England for the spiritual capital the nation had accrued over the centuries as a result of their work. In 1939, Minister of Health Walter Elliot told the NFWI's AGM: 'The land is the mother of us all, but the members of the Women's Institutes are the mothers of the land. Here we have the wives and daughters of the farmers of England and Wales, who have really made the land of England and Wales in thousands of years of patient toil.'[3] It did not matter that the majority of its members were not farmers' wives. By the 1940s, the association between ruralism and the WI was firmly embedded in the conscious-ness of England's political elites. It was also embedded in the WI itself, for despite the purely domestic role ruralism accorded women and the frequently patronizing way it was presented to them, it did grant them an important role in the nation-building process.

Moreover, to many WI members, their enthusiasm for this traditional construction of Englishness was consistent with a feminist concern for 'responsible citizenship' in the post-suffrage era. Having supported votes for women, it was not unusual for the organization's monthly magazine, *Home and Country* to contain articles entitled 'Voters Awake', which instructed the membership on parliamentary legislation of significance to women and encouraged them to partici-pate in all layers of the political process.

The identification of the good of rural women with the good of the nation, signified in the motto 'For Home and Country', allowed the WI to develop a radical stance on a variety of issues. Campaigns for rural phone boxes, women police, better housing, sewage and water facilities, rural libraries and analgesics for women during childbirth were fuelled both by the immediate needs of women at local level and by a fundamental belief in the importance of rural womanhood to the modernization of the nation. Such activities, discussed and debated at the WI's annual general meeting at the Albert Hall, led it to be described by the press as the 'Countrywoman's Parliament' — a term which expressed the absence of women from the state Parliament at Westminster but also the serious political nature of these alternative meetings and their potential to influence govern-ment policy-making. Thus, the WI adapted itself to the era of women's suffrage and reflected the new confidence and sense of choice and possibilities many women felt.

A key spokeswoman of this change was Janet Courtney, a writer on women's issues, who likened the WI to a trade union. Drawing on the Hammonds' work on the exploitation of rural workers, she claimed that 'the remedy sought by the agricultural labourer in [Joseph] Arch's day is the remedy women were seeking when war broke over our heads — combination, cooperation, strength in union.'[4] Courtney presented the WI as part of a wider women's movement. However, she distanced it from socialism and feminism, which she identified as narrow, marginal concerns that sought to stir up conflict between the classes and the sexes. Instead, she saw the WI as an exemplar of English democracy, a pressure group that campaigned for measures to readjust the prevailing political system without substantially threatening the power structures of the class and gender relations that maintained it. She reassured her readers that the WI 'take[s] no narrow feminist view . . . there is no trace of the sort of evils that have beset so many other movements. There is no "swerve to the left" or any other attempt on behalf of extremists to exert themselves.'[5] The boundaries she drew around acceptable and unacceptable political activity were generally shared by the WI's members, and remained the essence of its ideology.

I want to suggest, therefore, that there was tension between the WI's traditional articulation of rural womanhood as the heart of the nation and its aspiration to be a progressive feminist body, but that by juxtapositioning itself between these two discourses, it was able to bring about real improvements in the material circumstances of women's lives. In short, the WI saw itself as the 'acceptable face of feminism'. The nation is not a static concept and has been renegotiated to serve a variety of causes. The 1940s and 1950s were decades when meanings of both gender and nationality were particularly fluid. The state's emphasis on the home front, and on food production in particular, gave national significance to many of the everyday tasks performed by women.

Meanwhile, the wartime mobilization of women workers in a variety of spheres, from the forces to factories and farms, challenged traditional perceptions of women's role in society. Furthermore, postwar planning gave women's groups the opportunity to place what were previously seen as marginal feminist issues, such as family allowances, on to a national agenda of reconstruction. The conditions of women's belonging were renegotiated, shifting the emphasis from their role as mothers of the race and keepers of the rural home to an emphasis on domestic productivity and the cooperative democracy that was an emblem of the 'New Jerusalem' of the postwar settlement. Finally, I shall argue that in the affluent

1950s the WI's vision of women's right to belong increasingly came to be linked to consumption rather than production, as the organization identified itself as a consumer 'watchdog'.

The onset of war placed the WI in a quandary, which for a time threatened its close identification with the nation. The movement had a broad religious base, which included a number of Quakers. Due to this connection, many institutes were associate members of the League of Nations Union, while some, like the Chipping Camden WI, were formed out of a local peace group. As a result, the WI's national executive refused to allow the organization to partake in activities that directly contributed to preparation for war, or the maintenance of hostilities during the war, on the grounds that its activities could not exclude any members on account of their religious convictions. The WI's willingness to take seriously the religious convictions of a relatively small group like the Quakers was a measure of its determination to embrace all women rather than any prevailing religious ethos.

In the 1920s, the Church of England initially saw the WI as an unnecessary and mischievous competitor for the Mothers' Union. As the WI became more popular and received official recognition of its work from senior politicians and the royal family, a number of vicars' wives became chairwomen of local organizations. Despite this, the WI had resisted formal links at a local or national level with the Church, and attempts to start meetings with prayers were quickly stymied by the national organization. The WI's wartime position laid it open to criticism from inside and outside the organization, and it subsequently lost some of its members to the newly established Women's Royal Voluntary Service, which directly assisted the war effort by arranging the billeting of evacuees, running canteens for the armed forces and making camouflage equipment.

However, in jam-making the WI discovered an activity that preserved its reputation as one of the nation's essential voluntary organizations. The government was equally concerned for it to do so, and helped it set up fruit preservation centres across the country and supplied them with sugar. The centres also canned fruit, but it is for their jam-making skills that the institute became well known. In 1943, Cecily McCall, a member of the NFWI's executive, published a book — *Women's Institutes* — in the popular *Britain in Pictures* series, which pointed out its polysemic meaning:

> Jam-making was constructive and non-militant, if you liked to look at it that way. It accorded with the best Quaker traditions of feeding blockaded nations. For those who were dietetically minded, jam contained all the most highly prized vitamins. For those who were agriculturally minded the scheme saved a valuable crop from literally rotting on the ground, and it encouraged better fruit cultivation — though not, one can only pray, of plums only. And for the belligerent, what could be more satisfying than fiercely stirring the cauldrons of boiling jam and feeling that every pound took us one step further towards defeating Hitler.[6]

As *Picture Post* noted in 1943, work in the fruit preservation centres was often run on cooperative lines and it gave rural women's pro-ductive domestic labour national significance for the first time.[7] Indeed, to WI members, jam became the embodiment of the England that needed protecting from the prospect of a German invasion. Members of Langton Maltnevers WI, for example, discussed methods of hiding or destroying jam to protect it from jam-starved German paratroopers.[8] As a result of this work, the government came to look on the WI as a significant force in domestic food production. As well as sponsoring fruit preservation centres, the government contributed funds to the setting up of a national Produce Guild, trained its leaders to promote food production and allocated scarce paper resources to ensure the continuance of *Home and Country* during the war.

Women's domestic skills, which were not linked to food production, also took on national significance through the WI. The institute's tradition of competitions and exhibitions was continued to promote wartime crafts such as make-do-and-mend. A pair of trousers made by one woman in West Sussex went all the way up through the NFWI structure to an exhibition in London, where Mrs Churchill saw them.[9] Such exhibitions generated enormous personal and local pride because they validated housework through judging systems external to the home and because, for a short time, they left some public record of women's domestic productiveness, just as the weekly wage might record a man's productivity.

That housework should be recognized as a skilled profession became a recurring theme in the WI and other post-suffrage feminist organizations, right through to the wages-for-housework campaigns of the 1970s. Such women did not want to reject the domestic sphere, but to renegotiate its boundaries by questioning its marginal status as a solely female occupation that was not valued by the marketplace. An article in *Home and Country* in 1941 entitled 'The Nation's Cinderella' captured that aspiration. As well as improving the political position of women, the feminist movement had to:

> show that women doing their own traditional and specific job of running a household and bringing up a family should be considered as important, as responsible and as much worthy of respect as women doing the kind of job that can be done equally well by either sex; and that their work is just as vital if not more so.[10]

The importance of the home front during the Second World War, and the consequent elevation of women's everyday tasks to national significance helped English women in general to challenge the social construction of femininity.

Where the WI was concerned, the success of its jam-making and make-do-and-mend work encouraged a greater political consciousness among rural women. In 1944, the American film studio RKO produced a fictional melodrama entitled *The Great Day*, which focused on the preparations for Eleanor Roosevelt to visit Denby WI to observe the war effort of rural British women. Early in the film, WI members discuss why they have been chosen to represent the female war effort. The confident articulation of the importance of women's productiveness was coupled with a communitarian social agenda, which was a reworking of the radical English ruralism of the first half of the twentieth century:

> 'We're a community working together with no orders from anybody but ourselves.'

'We're a working village that's made itself . . . a powerful production unit. We're the beginning of something new, make no mistake. Look at our record, our production figures, 7000 lbs of jam for the troops last year — pure jam made in this hall not factory rubbish.'

'Fur coats for the Russians out of skins of rabbits we breed. And Lord knows, how much wool spun from the waste we collect from the fences where the sheep scratch themselves.'

'And where does that go? To keep our boys in the bombers warm on the long journeys and quilts for the wounded. Why there's no end to it.'

'There's no need to wonder why Denby was chosen . . . Where's your imagination? Doesn't it mean something to you that some of the defenders of Stalingrad kept themselves warm in the coats we made with our hands in this very hall.'

'How do we know that extra warmth didn't help somebody at some vital point.'

'Yes, how do you know that in some tiny way it didn't help the course of history. Fancy that now!'

The film is a powerful example of what Patrick Wright describes as 'the rags and tatters of everyday life being touched by the idealized nation'.[11] Despite the growth of political consciousness in the movement, the WI was careful not to adopt a party political stance, just as it had earlier been careful to avoid formal links with any particular church. A pamphlet published in 1941 presented it as an example of the English race's 'knack of being "clubbable"'. The pamphlet's author, Cicely Hamilton concluded: 'as these Institutes exist for the benefit of the neighbourhood in general, with the object of promoting sociability and friendliness, politics, that destroyer of peace and goodwill, is wisely barred from the list of subjects they discuss.'[12] Nonetheless, the war had given the WI an even higher national profile than it had previously enjoyed, and had galvanized many of its members. As Cecily McCall concluded, 'here was not only the perfect example of democracy at work but of training in citizenship.'[13]

The WI hoped that such training would be useful in the postwar period. The WI's many activities, together with its wartime work, led its members to believe that they had earned the right to belong fully to the nation, not simply as the embodiment of a timeless rural Englishness, but as active participants in the social, economic and cultural development of the nation. In particular, they sought to play a major part in equipping the countryside with an infrastructure that would guarantee a fair standard of living for its inhabitants, and would thereby ensure that the nation's heritage was a truly living entity. Cecily McCall, who resigned her post on the NFWI in 1945 to stand unsuccessfully as a Labour candidate in the general election, had this to say in *Women's Institutes*:

> Democracy has been well taught and practised in Institutes, and when peace comes there will be 300,000 women ready to say loudly and clearly that since country people are 'custodians of a heritage' that heritage must be living, not embalmed. It must be drained and electrified, equipped with modern school buildings and an adequate school staff; it must have up-to-date health services and recreational facilities; and working women must be given a fair chance to take their part in planning and building the village life of the future.[14]

Like many other groups that had campaigned for rural development with limited success in the interwar years, the government's ability to mobilize resources for the defence of the nation changed their perception of the government's ability and power to act in peacetime. For example, one woman wrote to *Home and Country* in 1940 to say that in the 1930s, her village had campaigned unsuccessfully for adequate water supplies in the area, only to discover that when a wartime army camp was placed nearby, it had promptly received water and drainage. Why, she wanted to know, couldn't such action be taken for ordinary people in peacetime?

The provision of public services was not the only concern of the movement. The WI actively supported the Beveridge Report, seeing the social welfare legislation it advocated as recognition of the importance of housewives' role as skilled workers. The activist Helen Judd, writing in *Home and Country*, proclaimed 'housewives have come into their own at last!'[15] Welcoming the family allowances, widows' benefits and maternity care the report promised, the WI's AGM of 1943 unanimously passed the following resolution: 'this meeting records its appreciation of Sir William Beveridge's great work for social security and particularly of his recognition that health insurance for housewives and family allowances are essential if family life is to be free from want.'[16] The members continued to discuss the report over the next two years, making suggestions as to how it could be built upon. Some of their more radical proposals, such as sick pay for housewives, did not reach the national agenda of reconstruction. But their discussions did much to gain acceptance of the welfare state and the managed economy in many otherwise conservative rural areas.

In the long term, the creation of the welfare state in the postwar period brought with it a mushrooming of both local and central government experts and officials. Consequently, like many other voluntary societies, the WI suffered a degree of marginalization as those officials took over a variety of welfare issues that were previously seen to be within the legitimate sphere of expertise of the NFWI. In the 1950s, the NFWI continued to give its opinions to a variety of government bodies, but found itself increasingly ignored by them. This trend contributed to a gradual waning of the WI's more overt political activities in the postwar period, and a greater concentration on the social activities of the organization.

The clear demands made in previous decades for legislation to improve the lives of rural women were replaced by AGM resolutions that concentrated on issues such as anti-litter campaigns, the removal of turnstiles in public loos, and uniform rental costs for telephones. Although of significance to rural women, they did not have the same level of gender specific radicalism of earlier WI campaigns. By concentrating on the politics of the possible, the WI reflected the consensual politics of the time, whereby to a large extent political differences were seen in terms of the most efficient administration of a mixed economy.

The WI's leaders became concerned that the movement was becoming complacent and sought to remind their members that many of the social provisions they now took for granted had been fought for by the WI since the 1920s. The chairwoman's address to the 1954 AGM was typical of this concern:

Does the public questions handbook penetrate into general reading in the Institutes? Are there a few perhaps rather earnest members who would like to see it, brushed aside in discussion by enthusiasts for basket making, cake icing and drama? Do we think public questions a rather dull sounding phrase? Yes it is dull to feel we have been concerned with bringing piped water to hard pressed countrywomen, who with aching backs and arms lugged buckets of water about until they feel old and battered before their time? Isn't it rather splendid that we can feel personal pride at the sight of the trim and resolute policewoman to be seen in our market towns and villages, for we asked for them as long ago as 1922, 1934 and 1940. Are we not proud that countrywomen take such a large part in local government on county district and rural councils, that they are constantly to be found actively engaged as school managers, and they are appointed as magistrates. In the public questions handbook you will find the roots of so many things that flower in our midst.[17]

Throughout the 1950s, social reforms the WI had been demanding for many years were celebrated as they were introduced, while the government was chivvied about the need for greater speed in implementing them. A survey carried out by the WI with results published in 1957 as a pamphlet entitled 'Our Villages'[18] may be seen in this light. It recorded the movement's views on amenities such as village halls, playgrounds and piped water, and highlighted improvements that were still needed. The NFWI chairwoman, Lady Brunner, instructed her members to buy a copy of the survey, compare their village to others and use it to pester parish councils.

Institutes were even established within mental hospitals in this period in an attempt to retain the movement's involvement in social policy. Some of the WI's membership responded to these attempts to stress the movement's more political past in order to reinvigorate its activities. Indeed, throughout the 1950s, some complained that they had done nothing more significant than make a few pots of jam in wartime.

However, such members were in a minority, and could not prevent the WI's retreat from the national political arena after the war. The WI's definition of its role in the community once again became predominantly social and localized. The function of monthly meetings was seen to be a well organized and structured exchange of domestic skills rather than an opportunity to discuss wider issues relating to women and the nation. Inez Jenkins's official *History of the Women's Institute Movement* published in 1953, reflected this change. Cooperative effort was still valued. But, in contrast with Cecily McCall's book a decade earlier, the stress was no longer on the importance of women becoming active citizens but on the ironing out of their individual differences in order to promote a peaceful, organic rural society.

> If in the modern village there is less need than of old for the Institute as a spearhead of activity, the need remains, pronounced as ever, for what it can provide as a meeting place where skill and knowledge may be exchanged in friendliness, where there may be discussion without bias, where differences may be reconciled, where conflicting points of view may be understood and respected, where the satisfaction and happiness of cooperative effort may be discovered and enjoyed.[19]

In part, this retreat reflected the renewed emphasis on the woman as home maker during the 1950s. As men came home from the war and ousted women from many of the traditionally male jobs they had briefly occupied on the home front, women were once again expected to take up their traditional domestic role. As a result, the number of women in part-time work rose substantially in the postwar period, but the number in full-time work remained static.

Although few WI members had become bus drivers, crane operators or welders, the removal of women from the male workplace lost them the central position in national life they had enjoyed during the war, and reduced the profile of the movement's leaders.

The change in the WI's outlook also reflected the class divisions within it. Ordinary members had always stressed the importance of the WI's provision of a social centre for women in villages. Generally, only those who could afford to engage domestic labour had the time and energy to participate in the leadership of the institute and in the political campaigns it organized. Rural working-class women were, at most, only able to attend the occasional campaign meeting. What exacerbated this situation in the postwar period was the increasing shortage of domestic servants (between 1931 and 1961, the number of women in residential service dropped from over two million to 200,000). This decline in domestic service substantially increased the burden of housework for middle-class wives. The increasing range of labour-saving devices available during the 1950s did little to halt the overall trend. The result was that middle-class women who had previously been the mainstay of the movement's political activities had little more time than their working-class counterparts to devote to them.

A related factor in this change was the influx of middle-class families from the towns and suburbs into the rural areas of the south of England during the 1950s. These families, who in the 1930s may have journeyed into the countryside on holiday, now came to live, encouraged by the spread of amenities — many of which the WI had campaigned for — such as electricity, drainage and public transport. Far from invigorating the working life of the countryside, their arrival was a continuation of the prewar reconstruction of England from a site of production to a place of recreation and consumption, for workers in these families usually commuted to nearby towns.

The migration from the towns to the countryside changed the social make up of many villages and their WIs. It is likely that an increase in the middle-class membership of the WI would previously have increased the level of its political activity. In the 1950s, it hastened the return to its original role as a social organization, for the priority of most new arrivals was to establish networks of friends to compensate for the dislocation they experienced as a result of their move from urban areas. In 1957, *Home and Country* carried a series entitled 'Letters to a Very New Member', which emphasized the companionship the WI offered such women.[20] The chairwoman's address at the AGM that year summed up the trend: 'You may have begun by feeling you didn't know a soul here, but WI fellowship breaks through that and we'll find new friends and good neighbours today all willing to help and be helped ... WI membership is the finest insurance there is against loneliness.'[21]

These changes did not lead to a complete disavowal of activism in the postwar period. Many women found a new area of power and expertise in consumerism, and they put a new emphasis on the right to leisure. While accepting a primarily domestic sphere, rural women were still forced into quasi-political activity in order to achieve the conditions necessary for them to carry out their domestic tasks efficiently. Women's domestic base was therefore used to justify their demands for reform, and consequently domesticity continued to be an assertive form of citizenship. In 1948, the WI passed a resolution 'deploring the poor quality of household goods and clothing' and demanding that action should be taken by the government to improve the standard of living in 'Austerity Britain'.[22] As affluence replaced austerity, mass production — though able to keep pace with consumer demand — did not always maintain the manufacturing quality the prewar generation had enjoyed. As a result, the WI's new role as a consumer watchdog became a firmly established part of its activities.

Members were encouraged to buy items that displayed the British Standards Institution kite symbol, and *Home and Country* contained frequent articles that sought to guide its readers about the best fridges, television sets and washing machines to buy. By 1955, the WI was involved in the staging of the Ideal Homes Exhibition at Olympia in London, where one of the homes was designed and furnished under the WI's direction. As well as a range of modern gadgets, it included William Morris wallpaper and patchwork bed-covers. The Morris revival in interior design did not get fully under way for another decade. But its presence at Olympia was an indication that the rural idyll of an earlier period, far from being redundant, was about to be harnessed to a new dream of 'England's green and pleasant land' in which country life was recycled for urban consumers as an antidote to the stresses of modern living.

Although criticized as a passive acceptance of advertisers' manipulation of popular fantasies, such consumerism was often pragmatically subversive. To quote Erica Carter, 'Consumerism not only offers but continually fulfils its promise of everyday solutions, albeit limited and partial ones, to problems whose origins lie elsewhere.' Thus, consumption was empowering for many women and, in the consumer boom of 1950s' Britain, it was a space from which women could again define themselves as part of the nation, with a right to belong as discerning citizen consumers.

If consumerism focused the WI's attentions once more on the domestic sphere, it did not mean the movement became insular. In the last chapter of Cecily McCall's wartime study of the WI, she looked to 'The Future' and predicted that, as well as teaching members about 'practical democracy' at home, its lectures had given members an opportunity to look beyond their villages and beyond the shores of England itself.[23] As the cold war developed, the WI espoused a muscular internationalism and formed links with other countries — particularly through their membership of the Associated Country Women of the World (ACWW), which held a triannual conference and a variety of fund-raising campaigns — 'pennies for friendship' being the most well known. Membership was open to all WI members and gave them a wider sense of belonging with foreign women and their cultures.

In interviews, members have recalled their excitement at identifying other ACWW members by their badge when abroad, and the sense of mutuality they felt as a result.[24] This internationalism had its roots in the interwar years when the WI supported the League of Nations and the Women's International League for Peace and Freedom. Indeed, in 1946, with the formation of the League of Nations' successor, the United Nations, the NFWI reaffirmed its commitment to peace with the following resolution:

The members of the NFWI, recognizing the important part women can play in promoting world peace and agricultural prosperity, pledge themselves to study the United Nations Organization, and to work by every means in their power for the promotion of friendship between nations by making contact with individuals and organizations in other countries, either direct or through international organizations such as the Associated Country Women of the World.[25]

In 1954, a resolution was passed that added a new clause to local WI rules giving them power to 'promote international understanding among country women'.[26] Understanding was facilitated in a number of practical ways. Writing to foreign pen pals and, for the better off, the adoption of refugee families, became popular with WI members in the postwar period. NFWI representatives visited other countries and welcomed foreign visitors to their AGMs and to their newly opened adult education college, Denman. The countries visited were as diffuse as the USSR and Ceylon, and the accounts of these trips in *Home and Country* were a significant facet of the movement in the 1950s. They were sometimes written in the tone of Victorian missionaries reporting events from the 'interior' to their bishop. One such was a visit to Germany by Helena Deneke — carried out, she said, to 're-educate German women into organizing themselves for the common good.'[27] However, on the whole, the WI rejected prevalent constructions of foreigners as a strange, amusing 'other', best avoided by all sensible Anglo-Saxons.

In particular, it rejected discrimination against black people, at a time in the late 1950s when discrimination was rife in Britain and spilling over into the Notting Hill race riots. Denman College ran a course on the history of apartheid in South Africa. A story entitled 'Black Beauty', published in *Home and Country* in 1958 is typical of the time. It tells of a mother taking her small child to hospital to have an eye operation. The mother walks up the long drive to the hospital; her son clutches her hand tighter as she prepares to leave him with the nursing staff. The nurse who is to look after her child approached: 'Coming down the corridor towards them was a nurse. She was black. A young African girl. And she was wonderfully beautiful, radiantly alive. Her white uniform emphasized her colour vividly.... Oh dear thought Mrs Martin nervously. Supposing

Andrew says something awkward. But Andrew gazed with awe. 'Oh, Mummy' he breathed ecstatically at last, 'Isn't she beautiful.'[28]

This story, which won first prize in a short story competition, concludes with both mother and son confident and reassured as the young boy has been handed into the nurse's safekeeping. It captures a voyeuristic love of the exotic, which is at best naïve. Yet, it also reflects the WI's overriding concern to promote an inclusive sense of citizenship among its members and in English society as a whole. When immigration controls became a major issue in the 1960s, the WI appears never to have discussed the subject at its AGMs. It may have been able to take a liberal approach because it felt that immigration was an essentially urban issue that was of no consequence to its members. However, for a resolution to be placed on the agenda of the WI's AGM, it had to jump through many administrative hoops, and other controversial suggestions, like nuclear disarmament did not make it through this process due to opposition. It is therefore reasonable to assume that the majority of the WI's membership were not in favour of controls.

In conclusion, though the WI eschewed radical feminism, its close association with traditional notions of Englishness was generally constructive. By the time it had established itself in the early 1930s, women were enfranchised and had a legal right to belong, but prevalent discourses of female rights still excluded them. By choosing to accept the elevated role given to rural women by the nation's male elites, it gained a position of influence at a time when meanings of gender and nation were becoming increasingly fluid. This influence enabled many rural women to improve the material conditions of their lives. Ultimately, they also succeeded in transcending the existing boundaries of their right to belong, first as producers during the war and then as consumers during the affluent 1950s. By 1960, rural women had become accepted, both as equal citizens of the English nation and as partners in an international women's movement. Consequently, they were able to reap some of the advantages of the next wave of feminism, which the 1960s and 1970s brought. A poem, written for *Home and Country* in 1923, captures the peculiar feminism of the WI:

Women of England, your country is calling,
Great is the choice that it gives you today,
Fair are the lines where our footsteps are falling
Grand are the chances, for work and for play.
Parts of one whole, we look forward together,
Sure of a welcome, wherever we roam,
Steady in a storm, or in sunny weather,
True to our watchword, 'For Country and Home'.
Follow on, follow on, follow on, follow on, follow on!
Till the country can blossom anew,
With the work that women do.
Follow on, follow on![29]

The tone of the poem today seems quaint. Yet its optimism, and some of the ideals that lay behind it, are perhaps not far removed from those of modern English feminists.

Notes

1. *Home and Country* (London, 1941) p. 17.
2. *Home and Country*, July 1925.
3. *Home and Country*, August 1939, p. 269.
4. J. E. Courtney (1937) *Countrywomen in Council*, London, p. vi.
5. Ibid., p. 150.
6. C. McCall (1943) *Women's Institutes*, London, p. 31.
7. *Picture Post*, vol. 18, no. 1, 2 January 1943.
8. 'Langston Maltnevers Wartime History' in the History File in the NFWI archive.
9. Mrs Anchor, a West Sussex WI member from the 1930s interviewed in 1986 (name has been changed for reasons of confidentiality).
10. *Home and Country*, June 1941, p. 114.
11. P. Wright (1985) *On Living in an Old Country*, London, p. 25
12. Cicely Hamilton (1941) 'The Englishwoman', in *British Life and Thought*, London.
13. McCall, *Women's Institutes*, p. 15.
14. Ibid., p. 48.
15. *Home and Country*, February 1943, p. 36.
16. *Home and Country*, July 1943, p. 112.
17. *Home and Country*, May 1954, p. 235.
18. C. McCall (1956) *Our Villages*, London, NFWI, in NFWI publications file at organization national archive.

19. I. Jenkins (1953) *The History of the Women's Institute Movement in England and Wales*, Oxford, p. 151.
20. *Home and Country*, February 1957, p. 52.
21. *Home and Country*, July 1957, p. 202.
22. *Home and Country*, July 1948, p. 59.
23. McCall, *Women's Institutes*, p. 48.
24. Oral interview with Sussex WI member Mrs Scott in 1987.
25. NFWI (1981) *Keeping Ourselves Informed*, London, National Federation of Women's Institutes, pp. 82–3.
26. Ibid.
27. Ibid.
28. *Home and Country*, July 1958, p. 205.
29. *Home and Country*, January 1923.

6. 'New vistas': the Labour Party, citizenship and the built environment in the 1940s

Nick Tiratsoo

In recent years, it has become fashionable to criticize the Attlee government for imposing a bureaucratic version of socialism on postwar Britain. Labour, it is argued, was only interested in top-down reform and ignored measures that would have fostered popular initiative and participation. What made this strategic orientation so damaging was that it produced passive rather than active citizens — a population variously described in the literature as 'welfare dependent' or 'alienated' according to taste. In more extreme versions, Labour is accused of creating social ills that have only finally been vanquished by Thatcherism.

This is a seductive interpretation, but I shall argue that it is nevertheless misleading. The problem is that the critics grossly overstate their case and so do much violence to Labour's ambitions as well as the social and political complexity of the postwar period. My objective is to establish this point by looking in detail at one particular example — Labour's policies on the planning of the built environment. Later sections will trace how Labour approached town planning; what it did once in office; and how ordinary people reacted when changes were introduced. First, however, it is prudent to look in a little more depth at the accounts I seek to revise.[1]

The charge that Labour imposed solutions after 1945 has been made with most vehemence by critics of the left. They argue that the British people were radicalized by the fight against fascism and stood ready to play an active role in reform by the war's end. However, they assert, the Attlee government refused to recognize this potential and

instead proceeded by administrative edict. The outcome was a
situation where 'the people' quickly lost all faith in 'the planners'.
The historian Jim Fyrth makes this point particularly clearly:

> The Labour governments . . . did a great deal for the people, but
> were not willing to see things done by the people. . . . It was a
> fatal flaw, which meant that the nationalized industries and the
> Welfare State were bureaucratic, and that the people's experi-
> ence of the bureaucracy did not enthuse them to defend the
> institutions of postwar Britain when they began to be savaged
> in the 1980s.[2]

More detailed work, for instance by Colin Ward and the feminist
Matrix collective, purports to show that this was just as true for town
planning and housing as any other policy area.[3]

Nevertheless, left-wing critics have been by no means the only
ones to raise these themes. Conservative commentaries on the Attlee
period naturally spend most time attacking the government's goals,
but they, too, also frequently criticize the way reform was engineered. In fact, polemics against 'socialist authoritarianism' began to
appear shortly after Labour had taken office. In a widely read book of
1948, for example, the economist John Jewkes raged against the new
system of state planning, both social and economic, and denounced
it as at once inefficient, unjust and undemocratic.[4] Later commentators have returned to these ideas. In the 1960s and 1970s, the
architectural critic Christopher Booker frequently argued that
Attlee's attempt to create an urban planning system had bequeathed a
poisoned legacy, not least because those involved in shaping the
reforms took no notice of the ordinary householder's common sense.
A recent pamphlet from the Social Affairs Unit, indicatively titled
'Planning Fails the Inner Cities', makes a similar point.[5] Indeed, this
kind of rhetoric was on occasion used by Lady Thatcher herself.
Addressing the 1987 Conservative Party Conference, she castigated
'the planners' for having too often 'cut the heart out of our cities' and
went on to launch a wide-ranging attack on the whole of the postwar
planning system:

They swept aside the familiar city centres that had grown up over centuries. They replaced them with a wedge of tower block and linking expressways, interspersed with token patches of grass. The planners didn't think: 'Are we breaking the pattern of people's lives?' . . . They simply set the municipal bulldozer to work. What folly, what incredible folly. . . . The schemes won a number of architectural awards. But they were a nightmare for the people.[6]

Of course, not all these various criticisms are wholly congruent, but there is a shared core of common propositions. The key point is the distance between 'the people' and the 'planners'. The former are portrayed as full of earthy common sense, clear in their choices, and yearning to participate. The latter are alleged to be self-absorbed and uninterested in consultation, driven by a fundamentally undemocratic ideology. The planners, it is declared, only ever wanted to apply their own ideas. All this sounds plausible but in fact amounts to little more than caricature, containing a grain of truth and no more. To give some idea of the real situation, I now turn to a detailed examination of the Attlee government and its policies for the planning of the built environment.

In the years before 1945, Labour developed a coherent analysis of what was wrong with Britain's urban fabric. There was no doubt, it was agreed, that Britain's cities suffered from a plethora of pressing problems. Many were so congested and poorly zoned that they hardly worked in economic terms. Most, too, had failed their populations. The poor were condemned to overcrowded slums without amenities. Better-off families had moved to a growing suburbia, but they also had problems. Housewives on the new estates, it was believed, felt imprisoned, isolated by poor public transport and alienated from social life. More fundamentally, there were good grounds for believing that the dominant pattern of living was itself unhealthy, since it prevented the emergence of shared loyalties. Aneurin Bevan, first Minister of Health in Attlee's government, spoke of 'castrated communities', which he felt were deeply undesirable: 'You have colonies of low-income people, living in houses provided by the local authorities, and you have the higher income groups living in their own colonies. This segregation ... is a wholly evil thing, from a civilized point of view. .... It is a monstrous infliction upon the essential psychological and biological one-ness of the community.[7]

Turning to the causes of this situation, Labour believed that the fundamental problem was lack of planning. As a pamphlet of 1944 concluded, nearly all the towns in Britain had 'just "happened"'.[8] They were shaped by the desires of disparate vested interests — landlords, developers and the business community — which had built when they pleased. Cities as they stood, therefore, essentially reflected a particular balance of power, in which the private dominated the public and the few benefited at the expense of the many.

The way to solve urban problems, therefore, was clear. Labour would have to augment the planning system. This must necessarily be achieved through national legislation, for experience had shown that local aggregations of the powerful were often too strong for town or even city councils to tame. However, within this overall objective, there was certainly considerable space for community-based action. Labour wanted to bring people together, and perhaps recreate 'the glory of some of the past English villages', where 'the doctor could reside benignly with his patients in the same street'.[9] There was no better way of attaining this end than by encouraging all citizens to be involved in decision-making about their own localities.

Once in office, Labour proceeded to introduce a number of specific reforms. The 1947 Town and Country Planning Act was the central piece of fresh legislation. Under previous statutes, any local authority could obtain powers to enforce planning, but only if it could afford to use a complicated and expensive set of procedures, aimed at obtaining a tailor-made parliamentary bill. The new act rationalized the number of planning authorities, devolving responsibility on to county boroughs or county councils, and instructed the new bodies to prepare development plans for their own areas, essentially blueprints outlining the future pattern of use. It also introduced complex procedures for dealing with compensation and betterment, allowing national monies to be used where necessary to overcome local ownership problems.

This approach certainly suggested an increased role for civil servants, councillors and professional planners, but it also provided several openings for popular input.[10] Planning authorities were instructed to consult as widely as possible when drawing up their plans. When completed, the plans could be challenged, with appeals being heard by an inspector at a public hearing. In this sense, it was hoped to strike a balance between the requirements for technical expertise in planning and the views of ordinary citizens.

Alongside this legislation, Labour also pursued various other policies aimed at increasing the sense of community and the desire to participate. After some discussion at the 1944 party conference, Labour formally adopted the Reilly Plan as a model for future estate development.[11] Reilly, who was Lever Professor of Civic Design, had been employed by Birkenhead Council to design an estate in the city. His final design was based on American neighbourhood-unit principles. What Labour liked about Reilly's ideas was their emphasis on community. The consultant wanted houses to be 'placed in friendly relation to one another'. He argued that homes should be built in fairly small numbers round village greens. Four or five of such groupings could then be arranged like the petals of a flower around a central area, equipped with appropriate facilities for education, recreation and shopping. Such neighbourhoods would then be aggregated into cities. The objective was to allow contact to develop between all classes in the population. As Reilly noted of his basic tier, the houses round a village green: 'with all the ways of meeting one's fellows such an estate would provide...a great many of the advantages of a residential university would accrue. It should make for a more intelligent community whose members do not rely on a single newspaper for their information.'[12]

Finally, there were a whole myriad of small initiatives by local Labour parties and councils aimed at educating and enthusing.[13] Some Labour groups completed their own planning surveys, drawing in other organizations as the work proceeded.[14] A number of councils held exhibitions on their ideas. A reviewer in the *Builder* during 1946 reported that a display on the Birkenhead plan was 'a great credit' to its organizers: it would 'educate the Birkenhead people to a civic awareness' and thus 'promote the effort necessary to carrying out this scheme'.[15] More ambitiously, a few authorities even made films about local town planning.[16] The objective, in every case, was to encourage participation. As the leader of Coventry Council explained in 1945, Labour must at every level promote a 'new democratic technique', which would 'make the citizen conscious of the vital part, the living part he [sic] has to play ... in a real democracy'.[17]

What did these various initiatives achieve in practice? Taking the 1947 Act first, it is clear that by the early 1950s there were good reasons for thinking that it had been in part successful. The financial provisions remained controversial. On the other hand, the appeals procedure appeared to be working quite well. As Table 6.1 shows, the number of cases disposed of was substantial, with the proportion of successful challenges by complainants never falling below 30 per cent of the total adjudicated on.

Table 6.1: Appeals under the 1947 Town and Country Planning Act

Year	Cases disposed of	Appeals allowed	Appeals dismissed	Appeals withdrawn
1947	2481	417	920	1144
1948	2750	424	831	1495
1949	4237	768	1169	2300
1950	3797	995	1271	1531

Source: Cmd. 8024, Ministry of Local Government and Planning, Town and Country Planning 1943–1951 (April, 1951), p. 179

Moreover, it was clear that the Ministry was making an effort to ensure that the hearings themselves were not intimidating. A US academic who studied the system reported:

The inquiry is governed by the traditional guarantees of due process: notice, representation by counsel, provision for witnesses, evidence on oath. ... At the same time, a refreshing freedom from procedural legerdemain exists. Inspectors ... permit gratuitous expressions of opinion. Objections to evidence on technical grounds are rather unpopular. Letters and petitions are admitted without formal authentication and substantial latitude is permitted in cross-examination. Expenses of hearing are nominal, making redress practically available to all.[18]

By contrast, progress in creating neighbourhood units was much less satisfactory. Almost all local authorities accepted the idea as an ideal but, particularly after 1947, the money was simply not there to build the required facilities. One observer commented in 1950: 'Most of the bigger new estates have been planned on neighbourhood lines. . . . In general, however, only the houses (and a few shops) are actually being built'. This meant, as he explained, that 'in many places conditions similar to those of the 1930s are unfortunately beginning to appear'.[19] What made this situation more depressing for Labour was the fact that, in several locations, there appeared to be no great enthusiasm for cross-class mixing.

Reporting from a town where neighbourhood units of middle- and working-class homes were being planned, the sociologist Mark Benney uncovered a familiar set of prejudices among the better-off inhabitants: 'the possibility that London slum-dwellers might have gardens adjacent to theirs, that squalling brats with intolerable habits of speech might corrupt the accents of their offspring, that visiting friends might assume they live in a working-class neighbourhood . . . such considerations outweigh the remote advantage of balanced communities far more than people will admit.[20]

Finally, what of more general attitudes in the population at large? Had Labour succeeded in making the British 'planning minded'? Foreign visitors tended to be impressed by what had been achieved. Coleman Woodbury, from the University of Wisconsin, toured the country in 1947 and felt the degree of popular interest in planning was 'remarkable'. 'Exhibits of planning charts, studies, and recommendations attract thousands in the larger cities,' he wrote, continuing: 'Documentary films, one at least that runs for more than an hour, are shown in commercial movie houses. Stories about public hearings on town plans or on the acquisition of land for larger projects are front page news.'[21] Seven years later, another US scholar, the Guggenheim fellow Leo Grebler, came to similar conclusions. He reported: 'city rebuilding in England has proceeded in an atmosphere favourable to planning. The citizens' interest in most communities is kept awake through speeches, lectures, and exhibitions.'[22]

On the other hand, local observers tended to be rather less sanguine in their assessments. The experienced garden city campaigner, F. J. Osborn, told the 1951 Town and Country Planning summer school that he was most struck by 'the paucity and thinness of public influences on planning'. 'The great mass of the people', he believed, were 'so far indifferent to the chance of rescue that planning could offer them'.[23] Some months later, a prominent political scientist from the LSE told a similar gathering that planning had only reached what he called 'the Third Programme stage of evolution': 'It probably appeals to about a quarter of a million people in this country out of forty million or so and somehow it must be made into the Home Service or Light Programme if it is to become politically important.'[24] The *Economist* came to similar conclusions. 'In less than five years', it editorialized in 1951, 'the town planners' dream had faded'. The position was unpromising in almost all possible ways:

Schemes for individual towns have been followed by broad regional blueprints. . . . This plentitude of plans has been matched by a multiplication of controls . . . and by the establishment of a hierarchy of officials having a vested interest in the planning process. But of concrete results, in the shape of an improvement in the living and working conditions of the people, there is little — pathetically little — to show. Popular enthusiasm for this brand of planning is turning rapidly to disillusionment.[25]

Taken together, to conclude, the evidence indicates that the impact of Labour's innovations was at best patchy. The government had created a new legislative system but there was little to suggest that the desired accompanying changes in attitude were occurring. What had gone wrong? To answer this question, it is necessary to look in a little more detail at the planning process itself and then turn to the more general question of what ordinary people wanted as regards the built environment in the postwar period.

The first point to make about the planning mechanism at this time is that it was dominated by professionals with very traditional practical skills. An official enquiry of 1949 reported:

> the majority of chief officers to local authorities responsible for planning are engineers, the remainder being architects and surveyors, with very few whose qualification is solely planning. Out of 153 planning authorities of all types, senior planning responsibility was held in 81 cases by engineers, in 34 by architects, in 32 by surveyors and in 6 by members of the Town Planning Institute who have qualified through examinations of the Institute without having a basic professional qualification.[26]

No doubt, some of these figures were sympathetic to Labour's goals, but the majority were not. Most civil engineers, for example, were ill-equipped, either by training or inclination, to deal positively with issues like consultation and participation. They saw themselves as experts doing an essentially technical job. There was deep suspicion of those who wanted to make planning more visionary — of planners who were 'up in the air or in dreamland instead of keeping their feet firmly on the ground'.[27]

Of course, alongside this cohort were small numbers of planning consultants, less rigorously grounded in narrow disciplines and more ready to admit that their work needed to have a sociological dimension. However, even in the few cases where such people dominated, the actual position in relation to Labour's objectives was not necessarily more promising. Most consultants were in favour of involving the local population in planning, but there was a wide spectrum of opinion about how and to what extent this should be done.

It was generally agreed that planning should start with research. Planners needed to know how people lived and how they wanted to live. Obtaining such information, as all recognized, was not easy. Commissioning special investigations required time and money, neither of which were usually available. The only really viable option, therefore, was to consult sociologists, but this, too, was fraught with difficulties. The disciplines of planning and sociology had grown up following very different paths and there was little sense of compatibility or dialogue among their practitioners. One observer characterized the gulf between the two professions as follows:

> If . . . the planner were to ask for advice about the planning of a railway, and the frequency with which trains should be run along the lines . . . the sociologist would give him a report on the colours of the socks worn by the engine-drivers . . . perhaps . . . embellished by a series of statistical correlations between those colours and the drivers' sex life and criminal propensities.[28]

Having completed the plan, the planners had then to decide how exactly the people should be consulted, a question which once again raised difficulties. One view was that the planners' work had been done if ordinary citizens understood and appreciated the schemes that were being proposed.[29] Against this, there was a more widespread feeling that the public needed to be granted the power of final veto.[30] Nevertheless, few were really certain about what this meant in practice. Plans usually contained many technicalities and so there was some doubt about whether the untutored mind would understand what was on offer. Moreover, there were few if any precedents to follow when constructing the machinery that would allow democratic decision-making. Planning consultants, like Labour politicians, were very aware of the power wielded by local vested interests. In the end, therefore, proponents of consultation and participation were often driven to place most emphasis on the need for educational programmes that would spread knowledge of planning — a solution which, quite obviously, was unlikely to alleviate their short-term problems.

Outside the planning departments, in the wider sphere of local authority life, there were also pressures encouraging caution and conservatism. Council bureaucracies were run on long-standing principles, with a strict division of labour between departments. Planners often found it difficult to fit in, particularly if figures like the local council treasurer or chief civil engineer were unsympathetic. The same tensions were evident at county level, with the eminent planning consultant Thomas Sharp going so far as to allege that good work by himself and others was being 'discarded' because of the 'professional jealousy' endemic among career local government officers.[31]

Politicians operating at this level were rarely much interested in resolving these difficulties. Some Labour councillors, drawn from industrial life via the trade unions, found planning concepts difficult to master and felt themselves to be out of their depth when confronted with novel ideas.[32] Many Conservatives were suspicious of planning in any form and campaigned against it. Moreover, the style and substance of city and county politics hardly encouraged experimentation. Councillors from across the political spectrum shared the objective of delivering a fairly restricted number of services in the cheapest way possible. They had been brought up to believe that the rate level was probably crucial in determining local voters' preferences. In the postwar situation, anyway, their room for manoeuvre was usually small. Many councils had large and urgent housing problems as a result of German bombing. In addition, some had lost considerable amounts of rateable value because of damage to commercial property or the forced evacuation of local industrial firms. The priorities, especially in urban areas, had to be housing and the quick restoration of business activity. Waiting for public consultation and approval sometimes hardly seemed an option.[33]

Given these pressures, it was not uncommon to find councils being very uncompromising and negative over planning issues during these years. In 1948, to give one example, the Ministry of Town and Country Planning in London became worried that some local administrations were enforcing regulations and fighting appeals with far too much vigour, disregarding the democratic spirit of the new legislation. Civil servants discussed how they could encourage more liberal attitudes, and some were in favour of producing a circular to remind local officials that the new planning process allowed openness and flexibility. Nevertheless, it was recognized, this would have to be worded with great care because of the delicate situation in many town halls. One official recorded some of the pitfalls that might arise if there were too much stress on the current lack of magnanimity and creativity:

1. It will be considered by most Councils, particularly the

reactionary ones ... as an admission of failure. Phrases like
... 'it is possible to attach too much importance to planning
for planning's sake' will be seized upon by the anti-planners
and hurled at the Planning Officer whenever he recom-
mends a refusal which conflicts with vested and sectional
interests.
2. Those Authorities still hesitating on the brink of whether to
plan properly and engage suitable staff will, on receipt of
such a circular, have no hesitation in withdrawing and
doing the minimum amount of work necessary to comply
with the Act.[34]

In the end, the Ministry decided to send out a circular but made sure
it was extremely mild in tone.

Given these various constraints and attitudes, there were relatively
few really creative attempts to democratize planning at a local level
during this period. The consultant Max Lock produced his Middlesborough plan after extensive research work among the local population, while there were also interesting experiments in involving
public opinion at Bilston and Knutsford. Several councils engaged
with rebuilding blitzed cities did their best to consult as widely as
possible, using citizens' groups as a conduit for communication and,
as has been noted, making real attempts to spread knowledge about
what they planned. Elsewhere, however, the situation was rather less
innovatory. Sometimes this was because councils remained wedded
to essentially illiberal principles, unwilling even to consider the idea
of allowing outside comment on their work. More often, however, it
simply reflected the difficulties of applying a relatively new set of
techniques in conditions that were far from optimal. William
Holford, professor of town planning at the University of London,
argued that both planners and politicians had made mistakes:

Countless plans vanish like pipe dreams because the planner
does not know how to bring his dream to earth nor how to
persuade people to take interest in it. But just as many practical,
imaginative and ... 'aesthetically pleasing' proposals are stillborn, because administrators do not appreciate their quality

and know nothing of the power of design in the battle for the improvement of conditions of living.[35]

One of the key assumptions of much recent literature, already referred to, is that ordinary people in the 1940s had quite clear views about what a future Britain would be like and desired to participate actively in its making. However, this is in fact a gross oversimplification, as a brief survey of attitudes before and after 1945 will demonstrate.[36]

Popular interest in planning and reconstruction was probably at its greatest in late 1940 and early 1941, fuelled by the blitz and a torrent of polemical literature about the possibility for a new beginning. However, by early 1942, observers were already beginning to notice that the situation had changed quite remarkably. Reviewing the past year's activities in January 1943, the columnist 'Astragal' told readers of the *Architects' Journal* that the British public appeared 'largely unconcerned' about reconstruction:

> The slackening in most areas of aerial bombardment has made the subject seem less urgent somehow, and certainly there was no room for its discussion in the tiny newspapers of 1942. A vague nostalgia for the suburban plot, a persistent aversion to blocks of flats and mild anger at the quality of the buildings which during the previous years had tumbled nightly about the people's ears, were the only active sentiments which occasionally, like barnacled but faintly remembered masters of the deep, broke surface in the placid pool of public opinion.[37]

During the rest of the war, a series of fairly detailed surveys about popular attitudes to housing and town planning confirmed this trend. The one thing people felt strongly about was the home. The war had been immensely destructive and disruptive to family life, and many longed to recreate what had been lost. They wanted a safe haven, occupied only by their immediate kin. Mass Observation's major survey of 1943, entitled *People's Homes*, stressed the common aspiration to be left alone: 'One of the paramount factors affecting people's feelings is the greater or lesser degree of privacy obtainable.

The "own front door" which can be shut, figures largely in people's ideas about the home. A garden that is overlooked, windows into which neighbours can see, balconies visible from the road or from houses opposite are all deplored.'[38]

In contrast with this quite definite choice, the ordinary person was very much less interested in, or enthusiastic about, the future shape of the wider built environment. One journalist claimed after reviewing the evidence: 'popular planning still ends at the garden gate.'[39] Most wanted to be near pubs, shops and schools, and among people of their own class, but few could add much more. Moreover, strength of feeling on such matters decreased down the income scale: as an enquiry in Middlesborough showed, 'among the poorer people the proportion of those without an opinion' was 'very much higher than in the highest income group'.[40]

By the end of the war, therefore, those who wanted radical solutions to Britain's planning problems felt anxious or depressed. Britain, it was believed, had a unique opportunity to rebuild creatively but majority opinion remained unconvinced of this and yearned only for the mundane and safe. Housing, as the editor of *Architectural Design and Construction* regretted, had to some extent become 'the enemy of planning'.[41]

The election of a Labour government in 1945 and its subsequent legislative innovations provided something of a boost for planning ideas. However, beneath the surface little had changed. In fact, among working-class people, there was only a hardening of attitudes already apparent in the war. The emphasis was once again on the personal rather than the collective.

The central popular imperative in the years of peace was to re-establish home and family ties as quickly as possible. Conversely, there was a strong reaction against having to share private space or respect petty regulations laid down by bureaucrats. Sacrifices might have been necessary in the war, it was believed, but Britain had won, and people should in future be left alone to get on with their lives, associating with others only if and when they pleased.

Typical aspirations were observable in relation to several different issues. Some observers claimed that there had been an increase in good neighbouring under the German bombs, but it was rapidly recognized that this had only been a very temporary phenomenon. J. B. Priestly, the great celebrator of Britain's wartime spirit, told listeners to the BBC in 1947: 'We are always hearing complaints now that people are becoming self-centred and selfish, unhelpful to others, disagreeable rude and callous. . . . There seems to be far less kind and neighbourly cooperation than there was a few years ago. . . . People are harder, more selfish, more intent upon looking after Number One.'[42] Mass Observation, approaching the matter with more rigour during 1948, came to identical conclusions:

> Relationships are awkward things to grade and attempts to measure them must inevitably be taken as rough estimates only. Even so the results of our latest investigations leave little doubt that flimsy and often almost non-existent relationships between neighbours are surprisingly widespread; moreover, in many cases, this unsociable state of affairs seems to be the product of a reserve that has been deliberately maintained.[43]

Those who worked to promote community cohesion registered similar impressions. Isobel Menzies talked to more than 400 people from two London boroughs in her work for the Family Welfare Association and reported that many of them 'had been frustrated in their attempts to make effective relationships in their community' and 'had given up trying'. 'The normal family', she observed, 'appeared to lead a fairly isolated life'.[44] A social worker who operated on estates in Bristol recorded his gradual realization that being working class did not mean being naturally 'community-minded'. Over time, he noticed, there was a 'continuous process of residential segregation' going on, as people sought to move away from those they judged inferior according to a range of micro-social distinctions.[45] More detailed work by the sociologist Leo Kuper for Coventry Corporation reached the same kind of conclusions. Studying a small neighbourhood, Kuper found that most residents valued privacy and would only mix with those they judged of roughly equivalent status.[46]

Finally, the popular disengagement could also be viewed in the political sphere. Large numbers did not vote in local elections and showed little interest in town hall politics. Activists were forever bemoaning working-class apathy over issues they felt should be important. An employee of the Crown Film Unit who visited Middlesborough in 1947 found that Lock's plan had been held up by local political bickering. However, she reported, this had caused little local dissatisfaction because most people were quite oblivious to anything that went on in the city administration. Local politics came low down on their scale of priorities: 'The citizens could more easily quote the names of their football team than those of their Council. Indeed they have more understanding and loyalty to this team than they have for the Council.'[47]

What did this mean for choices about town planning? As before, most people remained highly enthusiastic about securing their own houses, even if this meant buying property. The Hulton Press market research report, *Patterns of British Life*, included the following summary: 'People like living in houses rather than flats, and they like having a house to themselves. They like their own private domain which can be locked against the outside world and, perhaps, as much as anything, they are a nation of garden-lovers. They want space to grow . . . and they want it to be private.'[48] On the other hand, far fewer were concerned much about the particularities of how a city might be redesigned.

As has been shown, appeals under the new act mushroomed. Characteristically, however, there was much less interest over hearings about development plans themselves. The Berkshire plan was put on display, but only 87 people viewed it at the shire hall and an average of 32 people at each of the various district council offices. Forty objections were received, though eight of these had been withdrawn before the public enquiry began work.[49] A similar chain of events occurred in Coventry, even though the local plan proposed much comprehensive redevelopment.

The conclusion that emerges from such evidence, therefore, is rather different from that confidently proposed in some of the existing literature. There was no folk wisdom about how cities should be planned after the war. Most working-class citizens wanted the best for their immediate families and were quite happy if this could be achieved using either the public or private sectors. On the other hand, only a very small minority really felt very strongly about wider questions of development and all of them did not necessarily agree on questions of detail. Public opinion, like the character of the local planning process, could easily act as a break on central government initiative.

As a coda to the argument presented in the preceding paragraphs, it is perhaps appropriate to ask how those most intimately involved felt the new planning system had worked after the war. What did they see as the problems and successes? Most pertinently, did such people feel that the system might have been constructed differently?

There is no doubt that Silkin, the minister responsible for the 1947 Act, felt a sense of disappointment at the way the legislation had worked when applied. In a lecture during 1953, he was critical of 'the bureaucratic administration of planning' — the fact that plans were often written in technical language and championed by local government officers with excessive zeal. Nevertheless, Silkin recognized that there were no easy solutions. Any fair planning system needed to find some way of accommodating those 'concerned only with the way in which the plan affects their personal interest and not whether the plan is of benefit to the community as a whole'. Moreover, it had to be accepted that attitudes to planning could easily change because of a wide variety of outside factors. In the Attlee government's case, Silkin argued, popular antipathy had spread because of the slow rate of progress with reconstruction and then been encouraged by the Conservative assault on every kind of state direction. All things considered, the only possible answer seemed to be a maximization of consultation and discussion. For Silkin, indeed, it was worth delaying the production of the final plan to accommodate popular choices; then it would truly be a 'people's plan — one which they . . . had a real part in producing'.[50]

These views pointed to the wider truth that democratic planning would only be finally possible in a society that had already been much transformed. In this perspective, there were some who responded to Silkin's self-critical honesty by pointing out that the achievements of the postwar years were, given the circumstances, quite remarkable. F. J. Osborn agreed with much of what the ex-minister had to say, but believed that he was being too modest.

Osborn's judgement was clear: it had been 'a *tour de force*' in the 'then political situation' to get the 1947 Act passed and working.[51]

The analysis that has been presented, to conclude, seriously qualifies much of the existing literature about Labour and the question of participation after 1945. To begin with, as has been shown, Labour was not a party of 'top down' bureaucrats. Most socialists of the time believed in experts, but there was also a fundamental assumption that real reform could only be achieved with democratic participation. In the eyes of activists and ministers, progress needed to be engineered using a judicious mix of inputs from different sources.

Second, it is wrong to assume that the popular political climate was highly favourable to change in the years to 1951. Much of Britain sympathized with Labour's general political aims but this did not mean that many wanted to embrace socialism as a way of life. Both middle- and working-class cultures were fairly conservative during these years, centred on long-standing concerns with the home and family. The impulse to community and collective identity often remained subordinate, much less important than personal or kin advancement. There was no widespread desire to become involved in running society, nor any shared vision about how things could be made different. In this sense, popular attitudes acted to constrain rather than facilitate Labour plans.

Against such a background, and given the deepening economic crisis after 1947, Labour's actual achievements were bound to be mixed. More studies are needed to show how accommodations over encouraging active citizenship were reached in other areas. What complementary research there is at present tends to reinforce the conclusion reached here. The Attlee government did not create the great change it had envisaged, but its record was certainly nowhere as bad as critics of the left and right have suggested.

Notes

1. I would like to thank the following for their help in developing the arguments presented during the following pages: Stephen Fielding, Junichi Hasegawa, Hideo Ichihashi, Tony Mason, Peter Thompson and Tatsuya Tsubaki.

2. Jim Fyrth (1993) 'Labour's bright morning – and afternoon', in Jim Fyrth (ed.) *Labour's High Noon: The Government and the Economy, 1945–51*, London, p. 270.

3. Colin Ward (1985) *When We Build Again*, London; Matrix (1984) *Making Space*, London.

4. John Jewkes (1948) *Ordeal By Planning*, London.

5. Christopher Booker (1977) 'Physical planning: another illusion shattered', *National Westminster Bank Quarterly Review*, February, pp. 56–64; R. N. Goodchild and D. R. Denman (n.d.) *Planning Fails the Inner Cities*, London.

6. Lady Thatcher (1989) *Speeches to the Conservative Party Conference 1975–1988*, London, p. 128.

7. Hansard, no. 414, 17 October 1945, col. 1222.

8. Labour Party (1944) *Your Home*, London, p. 4.

9. Bevan, quoted in *Architects' Journal*, 24 June 1948.

10. R. Vance Presthus (1951) 'British town and country planning: local participation', *American Political Science Review*, vol. 155, no. 3, pp. 756–69.

11. The following paragraph is based on material in Stephen Fielding, Peter Thompson and Nick Tiratsoo (1995) *'England Arise!' The Labour Party and Popular Politics in 1940s Britain*, Manchester, pp. 103–4.

12. *Tribune*, 16 February 1945.

13. See, for example, the detailed discussion for Norwich in Norman Tillett (1947) 'Planning and the Citizen', *Report of Proceedings*, Town and Country Planning Summer School, London, pp. 10–31.

14. See for example L. McNae (ed.) (1946) *Your Barnes*, London.

15. *Builder*, 19 April 1946.

16. Toby Haggith (forthcoming) 'Film and the built environment, 1939–51', Ph.D. thesis, University of Warwick.

17. *Coventry Evening Telegraph*, 12 June 1945.

18. Presthus, 'British town and country planning', pp. 765–6.

19. L. E. White (1950) *Community or Chaos*, London, p. 27.

20. M. Benney (1947) 'Storm over Stevenage', in A. G. Weidenfeld (ed.) *The Changing Nation*, London, p. 49.

21. Coleman Woodbury (1947) 'Britain begins to rebuild her cities', *American Political Science Review*, vol. 151, no. 5, p. 906.

22. Leo Grebler (1955) 'Planners and planning in the rebuilding of West European cities', *Journal of the American Institute of Planners*, vol. 21, nos 2–3, p. 79.

23. F. J. Osborn (1951) 'Public influences on planning', *Report on Proceedings*, Town and Country Planning Summer School, London, p. 81.

24. W. A. Robson (1952) 'Town planning as a problem of government', *Journal of the Town Planning Institute*, vol. 38, no. 9, p. 219.

25. *Economist*, 3 March 1951.

26. Cmd. 8059, Report of the Committee of Qualifications of Planners (P.P. XIV, 1950), p. 25.
27. Public Records Office [hereafter PRO], HLG 87/2, Q.P. (8th meeting), min. 3 December 1948, evidence from the Association of Municipal Corporations.
28. T. S. Simey (1953) 'The contribution of the sociologist to town planning', *Journal of the Town Planning Institute*, vol. 39, no. 6, pp. 126–7.
29. Monica Felton (1949) 'Democracy in town and country planning', *Political Quarterly*, vol. 20, no. 1, p. 79.
30. Thomas Sharp (1945) 'Presidential address', *Journal of the Town Planning Institute*, vol. 32, no. 1, pp. 1–5.
31. PRO, HLG 87/2. Q.P. (7th meeting), min. 25 November 1948, p. 1.
32. See, for example, Nuffield College, Oxford, Nuffield Social Reconstruction Survey, Section A Box 21, File on West Ham, memo on 'Councillor Fox LPTB', (n.d. but 1941).
33. I have traced in detail how these pressures worked in one, perhaps rather extreme case; see Nick Tiratsoo (1990) *Reconstruction, Affluence and Labour Politics: Coventry 1945–60*, London.
34. PRO, HLG 71/280, Memo by Regional Planning Officer, 21 December 1948.
35. William Holford (1951) 'Qualifications for town and country planners', *Town Planning Review*, vol. 21, no. 4, p. 359.
36. For a more detailed exposition of the arguments in the following sections, see Stephen Fielding et al., *'England Arise!'*.
37. *Architects' Journal*, 21 January 1943.
38. Mass Observation (1943) *Peoples' Homes*, London, Mass Observation, p. xix.
39. H. Pilcher (1943) 'Planning Propaganda', *Town and Country Planning*, vol. 11, no. 42, p. 76.
40. D. Chapman (1946) *A Social Survey of Middlesborough*, London, p. 11.
41. Editorial, *Architectural Design and Construction*, vol. 15, no. 7, 1945, p. 153.
42. *Listener*, 23 October 1947.
43. Anon (1948) 'Next door neighbours', *M-O Bulletin*, vol. 15, p. 1.
44. Isobel Menzies (1949) 'Factors affecting family breakdown in urban communities', *Human Relations*, vol. 2, no. 4, pp. 370–1.
45. H. P. Dow (1955) 'Can a community be created?', *Housing Centre Review*, vol. 1, pp. 20–4.
46. W. Burns (1954) 'The Coventry sociological survey: results and interpretation', *Town Planning Review*, vol. 25, no. 2, pp. 128–48.
47. PRO, HLG 108/5, D. Fine 'Two Towns: Middlesborough and Malvern. Preliminary Report', May 1947, pp. 18–19.
48. Hulton Press (1950) *Patterns of British Life*, London, Hulton Press, p. 24.

49. Thomas Houghton (1952) 'Public inquiry into a development plan', *Journal of the Town Planning Institute*, vol. 38, no. 4, p. 87.
50. L. Silkin (1953) 'Planning and the public', *Journal of the Town Planning Institute*, vol. 39, no. 2, pp. 26–33.
51. Ibid., p. 30.

7. 'Building a new British culture': the Arts Centre Movement, 1943–53

Richard Weight

Every town should have some particular art centre in it. Without that centre you will not find your factories of great use in producing a high and noble life, and what is more you will not find your churches and schools of much use. If you have these things without art, you will have affectation, dilettantism, hypocrisy and brutality.

George Bernard Shaw
Speech to the Leeds Art Club 21 October 1905

On St George's Day 1940, after more than a century of campaigning, state funding of the arts formally began in Britain. That day, the first meeting of the Council for the Encouragement of Music and the Arts (CEMA) took place. CEMA had been founded by the Board of Education the previous autumn. Previously, the overwhelming view had been that the state had no right to interfere in the production and consumption of the arts, on the grounds that they depended more than any other human activity on the freedom of individuals to express themselves as they wished. This right was only limited by the duty of the artist to 'protect' public morality by not publishing, displaying or performing anything sexually obscene or politically controversial.

The generic aim of CEMA — encapsulated in the slogan 'the best for the most' — was to disseminate high culture to the masses. But, its creation also marked a specific determination by Britain's political elites to foster national culture using the organs of state. During the war, the government hoped that by raising popular sensibilities, ordinary Britons would become more aware of the common heritage for which they were fighting. In the short term, they hoped this would raise wartime morale and in the long term they hoped it would produce a cohesive society of patriotic citizens capable of rising to the challenges of postwar reconstruction. To achieve this ambitious goal, CEMA organized nationwide tours of theatre companies, art exhibitions and orchestras, and to reach a population that had become dislocated by the war, many performances took place in air-raid shelters, rest centres and factories. CEMA's efforts were amplified by the BBC, which broadcast talks by many of Britain's leading writers, artists and composers. Since its seminal years under the directorship of John Reith, the BBC had tried to take the arts to a wider audience, and its work was intensified during the war for the same reasons that prompted the creation of CEMA.

Within two years, the project seemed to be a success. Performers discovered a captive audience, hungry for the spiritual sustenance the arts offered amid the hardships and uncertainty of war. In addition to providing the 'best for the most', CEMA also encouraged 'music-making and play-acting by the people themselves',[1] by sending groups of unemployed professionals like the Pilgrim Players around the country to stimulate amateur activity. It seemed to many observers that the gulf between popular amusement and the arts had been bridged for the first time since the Elizabethan era. The chairman of the Communist Party's cultural committee, Jack Lindsay, undertook a survey of the arts in wartime Britain, at the end of which he concluded: 'We have . . . create[d] for the first time in England since folk days a genuine mass-audience for drama, song, music. The British people have begun powerfully to claim their cultural heritage. A cultural revolution has been initiated.'[2] Few of Britain's political elites were as optimistic as Jack Lindsay and there remained some reservations about the state becoming involved in such a sensitive area. Nonetheless, by the middle of the war a consensus began to emerge that state patronage of the arts had a vital and permanent role to play in British society.

The architects of that consensus were Rab Butler, who became president of the Board of Education in July 1941, and John Maynard Keynes, whom Butler appointed CEMA's first chairman the following April. Butler regarded the new organization as an essential part of his plans to improve education in Britain. Keynes, though more famous as an economist, had campaigned since the 1930s for the state to patronize the arts and his long association with the Bloomsbury group had given him a wealth of connections in the arts world. All they needed was a sufficient grant from the Treasury. They found a willing chancellor in Sir John Anderson, and it was he who announced the founding of the Arts Council of Great Britain in the House of Commons on 12 June 1945. A month later, just before Churchill's caretaker government gave way to a victorious Labour Party, Keynes discussed 'The Arts Council: It's Policy and Hopes' on the Home Service. He told his listeners 'we look forward to a time when the theatre and the concert hall and the art gallery will be a living element in everyone's upbringing.'[3]

How was this to be achieved? Keynes believed that for the state to stimulate a steady, long-term rise in Britons' demand for the arts, the current method of supply had to be drastically improved. He recognized that the success of CEMA's wartime operation owed much to the wider dispersal of exhibitions, orchestras and theatre companies, which the war had necessitated. The most effective way to democratize British culture, therefore, was for CEMA to encourage an appreciation of the arts at local level. Unfortunately, few British towns had adequate arts buildings, and a bad situation had been made worse by the blitz.

The provision of bricks and mortar in the provinces thus became CEMA's priority in the immediate postwar years. The move towards decentralization also sprang from a belief that the diversity of regional customs was proof of the pluralism that underpinned the British way of life. In short, a healthy national culture depended on the nurturing of its idiosyncrasies. Keynes told his listeners 'We of the Arts Council are greatly concerned to decentralize ... the artistic life of the country. Nothing can be more damaging to the nation than the excessive prestige of metropolitan standards and fashions. Let every part of Merry England be merry in its own way.'[4] His initiative led to the creation of the Bristol Old Vic, the Aldeburgh and

Edinburgh festivals. Furthermore, although he resisted calls for Scotland to have a separate Arts Council, Keynes granted one to Northern Ireland and he established 12 regional arts boards in mainland Britain.

Despite these achievements, Keynes has been criticized by a number of historians. His appointment, they say, marked the end of the 'people's culture' the war had spawned and the triumph of an elitist arts policy. The core of that policy was a belief that the right to belong should be determined by the citizen's level of education, sensibility and taste. In other words, nationhood was no longer seen to be a natural right, but something that had to be acquired from a cultivated elite who were the final arbiters of what constituted British culture. Keynes certainly was an elitist. As his ally, the art historian Kenneth Clark, once put it, 'he was not the man for wandering minstrels and amateur theatricals. He believed in excellence.'[5]

He saw the support of amateur organizations as a temporary wartime measure and as more resources became available, they were directed towards grand metropolitan projects like the Bristol Old Vic, and most contentiously of all, the Royal Opera House in London. The Arts Council charter, which received royal assent in July 1946 made no mention of 'music-making and play-acting by the people themselves'. Instead, it promised to develop 'a greater knowledge, understanding and practice of the fine arts exclusively'.[6]

Labour Party leaders shared Keynes's belief that standards should not be sacrificed in the attempt to democratize British culture and they encouraged the policy change the charter enshrined. Andy Croft has concluded that an anxious ruling class, intent on maintaining its hegemonic supremacy, acted swiftly to avert a cultural revolution. 'It was', he says 'the lasting achievement of the Labour government to re-establish authority in the well-kept gardens of cultural privilege. This was Bloomsbury's finest moment'.[7] Such conclusions are compellingly simple, yet they are a crude distortion of the cultural politics of the 1940s and 1950s. In this chapter I will argue that the Labour government and the Arts Council did continue to nourish popular participation in the arts and that the failure of their attempts to do so owed more to the changing aspirations of Britons in the postwar era than to a betrayal of wartime ideals by the nations' elites.

The supremacy of Keynes was not as great as his critics have sometimes supposed. Several senior figures in the Arts Council believed that his metropolitan projects, though worthy, would not place the arts at the heart of community life in Britain. They included Ivor Brown, the Arts Council's director of publicity, and its secretary-general Mary Glasgow. Prime among the dissenters was the leading adult educationist of the period, W. E. Williams. A charismatic socialist, Williams was editor-in-chief of Penguin Books and in 1941 he had established the Army Bureau of Current Affairs, whose work in promoting discussions of citizenship among British troops many on the right blamed for Attlee's victory. Most of his time and energy, however, was devoted to the arts. He was one of the Arts Council's founding members and, as director of the Institute of Adult Education in the 1930s, he had begun an 'Art for the People' scheme, which provided the model for CEMA's travelling wartime exhibitions. Williams noted that Keynes possessed 'a streak of donnish superiority and a singular ignorance of ordinary people',[8] and it was not long before the two were clashing over policy. In July 1943, he wrote an article for *Picture Post*, which, though it did not explicitly attack the chairman, set out an alternative plan for the arts.

Williams asked his readers 'Are we building a new British culture?' His reply was an emphatic 'Yes' on the grounds that popular appreciation of the arts had made them 'really national' for the first time. To continue that work, he proposed that centres should be built in every small town with a population of between 10,000 and 60,000 to house drama, music and art under one roof. The scheme would make it economically possible for local authorities to provide a wide range of cultural activity, and would also help to draw citizens together in a common pursuit. His proposal differed from Keynes's vision of the new British culture in one other crucial respect.

Williams was determined that the centres would not be earnest temples of high culture where Britons would be exhorted to improve themselves. As well as the arts, they would house forms of leisure normally pursued in pubs, music halls and working-men's clubs. In effect, the Arts Council would combine the work of CEMA with that of the Entertainments National Service Association (ENSA), which during the war provided Britons with popular entertainment on a similar basis before it was wound up in 1945. This was not a pragmatic way of enticing people through the foyer in order to convert them to better things. Williams, who had an 'unfettered capacity for hedonism',[9] believed that the arts had to be integrated with the whole spectrum of popular leisure. Only thus would a truly common culture emerge:

> [We] must no longer be content with the Calvinist notion that any old upper room will do for cultural purposes — an attic over the Co-op, or an Infants' School classroom. And instead of our present dispersal of the Public Library down one street, the art gallery (if any) down another, the Workingmen's Club somewhere else and so on, let us plan the Civic Centres where men and women may satisfy the whole range of educational and cultural interests between keeping fit and political argument. Let us so unify our popular culture that in every town we have a centre where people may listen to good music, look at paintings, study any subject under the sun, join in a debate, enjoy a game of badminton and get a mug of beer or cocoa before they go home.[10]

Later that year, the proposal was enthusiastically taken up at a conference on postwar leisure organized by the Town and Country Planning Association. Attended by local authorities, amenities groups and arts organizations, its discussions on local initiatives produced the revealing slogan 'Our Goal a National Culture'. By the end of the war, arts centres had become a prominent consideration in planning circles.

Like the Women's Institute, the idea for arts centres seem to have originated in Canada. There, the federal structure of the dominion, and the strong sense of regionalism that went with it, provoked intense cultural rivalry between the provinces which resulted in high levels of spending on the arts. Some planners saw arts centres as an extension of community centres, which had appeared on municipal housing estates erected in the 1930s in an attempt to recreate the organic communitarianism of rural Britain in towns and cities.

These urban village halls were largely the responsibility of the philosopher Ernest Barker, who as a leading member of the National Council of Social Service, had encouraged local authorities to build them. Writing a wartime survey of Britishness, Barker remarked that 'the cultivation of the arts is not only a matter for artists: it is also a matter for the whole community, which has to build for itself a house of beauty in which its communal life can be happily and finely spent. This is what the Athenians built on and around the hills of their city.' He believed that 'each community should take care of its own cultural well-being' and that, like village halls, a range of activities should be on offer from basket-weaving to string quartets.[11] Yet, community centres remained wedded, if not to the austere Calvinist view of culture condemned by Williams, then at least to a slightly chilly atmosphere of self-improvement, as Barker's neo-Classical imagery indicates. More importantly perhaps, community centres were generally too small to be able to stage any significant events.

The closest relations of the arts centres in Britain were probably the pioneering interwar health centres at Finsbury and Peckham. The centre at Peckham, for instance, offered free health care to local people through a small subscription. The ethos of both centres was an informal social one, in which people were encouraged not only to see a doctor regularly, but also to drop in to meet friends, drink, play games and dance as well as use the swimming pool or gymnasium. To some extent, the forerunner of modern leisure centres, their purpose was to transform health care from a regimented expert interrogation of the sick into a fun part of daily living.

Like the health centres, arts centres were to be large, bright and spacious modern buildings designed by the best architects in the country (Finsbury had been designed by the Russian constructivist, Berthold Lubetkin). This concern for the appearance and ambience of the buildings went even further than those involved with Finsbury and Peckham. It sprang from an acute awareness that while their counterparts in public health only had to compete with dank, Victorian hospitals, cultural reformers had to compete with all the glamour and excitement the modern mass leisure industry had to offer.

In a collection of essays by major town planners such as Patrick

Abercrombie, Ivor Brown warned that 'the association of the Arts with stale buns, the tea-urn and tepid lemonade is a dreadful curse of British community life'. The centres, he said should be 'a cordial home of all the reasonable pleasures, and not some austere factory of uplift, betterment and grim educational routine'.[12] Perhaps aware that Victorian attempts to reform the social habits of Britons had been hampered by the myopic puritanism of the temperance movement, Williams and his supporters emphasized that centres must have a good supply of alcohol at all times. They were also keen that the arts themselves should reflect the gaiety of their new surroundings. Since the seventeenth century, the theatre had periodically been singled out by Church and state as a threat to public morals and, as a result, it came under special scrutiny by those who were eager not to appear censorious in the twentieth. The chairman of the council's drama panel reminded his colleagues on more than one occasion that 'the theatre is a social event that must have some glamour as well as high intentions.'[13]

In the mid-1940s, the cinema was the most glamorous form of entertainment available to the majority of Britons. With an annual audience of 30 million, it was also the most popular. Yet, as it stood, it was the one form of entertainment even the most radical champions of arts centres had difficulty embracing. Since the 1930s, Britain's elites had been concerned about what they saw as its degenerative influence on the working classes. The left, in particular, bemoaned the cinema's moral laxity, which it saw as a threat to the development of a constructive sense of citizenship. A Labour Party policy document on leisure in 1947, for example, listed its 'perversions' as a 'preoccupation with an unreal world of wealth and trivial emotions, its concentration upon the stars [and] its social and political inhibitions.'[14]

Reformers were particularly concerned about the power of Hollywood. As the main conduit of American mass culture, many feared that it was debasing native culture and might eventually erode it altogether. Keynes had announced the arrival of the Arts Council with the cry 'Death to Hollywood',[15] and this view was shared by most of his colleagues. Their concern was one of the factors in the Labour government's decision to impose a quota on the number of

American films shown in Britain and, later, its decision in 1949 to subsidize British production companies to make films that portrayed the 'British way of life'. Champions of arts centres believed they had a vital role to play in this battle.

As well as providing pleasant surroundings, the centres would show 'serious' films — either wholesome Crown Film Unit documentaries or features funded by the National Film Finance Corporation and so draw Britons away from the commercial cinema. Nonetheless, the hostility of reformers towards Hollywood did not weaken their resolve to build a pluralistic native culture. This was apparent when the Third Programme was launched in September 1946 by the director general of the BBC, William Haley. The Third Programme, to which Keynes gave his support shortly before he died, was devoted entirely to the arts.

Haley was confident that the arts had gained a mass audience as a result of the war and that Britons no longer needed to be spoon-fed by slipping 'serious' programmes in with more popular ones on the Home and Light Services. Williams and his supporters, however, had deep reservations about the new separation of the arts and entertainment. In the *Listener*, Williams expressed his wish that 'if only its austere features would sometimes relax in a broad human grin!'[16] And Ivor Brown, who had become editor of the *Observer*, warned that the Third Programme would lead to a 'closed shop in the dissemination of culture', alienating those whose sensibilities were still in an embryonic stage.[17] Their warnings went unheeded and, a decade later, the programme became the focus of a concerted attack on cultural reform by the popular press.

As well as relaxing the austere features of the 'highbrow', a main concern of the arts centre movement was to encourage a more participatory national culture. Useful though pluralistic broadcasting had been in getting the arts to a mass audience in the pre-Haley era, it was still seen to have encouraged passivity as much as any Hollywood epic. Though keen to rouse the nation from its aesthetic torpor, reformers — Keynes included — were wary of patronizing ordinary Britons. The chairman implored listeners to his BBC broadcast 'not to think of us a schoolmaster'[18] and, in May 1946, Mary Glasgow reminded delegates to the council's northern regional conference that 'it is not the function of the council to dictate to the community'.[19]

The encouragement of popular participation took several forms. First, it was hoped that some citizens would promote the various activities of the centres. Mary Glasgow declared that 'in this world of planning, civic enterprise and government grants it is still the ordinary individual advertising, selling tickets, finding billets for visiting artists, who counts.' By doing so, they would 'maintain a continuity of interest in the arts in the community from one event to another'.[20] Second, and most importantly, it was hoped that communities would stage their own productions.

The attitude of reformers towards amateur activity was ambivalent. The composer Ralph Vaughan Williams believed that wartime 'music-making' in rural areas represented a nascent 'folk culture'. Advocates of arts centres were less certain. 'Let the people sing, by all means' commented Ivor Brown in 1945, 'but let them learn to sing . . . in tune.'[21] Such sentiments were not usually the result of a snobbish disdain for popular or 'folk' culture. They sprang from well-grounded fears that too much amateur activity, far from involving ordinary citizens, might put them off.

The chairman of the council's drama panel observed that 'with the coming of peace, people expect higher standards all round. In wartime a play in a school hall was part of the strange new life we all led. In peace it smacks of "welfare" and is unlikely to increase the public's respect for the theatre, or its popularity'.[22] Many people gained great pleasure from staging their own productions, but reformers realized that the majority would rather be entertained as a welcome release from the rigors of working life than use valuable leisure time participating in shows in order to enhance their sense of community.

Moreover, reformers knew that the majority would rather be entertained by professionals, however novel it might be to see their local butcher dressed up as 'The Lord High Executioner' once a year. With this in mind, it was clear that a constant round of ropy productions of *The Mikado* cast by the vicar's wife would do little to form queues outside an arts centre box office, when Stewart Grainger, Joan Crawford or Max Miller were appearing nearby. The spectre of Ivor Brown's 'tea-urns, stale buns and tepid lemonade' had to be constantly warded off. But it was a spectre that was seen to haunt all forms of cultural activity, whether it was a Gilbert and Sullivan operetta, a Shaw play, or a Gang Show that was being staged. In short, not only was the Arts Council wary of amateur activity for sensible strategic reasons, but it also rarely equated amateur activity with popular culture in the first place.

A related concern among reformers was the ethos of existing arts clubs. Most of these clubs had been founded in the Edwardian era at the height of guild socialism. While it was hoped that new ones would spring up in response to the scheme, the Arts Council was keen to use the experience of their Edwardian predecessors. The plan was to build a centre and for the local authority to employ a full-time professional to manage it on a daily basis. The Arts Council, meanwhile, would subsidize a club whose members would help the manager plan and organize a programme of events.

However, many clubs were hostile to the arts centre movement. Still inspired by the teachings of William Morris, they saw the arts as a moral and spiritual antidote to the materialism of the industrial age rather than as one component in a modern, eclectic national culture. George Bernard Shaw's belief that an arts centre should complement the work of a community's church and school to produce a 'high and noble life' shorn of 'hypocrisy' captured an aesthetic outlook to which even Keynes, for all his 'highbrow' tastes, was not prone. Clubs that retained that outlook were generally less enthusiastic than W. E. Williams about the prospect of a drunken game of bingo taking place after a poetry recital. Furthermore, they were often fiercely protective of their voluntarist heritage.

Like many other voluntary organizations in the 1940s, they were suspicious of the state and, in particular, feared that state patronage of the arts threatened creative freedom, however independent the Arts Council claimed to be. More often than not, they were simultaneously jealous of the relatively large sums of taxpayers' money the Arts Council had at its disposal. B. Ifor Evans, the educationist and founding member of CEMA, observed that:

Human nature being what it is . . . a jealous arts club may

actually wish to keep out the ordinary citizen who is not one of its own original members ... small towns are small towns and people who are enthusiasts for the effective organization of the arts may not always be the best inheritors of the great artistic revival which began in 1940.

In the face of such 'exclusive, partisan company', Evans warned that the sheer anonymity of the darkened cinema might make it even more attractive to the citizen than it already was.[23]

To ensure that the social prejudices of arts clubs and the slipshod nature of much of their work did not hamper the movement, the Arts Council was keen for professionals to be involved in the centres as much as possible. Touring theatre companies and orchestras would perform at them and, it was hoped, local people could be given parts in some shows — a practice the Old Vic had pioneered during its tours of the north of England during the blitz. Another wartime practice the Arts Council hoped to continue was for unemployed professionals or those on temporary loan from their companies to act as 'animateurs', assisting local productions technically and creatively. Many professional bodies were keen to help and there was a widespread hope that the gulf between the 'people' and the 'artist' might be bridged as a result. The director of one leading repertory theatre told Mary Glasgow:

for too long we have thought of the artist as a misfit ... but we must surely recognize that his place is as important as the doctor's or postman's and that his work is an essential element in the life of the town ... without the artist's good will, our scheme will be unworkable: without the bees our beehive will be derelict.[24]

The means of production were not the only concern of professionals. J. B. Priestley, who took a keen interest in the movement, advised that where possible the work of local playwrights who 'suggest the character of their several regions' should be performed to nurture 'local patriotism'.[25] The Arts Council hoped that, whether from the community or merely visiting, actors, writers, artists and musicians would help its citizens establish an empowering but also entertaining democratic national culture, which might become a cornerstone of the 'New Jerusalem'.

Keynes's response to the arts centre movement was generally hostile. Mary Glasgow attempted to reassure him that it was merely an extension of his desire to 'let every part of England be merry in its own way'. The chairman, however, thought the centres smacked of a return to the amateurism of the war and feared that his work was being hijacked by what he called the 'welfare racket', which he had kept at bay since his appointment. Ironically, he was partially responsible for the plan getting off the ground. His Home Service broadcast had called for a cultural building programme as ambitious as that of the Soviet Union's. Although he had in mind projects like the Bristol Old Vic, the response to his broadcast came largely from supporters of arts centres.

Keynes received many letters from voluntary groups praising his 'initiative' and asking for financial help to set up centres in small towns or in working-class areas of cities. Some came from established civic societies such as that in Sevenoaks, Kent, whose chairman had been president of the Royal Institute of British Architects during the war. Others came from unknown individuals such as the Battersea vicar, the Revd Stephen Hopkinson. Hopkinson reminded the chairman of the Arts Council that 'with the return of men and women from the forces, where they have grown accustomed to well-equipped clubs and to opportunities of free discussion ... there should be an influx of people interested in democracy and anxious to make experiments in self-education'. Hopkinson concluded his manifesto by telling Keynes that, like the Peckham health centre, 'the family will be the normal unit of membership, but emphasis will be laid on social and mental rather than physical development'.[26] Keynes did not reply and, soon after, he left Britain with his Treasury team for the United Nations monetary conference at Bretton Woods in the USA.

While Keynes was away, Williams discussed the centres with the Ministry of Town and Country Planning. The cultural policy of the Labour governments of 1945 to 1951 was a clear and determined one. A party policy document on the whole question of leisure saw dangers in 'state intrusion in a domain hitherto preserved for the individual' such as 'regimentation, lifeless conformity, lack of initiative and enterprise, and an unhealthy scope for pressure groups and cranks of all types'. These fears were exacerbated by concern that state intervention in the arts might raise comparisons with the abuse of culture in totalitarian regimes. Nonetheless, the document declared, 'the development of recreation' remained 'the ultimate goal' of the party's social, economic and political reforms and could be democratically achieved. The state's role was to 'supply services . . . and encourage citizens to use them'.[27] Labour's general election manifesto of 1945 was even clearer. It promised 'by the provision of concert halls, modern libraries, theatres and suitable civic centres, we desire to assure to our people full access to the great heritage of culture in this nation.'[28] Consequently, the Ministry was enthusiastic about the centres and, with the help of the Arts Council, it drew up an illustrated booklet to promote the scheme.

The building that *Plans for an Arts Centre* sketched had three main features, reflecting the desire of those in the Arts Council and Labour government to bring popular and elite forms of recreation closer together. First, an exhibition hall with an adjoining reading room housing an extensive library on all the arts. The library might also lend original and reproduction paintings so that people could enjoy art in the privacy of their own home as well as in the communal setting of the centre. Second, a hall to seat 600 with a proscenium arch, orchestra pit and projection room where plays, film shows, concerts and lectures could be held. And third, a restaurant to seat 200, with a bar for drinks and snacks.

There would also be a large open-air terrace with a bandstand for dancing on summer evenings. The floor of the main hall would be a flat, hardwood surface so that it could be used for dancing in winter when the terrace was too cold. To all this was added a recommendation that the interiors of the building should have 'a touch of colour; taste and exuberance in furnishings and fittings; and a general air of well-being and comfort — these are essential to any centre . . . if it is to be a live one: and we must rid ourselves of the false idea that art is a palliative for social evils or a branch of welfare work'.[29]

The only earnest note the booklet struck echoed a widely-held sentiment among reformers that the popular reclamation of British culture was a memorial to those who had died saving it. It concluded that 'at a moment when our hearts are filled with gratitude that the war has been brought to a successful conclusion, what better form of memorial could be devised than a centre where present and future generations can enjoy in comfort their rightful heritage?'[30]

Soon after *Plans for an Arts Centre* was published, Keynes wrote to Mary Glasgow from the USA demanding to know 'who on earth foisted this rubbish on us?'[31] But, just as Churchill had ignored Beveridge's plan for the welfare state until it was too late for the scheme to be quietly disposed of, so Keynes ignored Williams's plan for the new British culture. In any case, the chairman did not have the opportunity to take his opposition much further. Barely four months after he returned to Britain, Keynes died at his country home in Sussex on Easter Sunday 1946.

Kenneth Clark was, to his enormous disappointment, passed over by the new Chancellor of the Exchequer, Hugh Dalton. The man chosen instead was not a visionary. A former master of the Draper's Company, Ernest Pooley was dismissed by Clark as a 'man of bottom' who had little interest in the arts.[32] But to Williams he was a man of 'common sense and courage' who handled the 'acute' differences of opinion within the Arts Council and the 'high voltage' discussions that ensued with 'quiet but emphatic authority'.[33] Pooley was more sympathetic to the arts centre movement than his predecessor had been, and what his 'courage' meant in practice was that Williams was allowed to retain the initiative he had wrested from Keynes during the economist's absence in the USA.

The result was that in the summer of 1946 the Ministry and Arts Council held a joint press conference at which they unveiled an architectural model of an arts centre based on the *Plans*. The model formed the basis of an exhibition that toured the town halls of Britain to publicize the scheme and to persuade local authorities to build the centres. The response was enthusiastic. After having seen the exhibition, several local authorities decided to build one. Others, in Plymouth, Bridgwater and Battersea decided to use existing buildings. New arts clubs sprang up across the country and, by the end of

1947, 35 of these had received subsidies from the Arts Council in preparation for the local authority building programme that was about to begin.

As had been hoped, some of the Edwardian arts clubs affiliated themselves to the Arts Council. Those that did not suffered a rapid decline in membership. Helen Munro, the Arts Council's regional director for the North of England believed that the arts centre movement 'has the backing of the younger people'.[34] She also noticed that the Teesside Guild of Arts was making a desperate bid to compete. 'Its rooms in Stockton are now painted in gay colours,' Munro reported, 'and the Guild is considering raiding the houses of its members for cushions, cups and saucers'.[35] The Arts Council's *Annual Report* in 1947 concluded that 'one of the most encouraging developments of the period was the rapid establishment of arts clubs in all parts of the country ... as a result of the public interest shown in the arts during recent years.'[36]

The movement received a further boost in 1948 with Aneurin Bevan's Local Government Act. Bevan believed in the 'emancipation of the arts' from the ruling classes and wanted to see them 'restored to their proper relationship with civic life'.[37] To that end, Clause 132 of his Act revoked the 1925 Public Health Act, which had forbidden local authorities to spend any of their rates on the arts. This released a potential £50 million and promised a new era of civic patronage of the arts. The large metropolitan museums, concert halls and libraries, which the local authorities already maintained, had mostly been built in the mid- to late-nineteenth century by industrialists at the height of Victorian prosperity, civic pride and regional identity.

Their legacy was regarded with some suspicion by a number of reformers who believed that, although private action was sometimes necessary, commerce and culture ultimately did not mix. Mary Glasgow, for example, saw museums as 'dark monuments to Victorian business success', and deplored their 'dusty collections of stuffed birds and casts of Roman Emperors'.[38] By contrast, the cheery, accessible arts centres would be a testament to the new era of state patronage, in which occasional, self-aggrandizing benevolence was replaced by a regular contribution from the rate-paying citizenry in every town and district across Britain.

Despite nearly a decade of state support and tireless voluntary work, the arts centre movement was nonetheless largely stillborn. Local authorities sporadically built centres throughout the postwar period and there are now more than a hundred across the United Kingdom. Many of them stage a range of events from orchestral concerts to hypnosis shows. But the hope that inspired the movement in the 1940s, that arts centres would become the focal point of popular leisure, has not been realized. The economic crisis of 1947 dealt the movement its first setback. Attlee's austerity plan wiped £800 million off the government's capital expenditure programme and those local authorities that had drawn up plans for centres were forced to shelve them.

Every Labour Chancellor of the Exchequer ensured that the Arts Council grant continued to rise substantially and, by the time the party left office in 1951, it had nearly trebled. This enabled the Arts Council to maintain its support for major companies such as the Old Vic. But, without substantial help from local authorities, it could not fund the massive building programme required to make the arts 'a living element in everyone's upbringing'. Bevan's Local Government Act proved to be little more than a declaration of good intent as it did not impel town halls to spend their allotted 6d. The arts were never at the top of town hall budgets and, in the face of continuing economic austerity in the early 1950s, plans for arts centres remained largely plans. A survey by the Arts Council in 1952 revealed that of the 206 major authorities in England and Wales, 45 per cent did not fund the arts at all, while 39 per cent spent only a fraction of the money allowed to them. Meanwhile, 16 per cent, did not bother to reply. For several years the Arts Council blamed the stalling of the new British culture on the reluctance of civic leaders to invest in it.

The main reason for the movement's failure, however, was that the wartime audience for the arts declined dramatically after 1945. By the late 1940s, the Arts Council's regional directors were reporting that the promised 'renascence of taste' had failed to appear. One wrote despairingly to Mary Glasgow saying that 'all our arts societies are desperately worried because of their failure to establish contact with ordinary folk.'[39] In the year of Elizabeth II's coronation, the Arts Council's associate drama director, Charles Landstone, looked back on the cultural revolution that might have been: 'At the end of the war, all of us thought that all that remained to be done was to provide new buildings for this vast audience, but, unfortunately, an extraordinary thing happened. The audience disappeared from their hostels, camps and their war centres, and in a flash appeared to have left their interest behind them.'[40]

Landstone estimated that the Arts Council had retained only 20 per cent of its wartime audience. Why had this occurred? The decline was partly due to a lack of funding. Many arts clubs, such as Bridgwater, which had emerged at the end of the war, continued to perform in makeshift premises thanks to the small subsidy they received from the Arts Council. But without a proper arts centre they were all dressed up with nowhere to perform and, because they could not attract professional touring companies of any worth, audiences were even less inclined to support them, despite the fact that ticket prices remained low. Britons who had accepted sub-standard, amateur performances during the war were simply not prepared to do so in peacetime, just as they were not prepared to tolerate the indefinite rationing of food and clothing. Indeed, the continuation of economic austerity made people seek out more glamorous entertainment to relieve the gloom. But the lack of funding does not explain why even metropolitan venues failed to attract working-class audiences.

It is usually argued that this was because of the elitism prevalent in the Arts Council, which had created those venues in the first place. F. M. Levanthal, for example, has written that 'the Arts council which emerged after the war bore the imprint of Keynes's conception of public patronage. Unabashedly elitist, he disdained those, mainly on the left, who extolled the merits of popular culture or sought to revive participatory folk traditions.'[41] Most of the changes Keynes made remained in place after his death. The bulk of the Council's resources still went into ventures like the Old Vic, the Hallé Orchestra and, most contentiously of all, the Royal Opera House.

Like the religious missionaries of the Victorian era, many of the cultural reformers of the 1940s fell upon their quarry with a wide-eyed utopian zeal that sent Britons running to the Blackpool Tower, the Clapham Odeon or the King's Arms. The strenuous efforts of reformers not to appear patronizing, didactic or regimental were sometimes little more than a patient waiting game, behind which lay a deep revulsion towards modern popular culture. Stafford Cripps, addressing the British theatre conference of 1948, at which he announced the government's intention to build the long-awaited national theatre, vividly expressed that feeling:

> we can educate and persuade the public to adopt the tastes which we believe to be right, but we have no more right to impose taste upon them than we have to impose propaganda. Sometimes we may be rather disgusted at the choice which the public seems to make, but we must be patient to prove to them that our views of what is good are better than theirs.[42]

This kind of attitude was also present among voluntary activists. The local arts clubs the Arts Council subsidized — both old and new — were often reluctant to embrace W. E. Williams's vision of a common culture. In 1949, the Arts Council's regional director for the west of England complained that 'we positively alienate sympathy because we give the impression of being intellectual superiors.'[43] Mary Glasgow, attempting to explain the haemorrhaging of popular support, identified the middle-class membership of the clubs as a major problem. 'The withdrawal of the working class', she concluded, 'may have been hastened by the growing interest of the middle-class which is shown in the rapid rise ... in the number of independent arts clubs. They ... are by tradition almost invariably middle-class and may, without meaning to, frighten away any would-be supporters from another sphere.'[44]

However, the twin charges of under-funding and elitism that are levelled at the Arts Council by its critics do not sufficiently explain the failure of the cultural experiment of the 1940s. As I have shown in this chapter, a central strand of that experiment was a serious and well-organized attempt to continue the radical aspects of wartime cultural policy by combining the provision of art and popular entertainment in local communities throughout Britain. It is not the case, as Robert Hewison has argued, that reformers missed an opportunity 'to embrace a wider range of activities and to include a broader definition of the audience for them' or that it did not 'encourage those audiences to be active rather than passive in their participation'.[45]

We must therefore look deeper into the social changes that were occurring after the war for a proper explanation. To begin with, the return to normal life in peacetime meant that wartime audiences simply dispersed. As well as the demobilization of the armed forces, the many civilians who had been relocated for economic reasons during the war left their temporary factory and farm hostels and rejoined their communities. Once home, leisure was again largely pursued outside the workplace with friends and loved ones rather than workmates. This made it virtually impossible to attract a large, regular audience by performing in the workplace. It was for this reason, and not elitism, that in 1945 Keynes and the Minister of Labour, George Isaacs, ended the factory concerts that for the left had become a symbol of 'people's culture'.

The second change was more psychological. Thanks to the enormous propaganda exercise mounted by the British state between 1939 and 1945, on VE day Britons were probably more aware of their national identity than at any point in their history. As the country's leaders had hoped, a basic knowledge of Britain's cultural heritage had given its people a sense of unity and purpose during the conflict, while for many the arts in general had augmented the spiritual comforts offered by the churches. Despite the crises that beset the nation after 1945, such comforts were not needed by Britons to the same extent. Many who during the war had, for example, eagerly pocketed the latest Penguin issue of a Dickens novel while sitting bored and anxious on a camp bed far from home, returned to more digestible recreation when it became available again.

This leads us to the third and most important change that occurred after the war: the affluence of the 1950s, coupled with shorter working hours and paid holidays gave people a far greater choice of leisure pursuits than they had ever enjoyed before. As early as 1947, the Labour Party acknowledged the threat affluence posed to the creation of a common culture. 'In modern civilizations', it concluded 'there is an infinitely larger choice of types of leisure pursuits, and the community inevitably splits up into small groups as individuals make their own personal choice'.[46] Sometimes Britons chose pursuits that had once been largely the preserve of the well-to-do, such as country house visiting; or they spent more money than before on existing pastimes like the cinema; or they did something new, such as watch television or go to a pop concert — indeed, the phenomenal youth culture, which emerged in the 1950s, probably did more than anything to short-circuit the attempt to enhance popular sensibilities. What Britons did not, on the whole, choose to do, whatever strategies reformers employed, was to visit art galleries.

By the early 1950s, some reformers had come to terms with these painful facts, including W. E. Williams himself. In 1951, Williams succeeded Mary Glasgow as secretary-general of the Arts Council. Although arts clubs formed a relatively small part of the annual budget, he decided to cut support for them and for the smaller repertory companies the Arts Council had supported since 1946. Williams, the passionate champion of a common culture, reluctantly turned his back on the idealism of the 1940s. He replaced Ivor Brown's motto of 'the Best for the Most' with the more realistic 'Few But Roses', and wrote to the new Labour Chancellor, Hugh Dalton to explain his change of heart. Introducing the Arts Council's financial estimates for the following two years he mocked the 'sentimentalists willing to send tatty little troops out into the provincial wilderness to perform in village fit-ups — when the villagers have gone off in droves to see a film twenty miles away. Our provincial saharas are littered with the bones of these good companions'.[47] A year later, Williams held a conference in Manchester with the leaders of Britain's local authorities, to establish what might be done to restart the new British culture. The reply was blunt. The Mayor of Chester was one of several who asked 'why should we spend the public's money on something that only a very small section of the public wants?'[48] It is a question that is still asked today, despite the abundance of non-tax funds provided by the national lottery.

Arguably, the only way reformers could have succeeded was to have halted the expansion of consumer choice. This could have been done by nationalizing culture on a Soviet scale, a process in which people were 'persuaded' to consume a more balanced cultural diet by strict state control of the mass leisure industry. Such a move was advocated by the Communist Party and occasionally by J. B. Priestley in moments of despair at the banality of the British theatre in the early postwar period. It was never seriously considered by the majority of reformers. Indeed, when the Arts Council was created, Keynes went out of his way to assure people that it was not merely a decorative cuff link on the long arm of an overbearing state.

State patronage of the arts, he told his Home Service listeners 'has happened in a very English, informal, unostentatious way — half-baked if you like. A semi-independent body is provided with modest funds to stimulate, comfort and support' the arts.[49] This speech has been seen by some critics as a disingenuous liberal conceit. Certainly, Keynes did disguise the scale of the cultural experiment begun in 1940, and the Byzantine power and influence of the elites behind it. Yet he also expressed a sincere belief, shared by a majority of Britons, that while the activities of the state were being extended for the common good of all citizens, the state should nonetheless remain within the parameters allowed it by the British liberal tradition. The right to belong, however much it was defined in gentlemen's clubs, committee rooms and country houses, remained a right and not an obligation. What this meant for the future of national culture was that if Keynes, Williams or any other reformers failed to persuade Britons that their lives could be enriched by contact with the arts, then there was ultimately little anyone could do about it.

Notes

1. PRO EL1/2, 'Memorandum in support of an Application to the Treasury for Financial Assistance', 6 March 1940.
2. Jack Lindsay (1945) *British Achievement in Art and Music*, London, p. 35.
3. Lord Keynes (1945) 'The Arts Council: Its Policy and Hopes', *Listener*, vol. 34, no. 861, 12 July.
4. Ibid.
5. Kenneth Clark (1977) *The Other Half: A Self-Portrait*, London, p. 26.
6. The Charter of Incorporation Granted by His Majesty the King. Ninth Day of August 1946, p. 3.
7. Jim Fyrth (ed.) (1995) *Labour's Promised Land: Culture and Society in Labour Britain 1945–51*, London, pp. 218–19.
8. W. E. Williams (1971) 'Pre-history of the Arts Council', in E. M. Hutchinson (ed.) *Aims and Action in Adult Education 1921–1971*, London, p. 22.

9. J. E. Morpurgo (1979) *Allen Lane: King Penguin*, London, pp. 120–1.
10. Williams, W. E. (1943) 'Are We Building a New British Culture?', *Picture Post*, vol. 18, no. 1, 2 January.
11. Ernest Baker (1942) *Britain and the British People*, Oxford, p. 112.
12. Ivor Brown (1945) 'A Plan for the Arts', in Gilbert and Elizabeth McAllister (eds) *Homes, Towns and Countryside: A Practical Plan for Britain*, London, p. 140.
13. PRO/EL4/50, Michael Macowan, 'Policy of the Drama Department', 20 July 1949.
14. Labour Party Archive [LPA] RD/43, 'The Enjoyment of Leisure', February 1947, p. 8.
15. Keynes, 'The Arts Council: Its Policy and Hopes'.
16. W. E. Williams (1947) 'Listening to the Third Programme', *Listener*, vol. 38, no. 9757, 2 October.
17. *Observer*, 22 September 1946.
18. Keynes, 'The Arts Council: Its Policy and Hopes'.
19. PRO/EL3/13, 'Report of the First North Regional Conference, Newcastle 17–18 May 1946'; B. Ifor Evans and Mary Glasgow (1949) *The Arts in England*, London, p. 114.
20. Evans and Glasgow, *The Arts in England*, p. 114.
21. Brown, 'A Plan for the Arts', p. 142.
22. PRO/EL4/46, Michael Macowan, 'Drama Policy', Arts Council Paper No. 221, 26 October 1946.
23. Evans and Glasgow, *The Arts in England*, pp. 117–18.
24. Stanley Baron (ed.) (1944) *Country Towns in the Future England: A report of the conference representing local authorities, arts and amenities organizations and members of the Town and Country Planning Association on the 23rd of October 1943*, London, p. 100.
25. J. B. Priestley (1947) *Theatre Outlook*, London, p. 59. Priestley was not an active supporter of arts centres because, although he shared W. E. Williams's belief that popular and elite leisure should be integrated, he wanted drama to be separately run, with a 'National Theatre Authority' managing everything from small civic theatres to a national theatre.
26. PRO/EL2/34, Hopkinson to Keynes, 17 July 1945.
27. LPA/RD43, 'The Enjoyment of Leisure', February 1947, p.2.
28. Labour Party (1945) *Let Us Face the Future*, London, Labour Party, p. 9.
29. Arts Council of Great Britain (1945) *Plans for an Arts Centre*, London, p. 6.
30. Ibid., p. 7.
31. PRO/EL2/40, Keynes to Glasgow, 7 November 1945.
32. Clark, *The Other Half*, p. 129.
33. W. E. Williams (1975) 'Pooley, Sir Ernest Henry', *Dictionary of National Biography: 1961–1970*, Oxford, Oxford University Press, pp. 851–2.
34. EL3/13, Helen Munro, 'North Region Parish Notes', n.d., *c.* 1946.

35. Ibid.
36. PRO/EL4/2, Arts Council of Great Britain (1947) *Second Annual Report*, p. 9.
37. Aneurin Bevan (1952) *In Place of Fear*, London, pp. 50–1.
38. Baron, *Country Towns in the Future England*, p. 82.
39. PRO/EL3/60, Cyril Wood to Mary Glasgow, 8 December 1947.
40. Charles Landstone (1953) *Off-Stage: A Personal Record of the First Twelve Years of State-Sponsored Drama in Great Britain*, London, p. 60.
41. F. M. Levanthal (1990) 'The best for the most: CEMA and state sponsorship of the arts in wartime, 1939–1945', *Twentieth Century British History*, vol. 1, no. 3, p. 317.
42. PRO/EL4/62, British Theatre Conference (1948) *Summary of the Proceedings. 5th–8th February 1948*, London.
43. PRO/EL3/60, Cyril Wood to Mary Glasgow, 8 December 1947.
44. PRO/Mary Glasgow, 'Audiences for the Arts'.
45. Robert Hewison (1995) *Culture and Consensus: England, Art and Politics since 1940*, London, p. 48.
46. LPA/RD43, 'The Enjoyment of Leisure', February 1947, p. 20.
47. PRO/EL4/55, W. E. Williams, 'Financial Estimates, 1952–3: Notes for a preliminary discussion', 24 July 1951.
48. PRO/EL4/85, Report of a conference between Regional Directors of the Arts Council of Great Britain and Local Authorities, 12 December 1952.
49. Keynes, 'The Arts Council: Its Policy and Hopes'.

8. Taking pleasure in England: landscape and citizenship in the 1940s

David Matless

As opportunities for leisure expanded after the First World War, with shorter working hours and higher pay, what was increasingly called 'the leisure question' came to be a major concern among Britain's elites. The war against Nazi Germany temporarily curtailed the leisure boom for many Britons, but it fired the British geographical imagination. As soon as buildings began to be flattened by German bombs, planners who had for years identified misuses of land, seized the opportunity to propose new orders of settlement.[1]

Their visions of a reconstructed town and country were also visions of citizenship, of healthy, fulfilling and improving recreation, which was seen to be a prerequisite for community life. What Alison Light has termed a 'conservative modernity' in relation to interwar formulations of Englishness and domesticity had its outdoor counterpart, a moral modernity of the landscape.[2] The attempt to improve places and people was a vision of Britain — and in particular of England — that allied tradition and modernity. The conflict between these terms, which has dominated debates on heritage since the 1960s, should not be projected back on to earlier periods.

Elements of an anti-modern heritage movement have emerged, particularly within bodies such as the National Trust.[3] However, they were a self-consciously embattled minority setting themselves against the dominant vision of a simultaneously planned and preserved nation.[4] The patriotic Britishness of wartime placed arguments about landscape on to a national map, for the countryside was seen to be a pillar of national identity. Most planning, far from being the activity of an overbearing state as its critics often suggested, was formulated and carried out locally and regionally. Yet, debates about the meaning and use of landscape were generally worked out nationally.

The campaigners for what might be termed 'recreational citizenship' did not, however, simply believe that the land should be opened up to the people for national benefit. Both land and people were divided: the land by property borders whose transgression by holidaymakers was a major point of contention, and the people by definitions of citizen and anti-citizen. Taking pleasure in Britain was a question not only of access rights but also of behavioural obligations. While particular types of conduct in the country were held to promote good citizenship via mental, moral, physical and spiritual health, others signified a lack of citizenship.

Citizenship became defined in relation to an 'anti-citizenship' represented by those members of the public, whose behaviour did not live up to environmental standards and who stalked the land, destroying the nation's heritage. While access to landscape might be promoted as a right, environmental citizenship emerged as a condition to which the individual should aspire through responsible conduct. Certain kinds of behaviour did not become the citizen; education would therefore be required to promote the right kind of popularity. Knowledge and appreciation of landscape's beauty, morphology and history were held to form a basis for good citizenship. Thus, the educated eye of the citizen was upheld as a potentially vital organ of reconstruction.

What might be termed 'recreational citizenship', whereby geographical knowledge was related to a scale of national belonging, played a key role in the articulation of Britishness within the social-democratic political culture of the 1940s. In short, an essential part of belonging to the nation was to take pleasure in the environment. In the 1940s, taking pleasure in England, whether through leisurely walking or concentrated field study could be a route to good citizenship.

Whether considering the planning of landscape or its appreciation, planners sought principles of visual order. Those considered here sought at once to extend the social power of beauty yet also to maintain it as a discrete category for controlled academic reflection and definition. Preservationist geographers, such as the influential Vaughan Cornish, formalized a social aesthetics, which informed such popularizing instructional texts as Tom Stephenson's *Country-side Companion*, with its guidance on 'How to See the Countryside' and 'Making the Most of the Map', and Harry Batsford's *How to See the Country*.[5] Such books asserted the cultural authority of the planner-preservationist, mixing a romantic care for the land with a modern expertise.

Matters of citizenship and cultural leadership were central to the wartime arguments of planner and architect John Dower, the key lobbyist for national parks: 'when I have been asked to explain the functions of the Ministry of Town and Country Planning in which I serve, I have found the best short explanation is to say that our job is, or ought to be, creative geography.'[6] Dower emphasized questions of value: 'the landscape is so fundamentally a thing of "values", of aesthetic and spiritual rather than scientific and material assess-ment.'[7] Landscape, 'rooted in the human senses', was 'a continuous relation or partnership between objective and subjective, between the countryside and ourselves',[8] and should be at the heart of a visual culture of citizenship: 'public enjoyment of the beauty and interest of the landscape is, in my view, one of the major uses of it.'[9]

Cornish had argued that 'the faculty of appreciating beauty is latent in the generality and merely requires educating',[10] and Dower followed his prescription, drawing from Cornish and from Words-worth a mixture of theories on latent sensory appreciation: 'The driving force of the aesthetic instinct is within ourselves; it needs only to be released by the attitude of receptive, disinterested love.'[11] Dower was quick though to distance such love from decadent aestheticism; the eye needed training like a rambler's body: 'it can, I am convinced, be greatly broadened and deepened if we train it appropriately and exercise it strenuously.'[12]

While for Dower any theory limiting beauty to the few had 'no place in democratic practice', his aesthetic implied certain standards of freedom: 'Needless to say, liberty should not mean licence; public enjoyment should be subject to a reasonable standard of good behaviour.' Planning should not cater for those 'ignorant and insensitive elements in the visiting public'.[13] With beauty open to all through the senses, such people had no excuse. Elitism and populism mix as Dower wrestled with the question of how, if landscape was a matter of values, such values should be defined:

> the key to success is that enough of us — and especially of those who have some relevant authority or influence as governors, administrators, technicians, and writers should care enough about the task, and should go humbly and seriously to school with Nature herself as mistress and inspirer, and with the great minds that have been applied to the loving study of nature as guides and interpreters. It is my robust faith that, if we do this with heart and mind, it will not be long before we are sufficiently sure and united to assume a leadership which the rest of our fellow-countrymen are sufficiently ready to follow.[14]

Dower called for 'a team of experienced landscape lovers' with a mixed geography of appreciation. Local landscape lovers would be useful, but were seen to have a limited sense: 'many of them are simple folk with little power of expressing their opinions, and most of them are more or less lacking in comparative experience, and therefore tend to be unreliable outside the region or regions in which they have lived and observed.' The key would be to mix the simple and local with those — Cornish is given as an example — who could bring a national aesthetic geography to bear, those 'very few who have visited, studied, and appreciated the whole of England and Wales'.[15] Aesthetic geography demanded mobility and education, for if a national space was to be planned, national geographical standards had to be exercised.

Promoters of the countryside were haunted by visions of the ignorant, insensitive, loud 'anti-citizens', who were usually seen to represent the 'vulgar' element of the working class. As Greta Jones shows in her study of the relation between the planning movement and conceptions of social hygiene, planners distinguished between those citizens who were open to improvement through education and environmental change and those confined to the 'social problem group' for whom neither would do the trick. Arguments for social welfare by writers such as Julian Huxley and Richard Titmuss and groups such as Political and Economic Planning often formed only one part of what Jones terms a 'double-sided exegesis', with eugenic arguments about the irredeemable poor as the counterpoint: 'the Social Problem Group . . . the source from which all too many of our criminals, paupers, degenerates, unemployables and defectives are recruited'.[16]

A liberal discourse of citizenship attained through a mixture of rights and obligations depended upon the identification of an unworthy, degenerate residuum for its self-definition. The creation of an inclusive nation therefore rested, in the short term at least, upon exclusion. Bad conduct in the country was generally presumed to emanate from the interior of the city, and from the capital city in particular, for anti-citizens were often labelled 'Cockney' regardless of how near to the sound of Bow bells they were born. Harry Batsford, writing a *Home-Front Handbook* aimed particularly at those evacuees 'now living in the country for the first time, that they may use their leisure constructively for their own benefit and for the benefit of the nation in general',[17] could combine helpful popular hints on seeing with a call to send back the alien and vulgar:

> We have most of us enough city-dreading Anglo-Saxon blood to feel a rejuvenating transformation at cutting adrift from the huddle of human habitations. But by contrast, take the case of the large party, presumably from the East End, who, a friend of mine said, disgorged themselves from motor-coaches under the Duke of Bridgwater's column on Berkhamsted Common above Aldbury. They produced a gramophone, and started fox-trotting on the turf. "Why couldn't they have done that at home, Daddy?" said my friend's little boy.[18]

During the interwar period, Batsford's publishing firm had been largely responsible for the explosion of topographical guidebooks which accompanied the arrival of mass tourism in the English countryside. Batsford was one of several influential figures who, having fed popular demand for the countryside, began to express concern about the effects mass tourism was having on it. Commercial topography had become part of a moral geography posing the question, what kind of public space for what kind of public?[19]

Many of the practical answers to this question came from the open-air movement, which during the interwar period had assiduously presented the countryside as the space where a mentally alert, physically fit and spiritually whole citizen could be nurtured. Organizations such as the Youth Hostels Association thrived during and after the war, membership moving from a low of 50,000 in 1940 to 100,000 in 1943, 150,000 in 1945 and 230,000 in 1948.[20] The mapping–scouting–fieldwork ethos was maintained through such works as Jack Cox's 1953 *Camping for All*.

Cox, who was editor of *Boy's Own Paper*, thanked his Manchester geography tutors Fleure and Fitzgerald for teaching him 'the value of field studies of all kinds and the way in which such studies could be carried out from bases under canvas or in youth hostels'. This, indeed, was 'camping with a purpose'.[21] The most significant attempt to promote recreational citizenship was the production of *The Country Code* in 1951. Its ten maxims guided visitors through the principles of gate-shutting, dog-controlling and plant-protection. The code, which was drawn up after consultation with the open-air movements as well as the farming lobby, gave glimpses of agricultural practice so as not to appear overly didactic. Thus, the friendliest and most subdued canine pet is shown to be susceptible to overexcitement in a field of sheep, thereby causing the sheep to fall into streams and drown, to give birth to dead lambs, to break into the road and stray into traffic. Some 70,000 copies of the code were sold by 1959, providing the basis of a wider campaign targeted in particular at Britain's youth.[22] *The Country Code*'s illustrations depict British youth as both country hazards and potential citizens, wandering through corn, clambering on walls, tossing litter, carefree and careless. Above the heading 'live and let live', two young couples sing their way through a night-time village street, provoking a dog to bark and a resident to shout from an upstairs window: 'The countryman . . . has to keep early hours'.[23] The city that never sleeps, with all its youthful energy, meets the country that goes to bed early.

The codification of rural conduct was central to the creation of national parks. During the war Dower had surveyed possible parks, reporting to the Ministry in May 1945.[24] Soon after, Lewis Silkin, the new Minister of Town and Country Planning, set up a committee chaired by Sir Arthur Hobhouse which included Dower and fellow conservationists Clough Williams-Ellis and Julian Huxley. Their report in July 1947 formed the basis for the 1949 National Parks and Access to the Countryside Act. National parks took their place in reconstruction legislation alongside the 1947 Town and Country Planning Act, the 1947 Agriculture Act, the 1946 New Towns Act and the establishment in 1948 of the Nature Conservancy, as measures towards an orderly social-democratic nation.

At the time, planning legislation was seen to be as vital to the 'New Jerusalem' as the National Health Service, the welfare state and the nationalization of key industries and utilities. Though no single political ethos determined planning legislation, a distinctly social-democratic environmental vision did run through it. From the interior landscapes of new homes, schools, hospitals and entire towns to a modernized agriculture and a preserved nature, a new country was envisioned. Among these landscapes, national parks emerged as the ultimate spaces in which planners hoped that citizenship might flourish. They provided a protective umbrella for all forms of rural life and the means for urban Britons to enjoy what was commonly regarded as the essence of the nation.

The Labour administration was enthusiastic about national parks from the beginning. In his 1946 budget speech, Hugh Dalton looked forward to their creation on the grounds that:

There is still wonderful beauty to be found in our country. Much of it has been spoiled and ruined beyond repair; but we still have a great wealth and variety of natural scenery in this land. The best that remains should surely become the heritage, not of a few private owners, but of all our people, and, above all, of the Young and the Fit, who shall find increased opportunities of health and happiness, companionship and recreation, in beautiful places.[25]

Dalton, 'the Red Rambler of the Pennines',[26] was well known as an open-air activist, acting as president of the Ramblers' Association in 1948 and walking the proposed Pennine Way with rambling activist Tom Stephenson and Barbara Castle, while Home Secretary Chuter Ede was president of the southern area of the Ramblers' Association.[27] From Stephenson's account, it is clear that Labour leaders were emotionally committed to the open air as a democratic right for the people. However, in practice, there were limits to their commitment. Stephenson and other activists were disappointed when the 1949 Act did not go as far as the Dower or Hobhouse reports in proposing free rights of access to uncultivated land. Priorities of food production, along with a sympathy among key figures such as Dalton with the rights of landowners, led Labour to seek accommodation with farming interests in both the key Agriculture Act of 1947 and in legislation on recreation.[28] Many in the administration happily followed the distinction made by bodies such as the National Trust between the 'nation' and the 'people' and argued for the preservation of the nation's heritage through the exclusion of some of its people.[29]

In his foreword to *The Country Code*, the historian G. M. Trevelyan, a key figure in the National Trust, warned of the consequences of conflict between town and country: 'If the simple rules of conduct laid down here are neglected by visitors to the country, food production and country life will be hampered, and the farmer will regard the holiday maker from town as his enemy. This must reduce the opportunities for free enjoyment of the countryside for visitors'.[30]

Introducing the second reading of the National Parks Bill on 31 March 1949, Lewis Silkin concluded: 'This is not just a Bill. It is a people's charter — a people's charter for the open air.'[31] What kind of popular space was this? The Labour government's vision of environmental and social improvement for the mass of the people followed the prescriptions made by open-air activists, preservationists and planners from the 1920s onwards. Even the most militant access campaigners had stressed the necessity for rules of country conduct.[32]

Dower's national parks report offered a particular scheme of popular beauty, with national parks accessible from all main centres of population yet preserved from certain public habits. Dower argued that he was not judging according to class or education, but he nevertheless set up qualitatively different classes of pleasure: 'it will be by no means easy . . . to resist the inevitable demand of the "urban-holiday-minded" that they should have their share in the National Parks programme.'[33] Quoting as 'the first shot in the campaign for British National Parks', Wordsworth's talismanic comment on the Lake District being 'a sort of national property, in which every man has a right and interest who has an eye to perceive and a heart to enjoy',[34] Dower excluded the hearts and eyes of the urban holiday-minded. This was not simply a zoning of pleasures for mutual tolerance, but the assumption of an unbridgeable cultural divide whereby the urban holidaymaker could not conceivably take meaningful pleasure in the non-urban. 'For all who want to spend their holidays gregariously . . . National Parks are not the place. They had far better keep away, and (perhaps, after an unsuccessful experiment or two) pretty certainly will keep away — provided that any proposals to establish, within National Parks, the kinds of facilities they desire are firmly resisted.' A close watch should be mounted for such monstrosities as 'a garden pleasure-ground (small bar attached)'[35] or facilities for ball games. Dower issued the usual warnings on the 'minority' of bad visitors, 'typically . . . charabanc parties, ill-controlled children's outings and other "excursion" groups'.[36] The establishment of a landscape for citizenship, thought reformers, demanded a rigorous policing of the anti-citizen.

Urban-minded holidaymakers were not entirely forgotten. Dower proposed 'more and better Blackpools and Brightons, and . . . popular holiday camps'.[37] Holiday camps were regarded as particularly important by planners. They were upheld as an interim pleasure zone, a staging post to recreational citizenship in which the people could begin to camp with purpose. Geographer Dudley Stamp, a key figure in these debates as the dominant voice on the Scott Committee on Land Utilization in Rural Areas praised 'properly sited and organized camps on a proper scale' because, he said, 'I would rather see five thousand in a camp than those five thousand spread about in two thousand bungalows.'[38]

PEP's 1942 report on *Planning for Holidays* examined the postwar problem of how to prevent the ideal of holidays for all from destroying the amenity itself. Quantitative increase threatened qualitative decline, but a planned reconstruction might 'permanently' check the prewar spoliation of the countryside.[39] Holiday centres, including converted large country houses 'no longer inhabited by their traditional owners'[40] offered a means to channel people.[41]

Rambling activist, philosopher and radio celebrity Cyril Joad's influential *The Untutored Townsman's Invasion of the Country*, whose terms of argument uncannily prefigure the terms of recent critiques of uneducated leisure in the heritage industry,[42] gave guarded praise for Butlins: 'A holiday camp supplies a certain sort of delight which is best enjoyed in company. I say "delight" but, in fact, it is a whole way of life that is offered, complete with riding and swimming, with tennis and dancing and shopping, with "mateyness" and heartiness during the week and religious services and more "mateyness" on Sunday'.[43] Here was an intermediate stage between vulgar and healthy leisure, an out-of-town 'interim canalization' aiming at 'the development and expression of personality'.[44] Spatial concentration in open country minimized scenic destruction while giving campers 'a chance to open their eyes to the fact and presence of beauty. You cannot, after all, jump overnight from the Blackpool holiday in a mob to the mountain holiday with two or three'.[45]

According to PEP, camps could also serve as a wholesome demographic space: 'they should be developed on sound lines under enlightened management. They will then become an important national asset, not least as places where young men and women who may have few social opportunities in their daily lives can meet, mix, and plan to marry.'[46] Campers and camp owners may not have discerned the wider intent of planners behind their social and sexual activities, but one should not automatically assume an opposition of scheming elite social engineering and unreflective mass pleasure.[47]

Camps boomed after the war, attracting half a million visitors by 1947, predominantly from the affluent working class. Aside from value for money, their success was based on a combination of the ethos of fitness and health with all the fun of the traditional resort. Fielding, Thompson and Tiratsoo have argued that 'such a controlled holiday allowed working people — and especially women — freedoms they had hitherto lacked'.[48] In the progressive weekly *Picture Post*, Hilde Marchant, reported Billy Butlin's own message that 'within such a highly organized setting, the individual gets a greater opportunity for self-expression.' Like many at the time, Marchant expressed a sympathy with the Butlin ethos of self-formation through communal dancing, roller-skating and rambling, Radio Butlin wake-up calls and mass keep-fit classes: 'They are expected to take part each morning in army style keep-fit exercises. They do so. And they like it.'[49]

Recreational citizenship was also championed by the doyens of biological field study. Moves to popularize natural science were part of the attempt to promote a culture of improving landscape. If conservation, whether of plant, animal or mineral, was a matter of national heritage, the study of the natural world could be a means to good citizenship. Geography, as an academic discipline centred on field study and survey, played a key role alongside the emerging field of ecology in the promotion of a popular field science.

Between April 1943 and April 1945 the physical geographer J. A. Steers surveyed the coast of England and Wales for the Ministry of Town and Country Planning, registering a landscape of national value: 'we have only one coast and it is neither a local, nor even regional, but a national possession. It is the consciousness of the coast as a whole which needs quickening.'[50] A key figure on the Wild Life Conservation special committee, chaired by ecologist Arthur Tansley, whose 1947 report laid the foundations for Nature Conservancy,[51] Steers sought to register a cultural value in coastal features, deploying both a moral geography of conduct and a rhetoric of scientific neutrality in the service of preservation. In June 1944, Steers addressed a Royal Geographic Society audience containing many key figures in reconstruction debates:

> The whole matter is basically one of geography ... people have a great desire to visit the seaside, either in vast numbers ... or in ... more manageable masses ... or as individuals on the remoter coasts. It is the last type of coastal region which is likely to become more and more popular in the right sense. Let us think of national authority as a coordinator and a judge.[52]

The national coast contained different cultural zones. The 'more popular' resorts had 'acted as safety valves', saving other parts for 'the walker and naturalist'.[53] 'Hideous settlements' in the form of plotland shacks and bungalows, however, threatened to spoil even these sites.[54] Here was coastal popularity in the wrong sense: 'education must begin at school, and might well be associated with the teaching of geography. This is the subject above all directly concerned with the study of landscape, and intelligent knowledge and appreciation of the local region by school pupils should do much to guarantee the proper use of the countryside in the future.'[55] Tansley responded that: 'If we want our future citizens to value our national heritage of natural scenery and wild life, it is up to us to see that the young get the necessary training.'[56]

Two books summarized Steers's survey, *The Coastline of England and Wales*, introduced by Dudley Stamp and leading planner-preservationist Patrick Abercrombie, and the popular format *A Picture Book of the Whole Coast of England and Wales*.[57] The text, photography and cartography of such surveys sought to register coastal features as objects of cultural value as well as asserting the authority of science. Likewise, the Wild Life Conservation committee argued for the preservation of 'geological monuments'[58] with features such as Steers's primary research site of Scolt Head Island in north Norfolk proposed as national nature reserves for aesthetic as well as ecological reasons.

Alongside Steers on the committee was the geological popularizer, Arthur Trueman. Trueman's 1938 *The Scenery of England and Wales*, originally issued by Victor Gollancz and reprinted by Pelican in 1949 as *Geology and Scenery in England and Wales*,[59] set out geology in straightforward text, sketch and diagram: 'For geology is pre-eminently the layman's science. In it more than in any other science there is opportunity for a beginner to make original observations, to weigh up evidence, to coordinate his facts and in general to acquire a truly scientific outlook.'[60] This was not a romanticized geology of mysterious fossils but a serious subject for the ordinary citizen-scientist who, through it, could become more aware of the physical shape of the nation: 'Many', wrote Trueman, 'never know an area until something of its shape becomes clear to them, just as some may never feel comfortable in a strange town until they have seen a map of its streets'.[61]

The body responsible for putting these aims into practice was the Council for the Promotion of Field Studies (later the Field Studies Council), formed in 1943. It established a number of field centres in areas of prime ecological interest, the first of which opened in 1946 at Flatford Mill in Suffolk. Flatford Mill was the subject of one of Constable's most iconic paintings of rural Britain. As such, it was an appropriate setting for an attempt to teach Britons more about the practical workings of the nation's environmental heritage and to encourage them to see it not simply as a scenic playground but as a living organism that required understanding and respect. A central figure in the Council for the Promotion of Field Studies was geographer S. W. Wooldridge, who parodied Wordsworth in his promotion of the Council's work:

> *One traverse in a Surrey Vale*
> *(or if you prefer it Yorkshire Dale)*
> *Will teach you more of Man,*
> *Of Man in his terrestrial home,*
> *Than all the text books can!*[62]

Wooldridge worked closely with Geoffrey Hutchings, warden of Juniper Hall, a field centre in the Weald opened in 1947.[63] Hutchings's dustjacket for their book on *London's Countryside* displays a classic scene of the time; students sit on a slope while a bearded rucksacked man discourses before a spread-out landscape.[64] Such field study was connected to a wider movement of popular natural history. This embraced conservation groups, pioneering nature photography and film and, above all, radio broadcasts, for here, as in other areas of British life in this period, the BBC did much to amplify the work of those who were seeking to increase Britons' awareness of their national heritage.

The BBC children's panel programme *Nature Parliament*, chaired by popular personality 'Uncle Mac' (Derek McCulloch), ran from January 1946 with a panel of naturalists such as James Fisher and Peter Scott: 'Here, then', listeners were told 'is a team of real experts that will leave no stone unturned, no reference book unthumbed in excited interest, combined with honest endeavour, to candidly answer the pertinent, complicated, exacting and penetratingly imaginative questions posed by young listeners'.[65] The Collins *New Naturalist* series, edited by Stamp, Fisher, Julian Huxley, bird photographer Eric Hosking and James Gilmour, provided a popular-scholarly focus for the movement. The series was modern in its commitment to the science of ecology, while the same time plugging itself into an English observational tradition of amateur naturalists dating back to Gilbert White.[66] As such, the series promoted a national nature, not by jingoistically asserting British ecological superiority, but by viewing nature as a network of organisms set within a unique national space, a space in which the reader, as a fellow organism, was a citizen.

Although the movement for recreational citizenship concentrated on the outdoors, the idea of orderly settlement ranged from the mountain top to the modern home, from communion with nature to the layout of indoor living space.[67] The organization that more than any other embodied the belief that citizenship must be understood as part of a wider design for life was the Council for Visual Education. It began life as the Council for Education in the Appreciation of Physical Environment in September 1942, following a deputation by the CPRE and the Town and Country Planning Association to the president of the Board of Education R. A. Butler.[68]

Renamed the Council for Visual Education (CVE) in October 1945 and with Patrick Abercrombie as its first president, the CVE campaigned for visual education in schools, guiding the 'instinctive interest of all children in the matter'[69] through 'drawing, history, geography, mathematics, hand-work and projects',[70] and beyond school and childhood towards 'a more beautiful and better planned environment for the everyday life of the people'.[71] In structure, the CVE strongly resembled the CPRE, founded by Abercrombie and others in 1926, with various architectural, planning, design and educational bodies brought together to create an informal visual establishment.

Constituent bodies included the CPRE, the Town and Country Planning Association (TCPA), the Architectural Association, the Royal Institute of British Architects, the Design and Industries Association, the Institute of Landscape Architects, the Society for the

Protection of Ancient Buildings, the British Film Institute, the Town Planning Institute and the Workers' Educational Association. The CVE co-opted members from the Ministries of Health, Education and Town and Country Planning, and the Arts Council. Art critic Herbert Read and garden city campaigner F. J. Osborn were vice-chairmen, while preservationist Clough Williams-Ellis was vice-president. The executive included planner W. G. Holford, and design writer and founder of Puffin Books Noel Carrington. Others active included director of the National Gallery Kenneth Clark, founder of the village college movement Henry Morris, architects Oliver Hill and Hugh Casson, planners Elizabeth and Gilbert McAllister, and poet John Betjeman.

The CVE worked through school exhibitions, toys, models, lectures, films, teacher training courses and pamphlets.[72] From 1954, a school essay competition attracted around 1000 entries each year on such themes as 'My Favourite Street' and 'Beautiful Buildings I Have Seen'. In 1947, the CVE anticipated the more sophisticated technologies of urban simulation computer games with their 'Matchbox Village', followed in 1949 by 'Matchbox Town', which it described as 'a fascinating and instructive game'.[73] Activity continued along the same lines through broadly the same personnel, give or take a few recruits, deaths and resignations, until at least 1960, with *Annual Reports* recording a perennial frustration over lack of funds.

The CVE philosophy was set out in W. F. Morris's *The Future Citizen and his Surroundings*, which suggested the need to raise 'the uneducated taste of the great majority'.[74] The pamphlet's cover showed a young boy and a young girl walking in the country by a stile, village and church. Just as CVE vice-chair Osborn had praised Cornish as one whose direct way of seeing could help the citizen 'regain something of the direct appreciation of the child',[75] so Morris judged that 'the capacity for good judgement in aesthetic matters is latent in most children, but is warped or suppressed by bad surroundings or strong misleading suggestions in youth or adolescence.' Children had an eye for landscape: 'There is a spontaneous response in normal children to the beauty of flowers, to vegetation and scenery generally.'[76]

As part of 'the endeavour to make of the pupil a good citizen ideally a citizen of the world, but in any case a citizen of his own country', the child 'should be taught impatience with things unnecessarily drab or sordid, and should be infected with a desire to remove or improve them'.[77] 'This is Regional Survey in miniature' commented Morris, before suggesting that 'The Hobbies Club could make a relief model of a given area, as it is and as it might be, to illustrate, for example, the differences between heterogeneous ribbon building and planned settlement.'[78]

R. A. Butler, by then in political opposition, provided a foreword to the 1946 edition: 'The teaching method known as "the project" has on occasion been used in order to familiarize children and young people with the history and topography of their own district. . . . Such a method can be used to even greater advantage if the aesthetic importance of the pupil's surroundings be ever stressed.'[79] For Butler and the CVE, such education had direct economic implication in a newly competitive postwar world. Visual pleasure should be placed in national service: 'We can prevail only through qualities of distinction, and what is more distinctive than originality of Design? The Art School far from being considered in the past the agreeable and rather light-hearted shelter for the dilettante, will become the Training Establishment for our Export Commandos.'[80]

Subsequent CVE pamphlets addressed art, architecture and design, interweaving preservation and modernity and relating them to citizenship: 'we cannot put the new wine of present day social and economic needs into the old bottles of old-fashioned appearances to which we may perhaps sentimentally cling in our love for the "olde-cosye-worlde". New needs, new materials, and new scientific discoveries inevitably create new kinds of appearances.'[81] As 'taste can be educated', so the nation could be raised from 'the muddle of suburbia' and urban ugliness.[82] Charles Reilly's *Architecture as a Communal Art* featured Charles Holden's modernist 1932 Arnos Grove tube station on the cover: 'Our younger architects are already ceasing to be commercial travellers in the past styles and are becoming instead prophets of the new,' it declared.[83] Reilly upheld the English village, the country town and interwar municipal estates as examples of communal art against the 'vulgar individualism' of speculative building.[84] The coming age would be 'the new cooperative era' of state and municipal authority expressed in a new mode of steel and concrete building.[85]

Reilly's work is an example of how central the promotion of visual culture was to the Labour government's attempt to make a new Britain. In December 1944, his 'Reilly Green' model of community planning had been adopted by the Labour Party,[86] envisaging future towns of fast arterial roads dividing pedestrian neighbourhoods with buildings grouped around common greens.[87] Once more, radicalism and conservatism, elitism and populism coexisted in Labour's cultural policy. Minister of Health Aneurin Bevan called up a village spirit in the service of socialism, arguing against monoclass 'castrated communities' as 'a monstrous infliction upon the essential psychological and biological oneness of the community'.[88] 'We should try', he said, 'to introduce in our modern villages and towns what was always the lovely feature of English and Welsh villages, where the doctor, the grocer, the butcher and the farm labourer all lived in the same street. I believe that is essential for the full life of a citizen ... to see the living tapestry of a mixed community'.[89]

In the CVE's final pamphlet, Nikolaus Pevsner addressed *Visual Pleasures from Everyday Things*. At the time, he was pursuing the connection of the modern and traditional through his formulation of a 'modernist picturesque' in the *Architectural Review*, and would go on to catalogue the country by county in the monumental *Buildings of England* series. For Pevsner, every element in the environment, however small or mundane, should be subject to visual order. And, just as Dower and Cornish had distinguished love of beauty from decadence, so Pevsner, in seeking to embed a feeling for beauty in everyday life, attempted to rid aesthetic appreciation of its associations with the 'soft' or 'cissy', which he identified as a consequence of the Puritan strain within British culture.[90]

Through his coeditorship of the *Architectural Review*, Pevsner promoted 'visual re-education', whereby a 'new keenness of perception' would enable an engagement with all past styles: 'To re-educate the eye — that is the special need of the next decade.'[91] The visually bright citizen should revel in a designed country: 'Visual education ... is concerned with things in nature as much as with man-made things. Possibly only one in a thousand today knows what to do with his eyes beyond using them for utilitarian purposes. . . . Very few realize that any tree, any leaf, any stone — and also any pot, any rug, any spoon — can be regarded aesthetically.'[92]

Beginning with questions of harmony in landscape, we have ended with the beauty of spoons. Coastlines, villages, holiday camps, the birds of Britain, tube stations, national parks and rugs were all embraced by those who sought to improve the visual culture of Britain. The Second World War provided an opportunity for plans nurtured in the 1920s and 1930s by the environmental movement to be developed at the heart of the state. In the 1945 general election campaign, Labour's most famous election poster displayed a new social environment of modern housing in a town near to preserved open country with a giant 'Victory V' on the skyline: 'And Now — Win the Peace'.

Unfortunately, despite all the planning legislation that appeared on the statute book in the 1940s, a combination of unscrupulous private developers, misguided or simply corrupt local authorities, and overzealous modern architects did much to undermine the attempt to amplify Britishness by improving the citizen's visual awareness of the nation. A critique of the planning movement of the 1940s began to emerge in the 1950s, via bodies such as the National Trust and the Civic Trust, formed in 1956 to counter the increasing brutalism with which many of Britain's towns and cities were being redeveloped.[93] Significantly, the CVE's annual report of 1956 welcomed the Civic Trust. The faith in public authority as a vehicle of cultural improvement, which drove the wartime and postwar planning movement, began to wane as that authority seemed ever less accountable. The attempt to promote recreational citizenship was more successful, as more and more urban holidaymakers ventured into the countryside in search of physical, spiritual and cultural fulfilment, lured by an increasingly commercial 'heritage industry', but also more aware of the need to respect the environment being sold to them.

However, the planning movement was riven by the growth in the late 1960s and 1970s of an angry conservation lobby, whose target was the perceived vandalism of the nation by the state and its development agencies. In short, the planner, both at local and national levels came to be seen as an enemy rather than an ally of Britain's environmental heritage. The disjuncture between planning and preservation, progress and heritage, modernity and tradition, was exacerbated by the new right towards the end of the century. Anxious to discredit the whole concept of planning, its spokespersons played on the mistakes of planners to fracture the consensual body of opinion that had once propelled reconstruction forwards. Wartime books such as James Fisher's cheap pocket-sized guide to *Watching Birds* now seem almost eccentric. Fisher presented his book as part of a struggle for a democratic culture of ornithology: 'Some people', he wrote:

> might consider an apology necessary for the appearance of a book about birds at a time when Britain is fighting for its own and many other lives. I make no such apology. Birds are part of the heritage we are fighting for. After this war, ordinary people are going to have a better time than they have had. It is for these men and women, not for the privileged few to whom ornithology has been an indulgence, that I have written this little book.[94]

Open-air movements may, like birdwatching, take off to new heights of popularity, and both may be bound up with visions of personal and even global spiritual improvement. But such activities no longer take their place within a moral geography of the nation whereby both citizen and nation are seen to progress in mutual improvement, under an expert eye seeking a complete design for life. As a result, many now believe that taking pleasure in England has ceased to be a matter of citizenship.

Notes

1. An earlier version of this chapter appeared in the *Journal of Historical Geography*, vol. 22, no. 4, 1996, under the title 'Visual culture and geographical citizenship: England in the 1940s'. I am grateful to the editors of that journal for permission to revise that article here. Thanks also to Felix Driver and Richard Weight for comments on earlier drafts.
2. Alison Light (1991) *Forever England: Femininity, Literature and Conservatism Between the Wars*, London; David Matless (1995) 'The art of

right living: landscape and citizenship 1918–39', in S. Pile and N. Thrift (eds) *Mapping the Subject*, London, pp. 93–122.

3.   Richard Weight (1995) 'Pale Stood Albion: the Promotion of National Culture in Britain 1939–56', University of London, unpublished Ph.D.; P. Wright (1993) *A Journey Through Ruins*, London.

4.   David Matless (1990) 'Ages of English design: preservation, modernism and tales of their history', *Journal of Design History*, vol. 3, pp. 203–12; David Matless (1990) 'Definitions of England', Built Environment, vol. 16, pp. 179–91; S. Rycroft and D. Cosgrove 'Mapping the modern nation: Dudley Stamp and the Land Utilization Survey', *History Workshop Journal*, vol. 40, pp. 91–105.

5.   On Cornish, see Matless, 'Visual culture and geographical citizenship'; David Matless (1991) 'Nature, the modern and the mystic', *Transactions IBG*, vol. 16, pp. 272–86; A. Goudie (1972) 'Vaughan Cornish: geographer', *Transactions IBG*, vol. 55, pp. 1–16; T. Stephenson (ed.) (1939) *The Countryside Companion*, London; H. Batsford (1940) *How to See the Country*, London.

6.   Quoted in the discussion following J. A. Steers (1944) 'Coastal preservation and planning', *Geographical Journal*, vol. 104, pp. 7–27, quote 25.

7.   J. Dower (1944) 'The landscape and planning', *Journal of the Town Planning Institute*, vol. 30, pp. 92–102, quote p. 92. On Dower's work see also John Sheail (1981) *Rural Conservation in Interwar Britain*, Oxford.

8.   Dower, 'The landscape', p. 93.

9.   Ibid., p. 95.

10. V. Cornish (1950) *National Parks*, p. 9.

11. Dower, 'The landscape', p. 96

12. Ibid., p. 94.

13. Ibid., p. 95.

14. Ibid., pp. 95–6.

15. Ibid., p. 97.

16. R. Titmuss (1938) *Poverty and Population*, London, p. 288, quoted in Greta Jones (1986) *Social Hygiene in Twentieth Century Britain*, London, p. 132. On exclusion see D. Sibley (1995) *Geographies of Exclusion*, London.

17. Batsford, *How to See the Country*, inside back cover.

18. Ibid., pp. 4–5.

19. On moral geography see F. Driver (1988) 'Moral geographies: social science and the urban environment in mid-nineteenth century England', *Transactions of the Institute of British Geographers*, vol. 13, pp. 275–87; David Matless (1994) 'Moral geography in Broadland', *Ecumene*, vol. 1, pp. 127–56.

20. Oliver Coburn (1951) *Youth Hostel Story*, London.

21. Jack Cox (1953) *Camping for All*, London, p. viii. On interwar mapping, fieldwork and geography see David Matless (1992) 'Regional surveys and local knowledges: the geographical imagination in Britain 1918–39', *Transactions IBG*, vol. 17, pp. 464–80.

22. HMSO (1951) *The Country Code*, London, HMSO; H. Abrahams (ed.) (1959) *Britain's National Parks*, London, pp. 119–20.

23. *Country Code*, p. 20.

24. John Dower (1945) *National Parks in England and Wales*, London, HMSO, cmd 6628); John Sheail (1995) 'John Dower, National parks and town and country planning in Britain', *Planning Perspectives*, vol. 10, pp. 1–16.

25. Hugh Dalton, 9 April 1946, quoted in Coburn, *Youth Hostel Story*, p. 120. Dalton's budget also established the National Land Fund, aiming to purchase elements of this heritage as a permanent war memorial.

26. Quoted in Coburn, *Youth Hostel Story*, p. 141 from the parliamentary debate on the National Parks Bill.

27. The following information is taken from Tom Stephenson (1989) *Forbidden Land*, Manchester.

28. Weight, 'Pale Stood Albion'; M. Chase (1993) '"Nothing less than a revolution"? Labour's agricultural policy', in J. Fyrth (ed.) *Labour's High Noon: The Government and the Economy 1945–51*, London, pp. 78–95.

29. Weight: 'Pale Stood Albion', p. 129.

30. *Country Code*, p. 3.

31. Quoted in Stephenson, *Forbidden Land*, p. 208.

32. On political tensions within the open-air and preservation movements, see J. Lowerson (1980) 'Battles for the Countryside', in Frank Gloversmith (ed.) *Class, Culture and Social Change*, Brighton, pp. 258–80; Matless, 'The art of right living'. On Labour and popular leisure, see Fielding, Thompson and Tiratsoo, *'England Arise!'*, Chapter 6.

33. Dower, *National Parks*, p. 23. Dower was made president of the Ramblers' Association in March 1946.

34. Ibid., p. 19; see also Cornish, *National Parks*, p. 30.

35. Dower, *National Parks*, p. 23.

36. Ibid., p. 31.

37. Ibid., p. 23. On the holiday camp as cultural landscape, see Colin Ward and Dennis Hardy (1986) *Goodnight Campers! The History of the British Holiday Camp*, London.

38. Steers, 'Coastal preservation and planning', p. 23.

39. PEP (1942) 'Planning for holidays', *Planning*, vol. 9, no. 194, 13 October, p. 6.

40. Ibid., p. 12.

41. Ibid., p. 6.

42. Joad had made similar arguments in the 1930s. The frontispiece of his

1934 *Charter for Ramblers* makes essentially the same commentary on the commodification of the past and the supposed stupidity of its consumers as the frontispiece of Robert Hewison's 1987 *The Heritage Industry*.

43. Cyril Joad (1946) *The Untutored Townsman's Invasion of the Country*, London, p. 229.
44. Ibid., p. 230.
45. Ibid., p. 231.
46. PEP, 'Planning for holidays', p. 8.
47. Rob Shields (1991) *Places on the Margin*, London.
48. Fielding, Thompson and Tiratsoo, *'England Arise!'*, p. 152.
49. Hilde Marchant (1970) 'Life in a holiday camp, *Picture Post*, 13 July 1946', in Tom Hopkinson (ed.) *Picture Post 1938–50*, Harmondsworth, Penguin, pp. 192–6.
50. Steers, 'Coastal preservation and planning', p. 15.
51. HMSO (1947) *Conservation of Nature in England and Wales*, London, HMSO, Cmd 7122. See A. G. Tansley (1945) *Our Heritage of Wild Nature: A Plea for Organized Nature Conservation*, Cambridge. Stoddart's obituary of Steers suggests the epitome of a particular culture of geography; outdoor, organized, committed to conservation and planning via state action, happy in the field. See D. Stoddart (1988) 'Obituary: James Alfred Steers', *Transactions IBG*, vol. 13, pp. 109–15.
52. Steers, 'Coastal preservation and planning', p. 17. See also Matless, 'Moral geography in Broadland', pp. 127–56.
53. Steers, 'Coastal preservation and planning', p. 8.
54. Ibid., p. 11. On plotlands, see Dennis Hardy and Colin Ward (1984) *Arcadia for All*, London.
55. Steers, 'Coastal preservation and planning', pp. 13–14.
56. Ibid., pp. 20–1.
57. Preface to J. A. Steers (1948) *A Picture Book of the Whole Coast of England and Wales*, Cambridge; J. A. Steers (1948) *The Coastline of England and Wales*, Cambridge.
58. *Conservation of Nature*, pp. 29–30.
59. A. E. Trueman (1949) *Geology and Scenery in England and Wales*, Harmondsworth, Penguin. Trueman was knighted in 1951, when chair of the University Grants Committee. On the progressive ethos of Penguin Books, see Steve Hare (ed.) (1995) *Penguin Portrait: Allen Lane and the Penguin Editors 1935–1970*, Harmondsworth, Penguin.
60. Truman, *Geology and Scenery*, p. 10.
61. Ibid., p. 12.
62. Ibid., p. 78.
63. C. C. Fagg and G. E. Hutchings (1930) *An Introduction to Regional Surveying*, Cambridge. See also Hutchings's 1961 presidential address to the Geographical Association, 'Geographical field teaching',

Geography, vol. 47, 1962, pp. 1–14, and his (1960) *Landscape Drawing*, London, based on an earlier Field Studies Council guide.

64. S. W. Wooldridge and G. E. Hutchings (1957) *London's Countryside*, London.

65. James Fisher (ed.) (1952) *Nature Parliament: A Book of the Broadcasts*, London, p. xv.

66. Peter Marren (1995) *The New Naturalists*, London. James Fisher's 1947 edition of Gilbert White's *Natural History of Selborne*, London, claims White as a proto-modern scientific observer against a sentimental romanticism. Fisher also produced an edition of White for Penguin in 1941. For another contrast of new and old naturalism see the 1944 feature film *Tawny Pipit*, for which Fisher, Huxley and Hosking were technical advisers.

67. See, for example, the range of topics in G. and E. G. McAllister (eds) (1945) *Homes, Towns and Countryside: A Practical Plan for Britain*, London, which includes essays by Stamp and Abercrombie.

68. *Journal of the Town Planning Institute*, vol. 30, 1944, pp. 74–7, 154–6. Also CPRE archive, University of Reading, file 398.

69. Ibid., p. 75

70. Ibid., p. 154.

71. Ibid., p. 74.

72. It is unclear whether the pamphlet by Dower on *Planning and the Countryside* listed in the CVE 1946 book list as soon to be published was ever issued.

73. Information from CVE Annual reports.

74. W. F. Morris (1946) *The Future Citizen and his Surroundings*, London (first published 1942), pp. 5–6.

75. F. J. Osborn (1943) 'Introduction', in V. Cornish, *The Beauties of Scenery*, London, p. 9.

76. Morris, *The Future Citizen*, p. 6.

77. Ibid., p. 8.

78. Ibid., p. 13.

79. Ibid., p. 3.

80. Ibid., p. 3.

81. Hervey Adams (1946) *Art and Everyman*, London, p. 12 (first edn 1944).

82. Ibid., p. 19; see also Hervey Adams (1949) *The Adventure of Looking*, London.

83. Sir Charles Reilly (1946) *Architecture as a Communal Art*, London, p. 17. The pamphlet's foreword by Giles Gilbert Scott is more guarded in its enthusiasm for modernism.

84. Ibid., p. 6.

85. Ibid., p. 16.

86. Harold Orlans (1952) *Stevenage: A Sociological Study of a New Town*, London, pp. 95–6.

87. Reilly, *Architecture*, p. 19. Reilly developed the idea in his plan for Birkenhead; Charles Reilly and N. J. Aslan (1947) *Outline Plan for the County Borough of Birkenhead*, Birkenhead.

88. Speaking in the House of Commons, 17 October 1945, quoted in Fielding, Thompson and Tiratsoo, *'England Arise!'*, p. 103.

89. Quoted in Peter Hennessy (1993) *Never Again. Britain 1945–1951*, London, p. 163. See also Fielding, Thompson and Tiratsoo, *'England Arise!'*, p. 104; and Silkin quoted along similar lines in Orlans, *Stevenage*, p. 82.

90. Nikolaus Pevsner (1946) *Visual Pleasures from Everyday Things*, London, p. 4.

91. 'Second Half Century', *Architectural Review*, vol. 101, 1947, pp. 21–6, quotes pp. 23, 25.

92. Pevsner, *Visual Pleasures*, p. 4.

93. I. Nairn (1955) *Outrage*, London; I. Nairn (1956) *Counter-Attack Against Subtopia*, London; J. M. Richards (1948) 'Failure of the New Towns', *Architectural Review*, vol. 114, pp. 29–32.

94. James Fisher (1940) *Watching Birds*, Harmondsworth, Penguin, preface.

9. Citizen defence: the Conservative Party and its attitude to national service, 1937–57

Nicholas Crowson

Owing to exceptional circumstances in the last decade voluntary recruitment has had to be supplemented by the continuance of national service . . . it [is] now possible to contemplate putting the services on to an all-regular basis. . . . It must nevertheless be understood that, if voluntary recruiting fails to produce the numbers required, the country will have to face the need for some limited form of compulsory service to bridge the gap.

Thus declared the April 1957 defence White Paper, *Outline of Future Policy*.[1] Although the last conscripts would not leave the army until 1964, this measure announced by Duncan Sandys, the defence minister, in 1957 marked a return to the principle of a small voluntary regular army. The deterrence factor of a large conscript army was no longer deemed effective and henceforth Britain would attempt to create an independent nuclear capability. Behind the abandonment of national service lay the irony that the two politicians most responsible for this decision, Harold Macmillan and Duncan Sandys, had 20 years earlier enthusiastically advocated its introduction.[2] Only with reluctance did the then prime minister, Neville Chamberlain, when faced with sustained pressure from the constituencies and backbenches, agree first to introduce a voluntary national service scheme and when that failed to produce the necessary recruits a measure of military conscription — the first time that conscription had been introduced in peacetime.[3]

The literature on peacetime conscription since 1945 has thus far evaluated the matter either from a strategical perspective or from the practical experiences of recruits, or else considered the political implications of such measures on the Labour Party.[4] Little, if anything, has been written from the perspective of the Conservative Party. This chapter is aimed at evaluating a hitherto neglected aspect of Conservative postwar policy. In it, I seek to examine the attitudes of the Conservative Party to the role a citizen should play in the peacetime defence of the nation following the Second World War. It in no way claims to be an exhaustive study, rather it is an overview — it will confine itself purely to the conceptions Conservatives held about citizenship, individualism and conscription. The mechanisms by which the decision to abandon national service were reached are beyond the scope of this work. It will be shown how and why the party was able to reconcile its support for the principle of individualism with the compulsion necessitated by conscription.

In his analysis of Clement Attlee's battles and tribulations with the Labour Party over national service between 1945 and 1951, L. V. Scott suggests that only a small section of the right wing of the Conservative Party advocated national service on domestic grounds and that, as such, they had little or no influence on the policy-makers. A theme that persists throughout Scott's work is the bipartisan approach Churchill and Attlee adopted to the issue of national service. In this chapter I shall not only demonstrate the Conservative Party's acceptance of national service, but also illustrate that the parliamentary Conservative Party widely supported the domestic value of national service and that this helped maintain the bipartisan approach to the issue. This does not deny Scott's central thesis that conscription was inextricably linked to foreign policy and viewed as a symbol of Britain's resolve and determination. Such attitudes were apparent in 1939, 1947 and 1950.

Britain, unlike her European continental counterparts with their large conscript armies, had a tradition of voluntary recruitment. The First World War changed all this. The introduction of conscription in 1915 and the realization that in the era of total war compulsion was the fairest means of ensuring the burden was evenly spread, meant that there existed a political consensus during the 1930s that should another war occur it would be legitimate to reintroduce conscription. The deteriorating international situation prompted Neville Chamberlain, in April 1939, to introduce limited measures of conscription. Though this brought outcries from the Labour Party and the trades union movement, the actual outbreak of hostilities in September meant that once more a consensus emerged.

Conscription during the Second World War naturally had an adverse effect on regular recruiting, while the war's duration meant that many of the prewar regulars had finished their tenures by 1945 — leading to concerns as the war in Europe drew to a close about the army's postwar manpower requirements and capabilities. Therefore, national service in 1945 involved two issues. First, whether the call-up should be continued for the immediate few postwar years to enable Britain to meet her vast peacetime requirements; and second, whether these commitments required the initiation of a permanent scheme of conscription.

It was accepted that national service was a mechanism for providing temporary forces for overseas commitments in Germany, the Middle East, and Asia, while it would also provide the means by which trained reserves would be available on mobilization — the principal military lesson to be learnt from 1939 if not indeed 1914. Labour won the 1945 general election and in 1947 introduced a National Service Bill. The bipartisan approach to national service during these years make it unlikely that the essence of British defence policy would have been much different if the Conservatives had won in 1945.[5]

Under the 1947 National Service Act, conscripts were called to the colours for 12 months (faced with a backbench rebellion the Attlee government had overnight reversed its decision to introduce 18 months' service). Throughout the passage of the bill, Churchill ensured that the Conservatives supported the government.[6] Unfortunately, Britain's declining economic situation during this period (for national service was an expensive scheme) contrasted with an increase in commitments as the cold war developed. The Korean War in 1950 persuaded Attlee to initiate a rearmament programme and to increase the length of service to two years.

Despite the Conservatives being returned to power in 1951, the status quo was maintained. However, the costs of national service, both in manpower and financial terms, led the government to consider devices to reduce the intake, such as increasing the call-up age and extending deferment.[7] The effectiveness of these methods was steadily eroded as the 1950s progressed and the government was faced with the need to consider devising a system of selective entry — a suggestion 'thought to be politically unacceptable'. Ultimately, concludes Richard Powell, a senior civil servant in the Ministry of Defence during this period, 'political requirements coincided with the need to cut costs and forced the government to accept the return to wholly voluntary recruitment to the armed forces.'[8]

Elements within the Conservative Party had in fact been attempting since 1954 to reduce the national service commitment in order to secure some measure of political capital. The Treasury under 'Rab' Butler had been anxious before the 1955 general election to reduce defence expenditure 'for electoral reasons, if no other', and saw the preferred option to be a diminution in national service. Likewise, Macmillan as foreign minister had similar desires to cut the length of service — though foreign policy commitments in the Suez area, Malaya, Kenya and Cyprus prevented this.[9] Consequently, the 1955 party manifesto could only point out that they did 'not regard the current two-year period of whole-time national service as necessarily having come to stay'.[10]

Conservatives seek to argue that their politics are based upon pragmatism rather than ideology.[11] This pragmatism is considered a source of strength for it enables the party to reinvent itself under different leaders — something no less apparent with compulsion. Although the party is not ideologically rigid, conservatism revolves around a certain ethos — the defence of institutions (state, monarchy and church) and traditions; the preservation of society; and the safeguarding of the individual.

This last aspect of the ethos is what impinges on the question of national service, for the adoption of such a compulsory measure would appear at first glance to contradict the apparent spirit of individualism. The individual, Conservatives hold, 'must have the opportunity to set free those creative forces which are latent in the human breast, and he must be given every chance to rise to the height of his greatest potentialities. To allow him to be swallowed up in the totality would merely be to court disaster.'[12] Conservatives feel that their role in society is to provide the conditions that will encourage the individual to play a role conducive to society — this usually entails the intention to remove restrictions, as with Lady Thatcher's 'rolling back the state'.

Conservatives are distrustful of planning. If the individual plans, it 'is an expression of his personality'; if it is the state planning then it is a 'denial' of his rights.[13] F. A. Hayek, the messiah of the new right writing in 1944, considered the British to have a number of virtues that were to the nation's benefit: 'independence and self-reliance, individual initiative and local responsibility, the successful reliance on voluntary activity, non-interference with one's neighbour and tolerance of the different and queer, respect for custom and tradition, and a healthy suspicion of power and authority'.[14]

The advantages of individualism manifest themselves in the desire of the citizen to excel and achieve. However, this should not be at the total expense of the state. Freedom may be the 'indispensable vitamins of human society' but the individuals most profitable to the community are those who are also citizens. In Leo Amery's words, 'the qualities of cooperation, of public duty, of willingness to sacrifice personal interest and even life itself for the common cause are essential.'[15] To promote this citizenship the state may have to adopt a limited role. Indeed, one Conservative protagonist writing in the mid-1980s pointed out that in this sense the promotion of individuality was not the highest imperative for a Conservative politician. Rather, it was to assist in 'the guardianship of institutions and the fostering of traditions which provide the cultural soil in which selfhood can flourish'.[16] In other words, preservation of the state from external and internal challenges is essential if the individual is to be provided with the conditions that enable freedom, and therefore in such circumstances the individual must be prepared at times to assist in this defence.

After 1945, communism presented a challenge to the traditions and institutions of the West and therefore conscription was a legitimate act of guardianship. Such an interpretation can be traced back to Edmund Burke. In his *Thoughts and Details on Scarcity*, he recognized that the state should keep interference to the minimum: 'the state ought to confine itself to what regards the state, or creatures of the state, namely, the exterior establishment of its religion; its magistracy, its revenue; its military force by sea and land; the corporations that owe their existence to its fiat.'[17] These aspects of interference may in some cases be occasional, in others permanent. This was the issue at stake in 1945: could the state justify the permanent institution of conscription or should a continuation of the call-up only be made for the immediate postwar years? Overall, Conservatives accepted the right of the state to interfere in certain aspects of society for its greater good.

When the National Service League campaigned for the adoption of compulsion in the Edwardian era, Conservative Party leaders shied away from advocating such policies, fearing they were electorally unpopular. Resistance to collectivism had been the principal function of the pre-First World War Conservative Party.[18] Similarly, Chamberlain and other members of his cabinet during the later 1930s argued against the government taking compulsory powers to assist in the rearmament programme and recruiting for fear that they were unacceptable to public opinion and the trades union movement, whose goodwill was crucial to assisting the defence schemes. Compulsion was not the British way. It was argued that more could be achieved through voluntary association under effective leadership than was ever possible by compulsory methods. Certainly Conservative polemicists have seen voluntarism as a strength of British society.

However, circumstances do change attitudes. The fourth Marquis of Salisbury had been dismissive of the benefits of compulsion in 1914 but by 1938, as a member of the Army League executive, was urging conscription.[19] Just as the First World War inclined politicians to accept the need for conscription in wartime, the Second War ultimately proved a vehicle for changing attitudes. Viscount Hinchingbrooke, speaking in Bradford in 1943, believed that there existed two means by which a state could improve itself — voluntarily, as was the British tradition; and compulsorily and collectively, as had been the German and Soviet experience before

1939. He agreed that the latter method was 'the quicker and more effective'. Looking forward to the ending of hostilities, he warned that Britain had to 'watch out' for other nations equalling and surpassing her standard of living because of the 'willingness of those nations to continue with compulsory and collective action, while we revert too quickly and eagerly to a voluntary and perhaps mutually destructive basis to our society'.[20] During the war, Hinchingbrooke favoured a social Toryism and admitted to being greatly influenced by Harold Macmillan's *The Middle Way* (1938), which argued for some form of state collectivist intervention, 'Tory corporatism', to assist the British economy of the 1930s.

In another speech in 1943 Hinchingbrooke tried to reconcile the apparent contradictions between urging compulsion and the threat it posed to the individual. He agreed that the expectations concerning liberty in wartime and liberty in peacetime were different: 'In peace we aim at maximum freedom for individual expression. In war we voluntarily surrender part of our personal liberty to fortify the state, in order that the state may carry out more effectively and expeditiously its purpose of ridding itself of an overwhelming external danger.'[21] He nevertheless warned against complacency in peace, for Britain 'must expect that external dangers will remain, though taking other forms [to Nazi Germany], and our definition of individual liberty will be conditioned thereby and be interpreted as something less free ranging and diversified, simpler, more straightforward and disciplined than our fathers would have understood.'[22] In the post-1945 chill of the cold war, the new external threat proved to be the Soviet Union and the communist challenge. National service recruits, whether serving with the British army on the Rhine, supporting the regulars in Korea or patrolling the jungles of Malaya, were actively entwined with this threat — large forces of manpower being perceived as the best deterrent.

The 1945 Conservative Party conference passed a resolution 'urging' the continuation of conscription.[23] At the time, this was a reaction to the recent cessation of hostilities. Both Eden and Amery, when serving in the coalition government, argued that while the extra-European commitments would be met by the regulars, conscription was required to meet Britain's continental requirements.[24] It was widely accepted that the presence of British forces in the defeated and liberated countries was required to preserve law and order and to re-establish democracy. However, as this immediate task subsided, the question arose of whether permanent conscription could be introduced.

Of course, the Conservatives were in opposition from 1945 to 1951 and this afforded them a rhetorical position from which to admonish the Labour Party about the sparseness of existing military capabilities. At the 1949 party conference, the motion on defence, which was carried, deplored the Labour 'government's wasteful and indecisive defence policy'.[25] Harrow East Conservative Association had also forwarded a motion to this conference critical of Labour's defence policies. Although this motion was not debated, its criticisms of the conditions of national service were widely accepted in the party.[26] These views were reflected in the 1950 party manifesto, *This is the Road*, which argued that with better administration it was possible to reduce the burden of national service. The party's campaign guide pointed out that there were only two moments when the country was prepared to accept peacetime conscription: in times of acute national danger and in the immediate aftermath of a war.[27]

The communist challenge in Korea in 1950 was the acute national danger that justified conscription's continuation. Although Churchill declared in 1947 that prolonged overseas service for conscripts could not 'be maintained as a permanency', he nevertheless contended that:

> the only way to make us a nation of fighting men in time of war is by national service in time of peace. As all our habits in the past have been to live in a peaceful manner, we have entered all our wars unprepared, and the delay before we are able to place an army in the field at the side of our allies has been a very serious weakness, not only in the physical but in the moral sphere.[28]

The stigma of 'guilt' for Britain's unpreparedness in 1939 was a powerfully potent force in the late 1940s. For Churchill and many other Conservatives the maintenance of a large standing army helped Britain to preserve her international prestige.[29] Already the signs of decline were very apparent: the loss of India and Burma, the reliance on Marshall Aid and the 1947 sterling conversion crisis all indicated that Britain was 'living at a more humble level'. As Hinchingbrooke had prophesied Britain faced new challenges in peacetime and this arose in the form of the USSR and the cold war.

Colonel J. H. Harrison specifically cited the threat of communism as the justification for national service.[30] This was indicative of the changing emphasis on national service. No longer were conscripts a trained reserve force for emergencies and a supplement to the regulars, they had become an integral part of Britain's active forces. The 1955 White Paper on National Service did indicate the Conservative government's intention to lessen the burden of conscription 'as soon as circumstances permit[ted]'.[31] This arose from the desire of senior Conservatives to gain political capital from a reduction in the commitment of national service. Unfortunately, circumstances failed to allow these reductions in time for the 1955 general election. Furthermore, as Iain Macleod later pointed out, 'we cannot urge the abolition of national service unless we are prepared either to rely for our protection for all time and in all circumstances upon a foreign but friendly country or are prepared to take the grim decision to make the bomb.'[32] Not until 1957 had the decision to build a bomb been finalized and only then was national service as a deterrent superfluous.

In the 1937–9 debate about the merits of introducing national service, it was evident that Conservatives who had been professional servicemen were more willing than others to advocate compulsion.[33] This was despite the contemporary military authorities' wariness of such measures. Did the experience of military service in the Second World War make Conservative MPs more willing to implement national service? Certainly, the core of Conservatives who spoke during the 1947 debates were reflecting their own service experiences in advocating the measures.

Oliver Stanley, a former Secretary of State for War, considered that all MPs who had undergone a period in the armed forces would agree that national service was 'an experience from which . . . a great amount of good can be drawn by an individual'.[34] It was an often stated point that military service provided a youth with the opportunity to improve his education, discipline and outlook on life. This theme was recurrent throughout the 1940s and 1950s. Nigel Fisher declared in 1953 that there were many benefits to a period of service 'such as pride in wearing the Queen's uniform, pride of regiment, discipline and so on which may bring out in a young man qualities of character which might otherwise have lain dormant'.[35] The perception that conscription was a means of disciplining youth cultures should not be underestimated. The emergence of rock and roll and the disturbances that accompanied the release of the film *Rock Around The Clock* in 1955 served notice to Conservative politicians that British society was dramatically changing. National Service offered a device by which the growth of juvenile delinquency could be stemmed and the traditional concepts of citizenship instilled upon a new generation. As Walter Monckton, Minister for Labour and National Service explained, the young conscripts had:

> an opportunity of leading a corporate life with others of various types and different backgrounds. They have opportunities of developing initiative and of experiencing leadership. They experience as good a comradeship as they are likely to get anywhere. They generally benefit a great deal in health and physique and put on weight. They have an opportunity of travel certainly in Great Britain and possibly overseas.[36]

Monckton's reference to the health benefits of conscription was not untypical either. Since the Boer War, conservative politicians had been concerned about the physical deterioration in British youth. Without healthy young men how could the British be expected to maintain and defend their world influence? Furthermore, some argued that national service was a reasonable exchange for the provision of a welfare state — an argument that even Attlee employed in 1947. However, former professional soldiers now serving as MPs often repeated that, though they accepted the need for national service, they disliked compulsion and found voluntary means of recruitment preferable. The priority for these Conservatives was to improve the pay and conditions of the regular forces as a means of increasing the manpower of the armed forces and thereby removing the need for conscription.[37] Indeed, between 1950 and 1960 the pay of the military regulars increased fivefold.[38]

More generally, among the party the acceptance of national service rested on the assumption that the scheme was based on the principle of universality. A universal system was believed to be fairest. In the 1947 debates, some, including Winston Churchill, objected on exemptions being introduced that excluded coalminers from service. Service to defend the nation was the 'first duty of the citizen'.[39] Conservatives saw universal liability as 'an understandable desire' and a principle that was 'generally accepted and approved'. However, they saw difficulty in translating this into practical measures. To this extent, party managers saw it as 'important' for the 1950 election campaign that it was realized that 'this equality is not being obtained now, nor is it possible.'[40]

While in office, the Conservatives did attempt to remove loop-holes that enabled youths to dodge the draft. In 1954, Walter Monckton introduced the second reading of a bill that extended the upper age limit of liability for service in certain cases with the aim of preventing the evasion of service by young men who were abroad for most of their last year of potential call-up. He admitted that this bill would only affect some 300 individuals a year, but 'it involves the important principle of the universality of national service, for it is important that the system should be fairly administered and be seen to be manifestly fairly administered.'[41]

Though Conservative speakers during this debate echoed the minister's concerns, their rhetoric also suggested growing dissatisfaction with the continuation of compulsion — thoughts of electoral expediency cannot have been far from their minds. Malcolm McCorquodale saw compulsion as 'only tolerable when people are assured that they are being treated fairly, and that everyone is being treated alike'.[42] Another backbencher, Kenneth Thompson, though convinced of the bill's necessity confessed that his satisfaction was limited. To him, the continuation of compulsory peacetime service was 'a great pity'.[43]

Privately, party managers were seeking either to reduce the commitment to national service or to remove it entirely. But, presented with the problems of manpower wastage, costs and overseas commitments, solutions were not obviously visible. One suggestion frequently mooted was conscription by ballot. During secret talks with the Attlee government in 1949, Churchill appeared taken with the idea of a ballot system.[44] One Conservative backbencher critical of compulsion during the 1947 debates had asked whether a form of conscription by ballot was not preferable.[45] Ultimately, the ubiquitous nature of such a system made party managers wary of translating the private support for this measure into a firm electoral commitment.

In the initial years of national service, Conservatives had little trouble seeking historical justification for the introduction of compulsion. Winston Churchill pointed out in 1947 that 'it had been defended and practised by all the most advanced democratic countries in Europe since the French Revolution.'[46] Although some, like Legge-Bourke and Price-White, believed that voluntarism was a special British tradition, many other Conservatives argued that there was a tradition of compulsion whenever the state needed to construct a militia.

Lieutenant-Colonel Sir Cuthbert Headlam considered peacetime conscription to be 'perfectly consistent with the tradition of this country'. His argument was that 'a conscript army would be more careful of the liberties of the country than a standing army, which would be entirely under the charge and control of the government of the day.'[47] Equally, while there was general acceptance of the need to adopt these measures, the 1947 debates reveal that this support was far from universal in the parliamentary party. Though only one Conservative actually voted against the 1947 Act, many others could barely disguise their dissatisfaction.[48]

Kenneth Pickthorn, while having no doubts about the general right of a government to introduce compulsion on its subjects, considered conscription to be a form of taxation. He pointed out that 'this House should never give a government the right to collect taxes, except after the plainest demonstration from the Treasury Bench why the tax is needed, how it is spent, and why not a penny less is needed.' In his view, the Attlee government had failed to provide this information, which led him to feel that it was 'dangerous that my party should be supporting it' and that he was personally voting for it 'so very dubiously, very dubiously indeed'.[49]

The professional servicemen, as already indicated, were also doubtful of the necessity for compulsion. It is apparent that behind the scenes the party was divided on the issue. Churchill and other senior Conservatives sought to gain political capital from the U-turn the Attlee leadership did on the issue of 18 months' service when faced with a backbench Labour revolt. Churchill chastised Labour's front bench for its 'failure to stand up for convictions and belief, to this sudden volte-face, change and scuttle of which the Prime Minister and his Minister of Defence were guilty. . . . The title of the Minister of Defence should be changed. He should be called the "Minister of Defence unless Attacked".'[50]

It was evident, however, that many Conservatives also favoured 12 months' service. Robert Hudson and Harold Macmillan both wrote to Churchill after the party's defence committee had agreed to support 18 months, suggesting they were liable to vote against this. Both men were anxious that the party should not commit itself to a stance that may 'incur any avoidable unpopularity'.[51] The 1922 Committee also met to discuss the decision and only the personal intervention of Churchill won the day. Much of the rhetoric on this matter was motivated by perceived public opinion. However, it is apparent that Conservatives consistently underestimated public support for national service and generally exaggerated concerns.

At no point did national service become an election issue. During the 1945 campaign only 10 per cent of Conservative candidates mentioned it.[52] More generally, in 1950 only 28 per cent of the party's candidates made reference to defence matters during their election addresses.[53] In 1955, the party manifesto had only an oblique reference to the unlikelihood of two years' service continuing. Opinion polls carried out in the late 1940s and during the 1950s revealed continued support for national service. In January 1949, 57 per cent of a sample agreed that conscription should be continued in peacetime. Some 18 months later, 55 per cent agreed with the increase in service to two years. When asked in May 1954 whether they agreed with Churchill's belief that it was unwise to reduce the length of service, 49 per cent of that sample concurred.

Not until July 1956 did polls begin to show public disillusionment with the continuation of compulsion.[54] The changing public attitude to conscription was due to a multitude of factors: growing affluence, especially of the middle classes; the evolving youth culture which sprang from the increased financial independence and educational opportunities enjoyed by postwar adolescents. Finally, détente with the Soviet Union, combined with the anti-imperial mood following the Suez débâcle, lessened the need for conventional deterrents in the public mind. Even then, Conservative MPs were liable to point out the lack of constituency correspondence they were receiving on the issue. In 1947, Cuthbert Headlam had told Parliament that he had received 'fewer letters of protest against this bill than I have had against any other bill of similar importance'.[55] Another MP explained that he had:

> represented a working class district for many years, and there is a streak of radicalism, even Bevanism, in the constituency. For several years I have urged a return to conscription or some form of selective service. I have taken the most careful pains to point out in speeches and the like just what my position is. I have also indicated that a selective service system would be unfair, probably hit them harder than the other economic and social groups. Despite this I have never had a single protest, question or letter, indicating any disagreement or concern with my position.[56]

When Sandys announced the abolition of conscription, Prime Minister Macmillan felt that a 'stern warning' was necessary that if voluntary recruitment proved inadequate, a compulsory system of some form would be introduced.[57] However, once gone, its loss appeared of little consequence to Conservatives. Although the annual party conference that year was anxious that the new emphasis on nuclear weapons should not be at the total expense of conventional forces, there were no calls for the reinstatement of conscription. A survey of local party members in Newcastle-under-Lyme found only 22 per cent prepared to reintroduce a scheme, while fears in that year that conscription might have to be adopted once more just as the last conscripts finished their service led the Bow Group to publish its alternative proposals for a voluntary reserve army.[58]

While it appears that for political reasons senior Conservatives had been seeking to end national service for some time, it did not mean they disputed the principle of citizen defence.[59] In fact, a number of those involved in the dismantling of the system retrospectively expressed regret that it been abandoned. One time defence minister, Anthony Head, felt it should have been kept on the statute books 'just in case a volunteer force couldn't produce the necessary manpower numbers'. Macmillan also felt that 'we made a mistake; we should have kept it for six months, something like the Swiss, just to teach soldiers the simple things.'[60] By 1957, a new form of deterrence was now favoured, the atomic bomb, and this 'grim decision' enabled ministers to scrap national service.[61]

In conclusion, it must be realized that national service was perceived by Conservatives as a necessary tool in the preservation of Britain's international prestige. More generally, the principle of citizen defence was not disputed. It was not seen to contradict individualism because of the acceptance that the state could adopt compulsion to defend itself. Without the preservation of British 'traditions' there would be no climate in which the individual could flourish. Furthermore, many believed that individuals benefited from a period of service — there was no harm in a little bit of discipline. However, there were always exaggerated concerns that support for compulsion was politically inexpedient. The apparent inability to ensure the universality of the system added fuel to these worries. Ultimately, as the nuclear age dawned, the justification for large-scale conventional forces diminished and the political arguments could be dismissed no longer.

Notes

1.   Ministry of Defence (1957) *Outline of Future Policy*, London, HMSO, April, Cmd. 124.

2.   Harold Macmillan (1938) *The Price of Peace*, London; Norwood Conservative Association (Lambeth Archives, Minnet Library), executive council, 24 June 1938, IV/166/1/15; *The Times*, 1 July 1938.

3.   See Nicholas J. Crowson (1995) 'The Conservative Party and the question of National Service, 1937–1939: compulsion versus voluntarism', *Contemporary Record*, vol. 9, no. 3, pp. 507–28.

4.   For the pre-1918 period, see Keith Grieves (1988) *The Politics of*

Manpower, 1914–18, Manchester; John Morton Osborne (1982) *The Voluntary Recruiting Movement in Britain, 1914–16*, London; Roy Douglas (1970) 'Voluntary enlistment in the First World War and the work of the parliamentary recruiting committee', *Journal of Modern History*, vol. 4, pp. 564–85; Rhodri Williams (1991) *Defending the Empire: The Conservative Party and British Defence Policy, 1899–1915*, London; R. J. Q. Adams and P. P. Poirier (1987) *Conscription Controversy*, London; For the pre-1939 period, see Brian Bond (1980) *British Military Strategy Between the Wars*, Oxford; Peter Dennis (1972) *Decision By Default*, London; Michael Howard (1972) *The Continental Commitment*, London; For the post-1945 period, see L. V. Scott (1993) *Conscription and the Attlee Governments: The Politics and Policy of National Service, 1945–51*, Oxford; William P. Snyder (1964) *The Politics of British Defence Policy, 1945–62*, Columbus; Frank Mayers (1984) 'Conscription and the politics of military strategy in the Attlee government', *Journal of Strategic Studies*, vol. 7, pp. 55–73; L. V. Wallis (1977) 'Peacetime conscription and the British army', Lancaster University: M.Litt.; David Greenwood and David Hazel (1977) *The Evolution of Britain's Defence Priorities, 1957–76*, University of Aberdeen, Studies in Defence Economics 9; Martin Navias (1989) 'Terminating conscription? The British national service controversy, 1955–56', *Journal of Contemporary History*, vol. 24, pp. 195–208.

5. Scott, *Conscription and the Attlee Governments*, pp. 42–4.
6. A total of 152 Conservative MPs supported the 1947 National Service Act and only one voted against it. This was Colonel Price-White (Caernarvon Boroughs) who explained that he felt it was his duty to represent his constituents' views. This Welsh seal had a strong non-conformist tradition. Hansard, 31 March 1947, vol. 435 cols. 1731–5.
7. *National Service*, London, HMSO, October 1955, Cmd. 9608
8. Richard Powell (1978) 'The evolution of British defence policy, 1945–59', in John Simpson (ed.) *Perspectives Upon British Defence Policy, 1945–70*, Southampton, p. 54.
9. Michael Carver (1992) *Tightrope Walking: British Defence Policy since 1945*, London, pp. 31–2.
10. David Butler (1955) *The British General Election of 1955*, London, pp. 18–19.
11. For example, David Stelling (1943) *Why I Am a Conservative*, London, p. 3; David J. Levy (1988) 'The politics of self', in Roger Scruton (ed.) *Conservative Thoughts: Essays from the Salisbury Review*, London, p. 83.
12. Reginald Northam (1939) *Conservatism: The Only Way*, London, p. 113.
13. Richard Law (1950) *Return From Utopia*, London, p. 80.
14. F. A. Hayck (1944) *The Road to Serfdom*, cited in Kenneth Baker (ed.) (1993) *The Faber Book of Conservatism*, London, Faber & Faber, p. 180.
15. Leo Amery cited in Baker, *Conservatism*, p. 91.

16. Levy, 'Politics of self', p. 82.
17. Edmund Burke, cited in Baker, *Conservatism*, p. 162.
18. See Matthew Fforde (1990) *Conservatism and Collectivism, 1886–1914*, Edinburgh. In his conclusion, Fforde suggests that the Conservatives under Thatcher have followed on from the Edwardian Conservative tradition of opposition to collectivist policies.
19. Compare Williams, *Defending the Empire*, pp. 147, 221, 223 with L. S. Amery (1955) *My Political Life: The Unforgotten Years*, London, p. 299n; Lord Salisbury, *House of Lords Debates*, 22 May 1939, vol. 113, cols. 24–30.
20. Viscount Hinchingbrooke (1945) *Full Speed Ahead! Essays in Tory Reform*, London, p. 33.
21. Hinchingbrooke, *Full Speed Ahead*, p. 62.
22. Hinchingbrooke, *Full Speed Ahead*, p. 66.
23. F. W. S. Craig (ed.) (1982) *Conservative and Labour Conference Decisions, 1945–1981*, Chichester, p. 57.
24. Scott, *Conscription and the Attlee Governments*, p. 24.
25. 70th Annual Conservative Conference, 1949, Programme of Proceedings, motion number 55.
26. 70th Annual Conference, motion number 57.
27. Conservative Central Office (1949) *General Election 1950: The Campaign Guide*, London, Conservative Central Office, October.
28. Conservative Central Office, *General Election 1950*.
29. Churchill wrote to Gifford Martel (a military expert and opponent of national service) in June 1949 explaining that he would consider its abolition 'a great blow to what is left of British prestige throughout the world' (Martin Gilbert (1989) *Winston S. Churchill: VIII: 1945–65*, London, p. 321n).
30. J. H. Harrison (1953) Hansard, 16 November, vol. 520 col. 1422.
31. *National Service*, p. 3.
32. Iain Macleod (1957) Hansard, April, vol. 568 col. 1958.
33. Crowson, 'Conservative Party'.
34. Oliver Stanley (1947) Hansard, 1 April, vol. 435 col. 1900.
35. Nigel Fisher (1953) Hansard, 16 November, vol. 520 col. 1483.
36. Walter Monckton (1953) Hansard, 17 November, vol. 520 cols. 1581–2.
37. Various, Hansard, 31 March 1947, vol. 435 cols. 1720–1, 1735; 7 May 1947 vol. 437 cols. 511–12; The Llandudno conference in 1948 passed an emergency resolution urging 'unqualified support for the present Armed Forces Recruiting Campaign'. 69th Annual Conservative Conference, 1948, Verbatim Report (London, 1948), p. 24.
38. Snyder, *Politics of British Defence*, p. 237.
39. Winston Churchill (1947) Hansard, 31 March, vol. 435 col. 1698.
40. Conservative Central Office, *The General Election 1950: Campaign Guide*.

41. Walter Monckton (1954) Hansard, 17 December, vol. 535 cols. 2300–2308 quote col. 2300.
42. Mark McCorquodale (1954) Hansard, 17 December, vol. 535 cols. 2315–16.
43. Kenneth Thompson (1954) Hansard, 17 December, vol. 535 cols. 2322.
44. Scott, *Conscription and the Attlee Governments*, p. 44.
45. J. J. Astor (1947) Hansard, 7 May, vol. 437 col. 493.
46. Winston Churchill (1947) Hansard, 31 March, vol. 435 col. 1695.
47. Cuthbert Headlam (1947) Hansard, 22 May, vol. 437 cols. 2550, 2551.
48. For the 1949 party conference a motion was on the order paper from West Gloucestershire Association, which pointed out that they would 'welcome' the abandonment of conscription. 70th Annual Conservative Conference, motion number 58.
49. Kenneth Pickthorn (1947) Hansard, 1 April, vol. 435 cols. 1919–1920.
50. Winston Churchill (1947) Hansard, 7 May, vol. 437 col. 458.
51. Gilbert, *Churchill*, pp. 321–2.
52. McCallum and Readman, *The British General Election of 1945*, p. 98. Only 1 per cent of Labour candidates spoke about the subject.
53. H. G. Nicholas (1951) *The British General Election of 1950*, London, p. 221.
54. Snyder, *Politics of British Defence*, pp. 54–5. For examples of polls between 1945 and 1947, see Scott, *Conscription and the Attlee Governments*, pp. 41–2.
55. Cuthbert Headlam (1947) Hansard, 22 May, vol. 437 col. 2552.
56. Snyder, *Politics of British Defence*, pp. 179–80.
57. Harold Macmillan (1971) *Riding The Storm, 1956–1959*, London, p. 265.
58. Frank Bealey et al. (1965) *Constituency Politics: A Study of Newcastle-under-Lyme*, London; R. A. Brearley et al. (1964) *A New Reserve Army: The Alternative to Conscription*, London.
59. Acceptance of the principle still persists in the 1990s. One Scottish constituency agent told the author that, in his view, many of the grassroots still harked back to the days of conscription as a means of 'improving' today's youth.
60. Robert Horne (1989) *Macmillan, 1957–1986: Volume II*, London, pp. 49–50. In fact Macmillan had sought to justify the abolition of conscription to Parliament for that very reason in 1957, believing that there were 'too many people under this system learning and then leaving when they have learned', Harold Macmillan (1957) Hansard, 17 April, vol. 568 cols. 2050.
61. Ian Macleod (1957) Hansard, 17 April, vol. 568 col. 1958. For further analysis of the decision to scrap national service see the article by Navias, 'Terminating Conscription?'

10. From subjects to immigrants: black Britons and national identity, 1948–62

Kathleen Paul

In June 1948, Clement Attlee's Labour government passed a new British Nationality Act. Of the variety of issues that lay behind this decision, one particular matter stands out for the light it sheds upon the contested nature of the politics of citizenship and national identity in postwar Britain. The Foreign Office and the Board of Trade approved of the new legislation because it would provide an opportunity, when signing international treaties, to identify more clearly those individuals in whose name the treaty was being concluded. As things stood prior to the act, both departments relied on the rather 'clumsy' and 'unsatisfactory' term 'belonging to' as a means of separating out those deemed to 'belong' to the United Kingdom from all other British subjects.[1]

This concern highlights some of the contradictions inherent in postwar British nationality. First, it suggests a lack of clarity in nationality law — if everyone was British why did some have to be separated out as 'belonging to' the United Kingdom? Why did British nationality policy not follow the simple logic of providing all-inclusive protection for all those who bore the title British and who carried a British passport? Second, it suggests that among the governing elite at least there was an understanding that the universal term British subject could be qualified to differentiate between those who bore the title and those who really 'belonged' to Britain. This differentiation suggests that some British subjects were perceived to be more British than others. The assumption of a tiered nationality was only implicit in the Foreign Office and Board of Trade literature:

over the course of the subsequent decades, as three different migrant groups entered Britain, the assumption of hierarchy became explicit.

Between 1945 and 1961, European refugees, citizens of Ireland and British subjects from the West Indies, India and Pakistan together constituted an addition of more than a million people to the British population. In some respects, this migration experience was similar to that undergone by continental Europe — migrant workers taking up jobs left vacant by an indigenous workforce moving up the ladder of economic and social mobility.[2] In other respects, however, the British case was very different. Labour migration to Britain began much earlier than to the Continent and was composed both of migrants who planned only a temporary stay and those who from the start accepted the resettlement as permanent. Further distinguishing the British and Continental experiences, neither government nor capital in Britain perceived the migrants as an undifferentiated mass but rather separated the migrants out into three clearly distinguishable groups with some migrants receiving better treatment than others.

Stemming from the politics of citizenship, this differentiated treatment ensured that each group underwent a different migration experience. Perhaps most like the Continental guestworkers in outward form were the refugees. Facing a labour shortage estimated at between 600,000 and one million, the Attlee Cabinet in February 1946 established a Foreign Labour Committee (FLC) charged with the responsibility of locating additional sources of labour that could help relieve some of the most serious shortages.[3] The first source of foreign labour to be considered by the FLC were members of the Polish armed forces who had fought under British direction during the war and who were currently the financial responsibility of Britain. It appeared logical to the Attlee Cabinet that the soldiers should be encouraged to take up work in the civilian labour force as a means of relieving pressure upon the domestic economy.[4]

Accordingly, over the course of the next two years more than 120,000 Polish veterans and their dependants took up permanent residence in Britain.[5] The FLC found an additional source of foreign labour among the refugees of Nazism currently housed in camps in Germany and Austria, many of whom were eager to emigrate out of continental Europe to start a new life elsewhere.[6] As in the case of the Poles, it appeared logical to the Attlee Cabinet that by bringing some of the refugees to Britain, the cost of the camps' maintenance could be reduced and the domestic labour shortage could be relieved.[7]

Over the course of its lifetime, in addition to the 120,000 Poles, the FLC was responsible for the direct recruitment of 78,500 refugees (a combination of Yugoslavian, Bulgarian, Romanian, Ukrainian, Estonian, Latvian, Lithuanian and other nationalities), 13,600 non-refugees and the civilianization of 25,000 former German, Italian and Ukrainian prisoners of war. In addition, still searching for additional sources of foreign labour, the Attlee administration restarted the work permit system by which aliens seeking to work in Britain acquired authorization. A generous distribution both under Attlee and later under his Conservative successors brought approximately 35,000 aliens to Britain each year from 1947 through the mid-1950s. All told, these foreign sources of labour added some 345,000 to the UK population between 1946 and 1952.[8]

In outward form at least, these foreign workers compare with Europe's later *gastarbeiters*. They were initially recruited on short-term contracts for particular, usually unattractive industries such as coalmining, textiles, foundries, agriculture and institutional domestic service. Unlike the *gastarbeiter*, however, who faced residential segregation and social and economic discrimination, these aliens found their entry into the British labour market smoothed by UK politicians and civil servants. Minister of Health Nye Bevan, Minister of Fuel Emmanuel Shinwell and Minister of Labour George Isaacs, for example, as well as numerous officials under their direction, all worked with the trade unions to ensure that the foreigners were accepted as equals on the shopfloor. As a part of these negotiations, both sides agreed that the incoming aliens would receive prevailing wages and conditions and would join the appropriate trade union.

Further discussions resulted in the agreement that aliens would be released from their commitment to specific industries after three years' work and would then be free to take up any employment available.[9] In addition to these workplace negotiations, the Attlee government went to a great deal of trouble to ensure that the aliens were accepted socially. Thus, the camps where aliens lived offered classes in English; several departments combined to conduct a publicity campaign on the aliens' behalf, distributing literature to women's magazines and newspapers that cast the aliens in a favourable light; and government ministers enthusiastically praised aliens' contribution to the relief of Britain's economic crises, while emphasizing the great good that could come of this alien immigration.[10]

The second migrant group of the postwar period hailed from Ireland. From an annual cross traffic of around one million, the UK labour market received an average of 50,000 new recruits each year. The level of migration was such that by 1961, just over a million Irish-born lived in Britain.[11] Like the refugees, these recruits were not British: unlike the refugees, however, they were given all the privileges of subjecthood immediately on entering the country. Indeed, according to the 1948 British Nationality Act, Irish migrants in Britain were to be treated exactly as though they were British subjects.[12] This position ensured free access to the territory, freedom to take up any job available and the opportunity to participate in the electoral process. Furthermore, to accelerate the flow of migrants from Ireland, the UK Ministry of Labour operated a liaison office in Dublin, which facilitated the whole process of migration by providing information and travel warrants and by placing Irish citizens in jobs in Britain.[13]

Though the Attlee government neither intervened in private job placements nor ensured bulk employment practices, as was done for the European refugees, the Irish still benefited from the value the UK Ministry of Labour placed on continued Irish migration. It was partly because of this perceived value that the Irish had been set apart in the 1948 Act and partly because of it again that a year later the Irish in Britain retained their unusual status, despite the Eire government's declaration of Ireland's republican status. On both occasions, representatives of the ministry emphasized the advantage to Britain of continuing undisturbed a regular migrant flow. Strengthening the case for distinction, other departments highlighted the practical difficulties that would result were Irish citizens in Britain to be made aliens.[14] Created in 1948 and retained in 1949, the Irish in Britain retained their unique position throughout the 1950s and indeed for all practical purposes continue to do so today. Thus, the Macmillan government resisted the few parliamentary calls for the control of Irish migration in the late 1950s and, in 1961 when some British subjects faced infringements upon their freedom to migrate to Britain, Irish citizens, though not British subjects retained that right.[15]

The third migrant group to enter Britain in the postwar period travelled from the West Indies, India and Pakistan. Between 1948 and 1952, between 1000 and 2000 people entered each year, climbing to 3000 in 1953 and 10,000 in 1954. For the next three years an average of 40,000 entered each year, while in 1958 and 1959 numbers dropped significantly to 27,000 and 22,000 respectively. In 1960, however, the net intake of colonial migrants increased substantially to 58,000 and more than doubled again in 1961 to 136,000.[16] Outwardly, at least, these migrants should have been the most favoured group of all, for under the terms of the 1948 British Nationality Act, those from the West Indies were citizens of the United Kingdom and Colonies and those from India and Pakistan subjects of the British Empire.[17] As a result, there was no special intervention required to provide them access to Britain nor any permits needed to facilitate entry into the labour market.

However, this group faced the least welcoming reception and had to overcome significant obstacles deliberately placed in the way of their entry to Britain. The Colonial Office cooperated with all three governments to limit the distribution of passports, and with India and Pakistan to increase application fees, to impose repatriation deposits and generally to make the process of migration to Britain more difficult.[18] For its part, the Home Office insisted on documentary proof of British nationality from all stowaways and since October 1954 ran an unofficial tally of all incoming British subjects of colour. The Colonial Office attempted to discourage colonial migration further by emphasizing the likelihood of unemployment for new arrivals, and by 1958 was sufficiently resistant to colonial migration as to be ready to propose that the West Indian governments impose a six-month moratorium on the issue of passports.[19]

The different experiences of the three migrant groups outlined above provides some clue as to why certain departments sometimes relied on the phrase 'belonging to' as a means of separating out the larger mass of British subjects. In doing so the experiences offer an insight into the politics of citizenship and national identity in postwar Britain. The policymaking elite, drawn from all sides of the House and including the appointed civil service, categorized each migrant group according to how that group was perceived to 'fit' within or against the constructed British national identity.[20] Policymakers presumed this constructed national identity to be a singular fixed entity, which it was their duty to protect and preserve. In reality, of course, the British national identity was and is neither singular nor fixed. Rather, there are many different identities in a continuous state of flux as new generations and incoming groups redefine what it means to be British. In the immediate postwar years, however, understanding their vision of the national identity to be the only identity, the policymaking elite judged each migrant group according to whether it could be incorporated into or whether it challenged that identity. The resulting 'fit' then determined what kind of welcome each group received and what level of encouragement was given to future migrants.

The postwar British national identity against which migrants were judged was composed of a number of factors. The heritage of imperialism, the favoured position of Anglican Christianity, the conviction that Britain should occupy a dominant place in international affairs, the strain of conservatism shared by both principal political parties, the fervour of anti-communism, the stratified understanding of gender which relegated women to an inferior, passive position and a pragmatic acceptance of the need to rebuild the domestic economy all played a significant role in shaping British nationality policy. Most relevant to the fate of the three particular migrant groups mentioned above, however, was the perceived significance of skin colour and the resultant 'races', which different skin colours were presumed to denote.[21] From the outset, the elected administrations and the civil servants under their charge placed postwar migration to Britain within a framework of demographic acceptability. This framework was perceived to be of greater significance in determining access to membership of British society than the legal nationality policy.

Thus, when judged according to this contextual background, alien refugees and Irish citizens fared better than colonial subjects. One may go so far as to suggest that the refugee aliens were so well treated because they were presumed to possess the genetic potential to become British and were in effect designated as future belongers. Similarly, the Irish received all of the benefits of subjecthood without having to become subjects because they were perceived to be just like the British and thus were assigned the status of parallel belongers. The West Indians, Indians and Pakistanis by contrast were deemed demographically to be most unlike the true Britons who lived in Britain and thus were conceived of in terms that labelled them non-belongers. By this criteria, West Indians, Indians and Pakistanis, though holders of British passports and though recently confirmed in their status as British subjects and in the case of West Indians as United Kingdom and Colonial citizens, were not regarded as real Britons. As a result, their presence in the United Kingdom in the postwar period was a contested one. Thus, according to this inter-pretation, two conclusions suggest themselves: first, colonials were presumed not to belong and second they were presumed not to belong because they were black.

The contested nature of colonial migration manifested itself despite the formal acknowledgements of their British subject status given by government representatives throughout the 1940s and 1950s. For, contained within a public rhetoric that accepted the West Indians and others as British was an informal message that it would be better for Britain and for the migrants themselves if migration ceased altogether or at least was severely limited. As early as 1948, Colonial Secretary Arthur Creech Jones upheld the right of British subjects to travel to Britain but sought to reassure the House of Commons that such a movement as the *Empire Windrush* (the first significant arrival of postwar colonial migrants) would be 'very unlikely' to occur again.[22]

A few years later, Henry Hopkinson, Minister of State at the Colonial Office adopted a similar tone as he coupled his office's pride in the universality of the imperial nationality with an assurance that his office was also 'well aware of the importance of the problem' caused by colonial migration.[23] In 1955, Prime Minister Anthony Eden formally acknowledged the colonials' status by asking the House to 'bear in mind the traditions by which we have always hitherto been careful to observe the rights of British subjects', but at the same time the prime minister stigmatized colonial migrants by declaring that 'whatever our feelings may be, the problem is not an easy one to solve.'[24]

A year later Colonial Secretary Alan Lennox-Boyd assured the House of Commons that 'without interfering with the right of British citizens to move freely within the British Commonwealth . . . all that can be done is now being done' with regard to immigration.[25] Six months prior to the outbreak of the postwar 'race riots' at Nottingham and Notting Hill when white Britons told black Britons to 'go home', Patricia Hornsby-Smith of the Home Office stated that the government was 'certainly not complacent about this problem [of immigration]'.[26] By 1960, Colonial Secretary Iain Macleod publicly referred to the government's attempts to make West Indian governments 'maintain and if necessary strengthen their efforts to reduce migration to the United Kingdom'.[27] The consistent implicit message through all these parliamentary statements was that while colonials had the legal right to migrate, their doing so caused problems for Britain. This manner of presentation contributed to identifying colonial migration itself as a problem — a problem which could most easily be solved by stopping the migration.[28]

In addition to problematizing colonial migration, the language and rhetoric of civil servants and politicians conveyed the implicit suggestion that these colonial subjects were not really akin to other British subjects. The first Colonial Office report of the *Empire Windrush* identified its passengers as 'Jamaican unemployed'.[29] This language placed a dual barrier between the migrants and the resident UK population: they were foreign (from Jamaica) and they were likely to be a drain upon public resources — they were unemployed. Speaking in Parliament in response to the ship's arrival, Under Secretary for Labour Ness Edwards made clear that while the government would do something to assist the migrants, it could 'do no more for these men than we do for our own men'.[30] With this language Edwards, as had the Colonial Office before him, publicly separated the West Indian arrivals from UK residents and effectively identified them as possessing different nationalities.

A few years later, Patricia Hornsby-Smith of the Home Office reassured her parliamentary colleagues that while certain 'coloured immigrants' did appear to be disproportionately prone to violence, it was generally directed 'against their own fellow countrymen'.[31] With this assurance, Hornsby-Smith re-enforced the image of colonials as citizens of another, presumably alien, country. Likewise, an inter-departmental committee of civil servants noted in 1948 that West Indians in Britain would have the same employment mobility as 'British workers'.[32] Through this comparison, West Indians were again denied their identity as Britons and placed instead in a separate sphere of nationality.

These separate spheres were maintained throughout the postwar period and indeed acquired re-enforcement from a variety of sources. Most noticeably, over the course of the 1950s, colonial migrants were linguistically transformed from British subjects to Commonwealth immigrants. Under the terms of the 1948 Act, these two titles were interchangeable and bore exactly the same meaning. In the imme-diate postwar period, ministers and civil servants tended proudly to refer to British subjects to describe all residents of the British Empire. By the end of the period, however, both ministers and officials had come to rely instead on the term Commonwealth immigrant to describe the class of people it was desired to exclude.

This reconstruction had two effects: labelling the migrants as immigrants categorized them as outsiders with no automatic right to enter the country and, by dropping the term British, the migrants' association with Britain was pushed into the background. While not assigning deliberate intent to policymakers in this reconstructive process, the net effect was the weakening of colonial migrants' per-ceived Britishness. Likewise, one result of naming the 1962 Act, which for the first time placed restrictions on the right of some colonial migrants to enter the United Kingdom, a Commonwealth Immigrants Act rather than a British Subjects Act, was a further continuation of the same process of distancing colonial migrants from UK residents, with the common nationality both shared over-shadowed by the suggestion that each group were citizens of different countries.

This distancing process or denial of the common nationality was also evident in the succession of interdepartmental investigations of colonial migration conducted throughout the postwar period. Even the very titles of these official studies robbed the colonial migrants of their true nationality as they were labelled 'coloured workers from other Commonwealth countries' rather than British subjects. Furthermore, apart from one supplementary study on the Irish in 1956, only the colonial migrant community became the subject of official study, suggesting that the other migrant groups were not perceived to present the same problems. The substance and the language of the interdepartmental reports repeatedly served to distinguish between the migrant and the settled populations.

Each working party, from 1953 through 1961, successively identified the 'problems' of colonial migration and successively conceived of a solution in terms of limiting further access. Even though throughout this period only housing could be identified as an immediate concern, committee members and the ministers to whom they reported dwelt on the future problems that would develop if colonial migration were allowed to continue unchecked. The focus on border control as the solution again re-enforces the argument that UK officials located colonial migration within an exterior framework — it was a domestic issue only in so far as poor border control caused problems in the domestic arena: it was not a problem caused by true domestic citizens.

This view of colonial migrants as 'false citizens' manifested itself both in the general existence of investigative committees and in the specific language employed by committee members. Arguing the case for legislation enabling the Home Secretary to deport colonial citizens convicted of an offence carrying a custodial sentence, the 1953 interdepartmental working party recognized that it was recommending breaking the principle of the universal nationality law, but believed that the violation was worth it to rid the United Kingdom 'of thoroughly undesirable people who cannot be said to belong to it in any real sense'.[33] Thus, the committee members, as the Attlee Cabinet before them, were able to differentiate between the formal nationality policy which accorded colonial subjects the status of British nationality and the informal, but no less real, constructed national identity which reserved inclusion within the real body of British subjects to existing UK residents who 'fit' within that identity.

The strength of the constructed national identity in the face of the legal nationality policy persisted throughout the decade with officials in 1955 asserting Britain's right to do as other countries did and 'control immigration from outside in the interests of its own citizens'.[34] This assertion blatantly ignored colonial migrants' status as citizens of the United Kingdom and once again placed them outside the sphere of Britishness inhabited by real Britons. Much the same impression was given six years later when Conservative Home Secretary Rab Butler presented the bill that would control the access of certain British subjects to Britain. By referring to the 'quarter of the globe's population' who were 'legally entitled' to come to Britain, the language presented an image of a legal error being corrected rather than existing rights being curtailed.[35]

The ostensible reason behind the 1962 Commonwealth Immigrants Act was the question of numbers — more migrants were entering Britain than could be absorbed.[36] In reality, the issue was not numbers but the skin colour of some of the migrants. The significance the political elite attached to skin colour in the postwar period cannot be overstated. It was the determining factor in deciding which migrants could be assimilated and which would always be perceived as an outsider group. Thus, regardless of their British passports, West Indians, Indians and Pakistanis were perceived as non-belongers because policymakers believed their possession of a black skin prevented them from merging into the domestic population. Furthermore, migrants' black skin was presumed by policymakers to carry with it certain prescribed behavioural traits which were also non-British.

Even before the *Empire Windrush* docked, an interdepartmental working party established to review the possibilities of recruiting colonial labour for jobs in Britain based its conclusions on the assumption 'that a large majority of any workers brought here would be coloured' and bore 'this fact and its repercussions' in mind throughout its deliberations.[37] Discussing the same issue, senior civil servant Sir Harold Wiles observed that 'Whatever may be the policy about British citizenship . . . [he did] . . . not think that any scheme for the importation of coloured colonials for permanent settlement here should be embarked upon without full understanding that this means that a coloured element will be brought in for permanent absorption into our own population.'[38] In both cases, the 'repercussions' and the 'full understanding' were presumed to be certain to produce negative outcomes.

In short, one may suggest that for many members of the policy-making elite, regardless of the formal nationality policy which declared equality and access for all, there was no room for blacks within the constructed national identity shared by 'real' Britons. Hence, in 1954 Lord President of the Council, Lord Salisbury argued that it was 'not merely a question whether criminal Negroes should be allowed in or not; it is a question whether great quantities of Negroes, criminal or not, should be allowed to come'. Taking this argument to its conclusion, Salisbury identified the 'coloured problem' as fundamentally important 'for the future of our country'.[39] Oliver Lyttelton as Colonial Secretary concurred with Salisbury's view, suggesting that something had to be done if there were to be 'any means of controlling the increased flow of coloured people who come here largely to enjoy the benefits of the welfare state'.[40]

Around the same time, Prime Minister Winston Churchill feared the growth of a 'magpie society' and civil servants warned that 'the real danger' of colonial migration 'lay in the prospect of a multiracial society'.[41] Likewise, within months of taking office, Home Secretary Gwyllim Lloyd George argued the case for controlling legislation on the grounds that it was no longer possible 'to look with equanimity on a large, increasing and uncontrolled flow of immigrants into the United Kingdom of a kind which does not readily assimilate itself to the native population of this country'.[42] For its part, the Ministry of Labour was prepared to argue against any programme of colonial migration on the general grounds that Britain's 'small coloured population' should not be increased and the specific proposition that 'the moral standards of the young women in the Isles are quite different from those that prevail in this country'.[43]

The Ministry's association of colour and behaviour was typical of other departments. The 1953 working party, for example, documented a 'coloured population' as 'more volatile in temperament than white workers and more easily provoked to violence'. 'Coloured women' were 'slow mentally' and not up to the speed of work in modern factories. In general, according to civil servants, 'coloured workers' were irresponsible, 'lacking in stamina' and generally not up to the standards required by UK employers.[44] More specifically, one Colonial Office representative wrote scathingly of Indians and Pakistanis as 'feckless individuals', illiterate, dirty and subject to ill-health.[45] These negative behavioural traits contrasted with the government's own information, which reported the majority of migrants to be gainfully employed, law-abiding and not posing a burden on the welfare state.[46] The persistence of the false image despite the available evidence conveys something of the strength of the negative connotations associated with colonial migrants' skin colour.

Policymakers' own deliberations make clear that skin pigmentation rather than numbers was the predominant factor behind the efforts to limit colonial migration. Successive Conservative administrations wrestled with the form of any bill that would be used to control British subjects' access to Britain. The essential dilemma was how to prevent the migration of British subjects of colour without imposing on the freedoms enjoyed by white British subjects.[47] While wishing to limit the entry of 'an excessive number of West Indians or West Africans', ministers had no desire to prevent the entry of those 'of good type from the "old" Dominions ... who come here with no clear plans in order to try their luck'.[48] A specific bill applying only to subjects of colour was dismissed on the grounds of political difficulty and embarrassment — ministers believed that it would be difficult to gain support for such a measure and feared that discriminatory legislation would reveal the emptiness of the principle of a universal British nationality.

As an alternative, ministers discussed the operation of a theoretically universal bill that could be operated with the 'minimum of inconvenience' to British subjects from the 'Old Dominions'. One version of a bill was presented as advantageous because 'there would be no need to regulate passenger traffic ... which we do not need to control for this particular purpose of restricting the immigration of coloured people'.[49] Officials assured ministers that immigration officers could 'without giving rise to trouble or publicity, exercise such a measure of discrimination as we think desirable' and that while all British subjects would formally have the right to gain access to Britain, 'the type of person whom it is desired to exclude would seldom be able to do so'.[50] As easy as this discrimination appeared, however, some ministers doubted that they would be able to 'conceal the obvious fact that the object is to keep out coloured people'.[51] Yet, the alternative of letting migrants of colour continue to enter unchecked risked the production of 'a significant change in the racial character of the English people'. Furthermore, 'a large coloured community' was not part of the constructed national identity to which 'British stock' throughout the world was attached.[52]

The Macmillan administration took the final decision to introduce controlling legislation on 10 October 1961. The act was formally colour-blind limiting the access to Britain of both black and white British subjects whose ordinary residence was other than the United Kingdom, Channel Isles or Isle of Man. Behind the façade of universality, however, the act retained the demographic emphasis of the discussions that had preceded it. Home Secretary Rab Butler justified the case for control to his Cabinet colleagues on the grounds that the immigration total for 1961 was likely to exceed 100,000 and his conviction that 'it was evident that the country could not assimilate coloured immigrants on the current scale'.[53] Furthermore, Butler believed that the act's 'great merit' was that while it could be presented as non-discriminatory, in practice 'its restrictive effect is intended to, and would in fact, operate on coloured people almost exclusively'.[54]

Thus, throughout the postwar decades, members of both major political parties as well as the civil servants under their direction sought an effective means of controlling the access of British subjects of colour to Britain on the primary grounds that, because such migrants were 'coloured', they posed a threat to the demographic purity of the constructed national identity which included as one of its constitutive elements an image of white-skinned Britons. The depth of the perception that migrants of the wrong sort posed a threat was evident as early as 1949 in the report of the Royal Commission on Population, which declared that immigration 'could only be welcomed without reserve if the immigrants were of good human stock and were not prevented by their religion or race from intermarrying with the host population and becoming merged in it'.[55]

Clearly, by this criteria migrants of colour did not qualify as migrants to be welcomed since their 'race' prevented them from intermarrying. Thus, by this same criteria, they did not belong in Britain.

The language of the Royal Commission suggests that the Labour and Conservative administrations, which sought to restrict the access of black Britons to Britain, did so surrounded by an informal consensus of support. In the 1940s and 1950s, however, this support was almost wholly private in nature and reflected on the public stage by only a very few parliamentarians and members of the press. Noticeably, the public rhetoric of the few extremists in the 1950s reflected very closely the private language and actions of some ministers and civil servants. Thus, Louth Conservative MP Cyril Osborne's reference to the 500 million people who were 'technically entitled' to come to Britain was a precursor of the language which, as we have seen, would shortly be employed publicly by the Home Secretary when bringing in the 1962 Act.[56]

Martin Lindsay, Conservative member for Solihull, forecast that Britain was 'becoming a country of immigration' and thus re-enforced the perspective of colonial subjects as foreigners.[57] Similarly, Osborne's claim that he spoke 'for the white man' whose country was under threat and Lindsay's profession to be trying to preserve the 'national character' fit well within the language employed by members of the civil service as they warned against a 'multiracial' Britain.[58] Thus, although the few parliamentary outsiders were repeatedly rebuffed by government representatives' formal and public acknowledgement of colonials' status as British subjects, the similarity of their public rhetoric with the governing elite's private rhetoric suggests that both drew their understanding from the same repertoire: black Britons did not belong in Britain because they were not true Britons.

While it is difficult to document popular conceptions of black Britons for the period prior to the taking of public opinion surveys in the 1960s, what sources are available suggest that the public did not draw from this same repertoire. As others have suggested, the resident population of the United Kingdom was quite welcoming toward African-American GIs and resented the American colour bar.[59] On a number of occasions in the 1950s, the media ran occasional alarmist stories about the growing 'coloured population', but it also ran articles in support of colonials' right to migrate and condemning discrimination.[60] Rank and file letters to the Trades Union Congress headquarters reflected this same ambiguity with some correspondents firmly supporting colonial rights, others seeking additional information and a minority calling for control.[61]

Early practitioners of the new field of 'race relations' recorded a domestic population uncertain and perhaps confused about the presence of blacks in Britain and ready to receive guidance.[62] Finally, perhaps the most significant evidence that the domestic UK population did not draw on the same repertoire as the governing elite is provided by the governing elite itself. One reason why successive administrations waited to impose controls was because ministers thought that a control bill would be unpopular and difficult to pass. A ministerial committee in 1956, for example, observed that the 'ordinary people of this country are by no means intolerant of coloured people in their midst.' In the light of this, legislation to control entry 'would come as a shock for which public opinion is still not prepared' and would likely provoke 'most people — certainly the more vocal elements' to express concern about the 'illiberal' nature of the government's proposals. The committee suggested that, before taking action on such a controversial matter, the government needed to count 'on a satisfactory volume of public support', which was unlikely to be 'forthcoming at present'.[63]

This noted dearth of popular concern with colonial migration appears to refute the traditional assumption that the 1962 Commonwealth Immigrants Act was the result of a racist public pushing a liberal government towards control. Instead, a governing elite determined to preserve the whiteness of the constructed British national identity by keeping out all perceived not to belong, waited anxiously for the time when public opinion would catch up. Thus, Cabinet secretary Norman Brook observed that the purpose of an official enquiry into colonial migration 'would not be to find a solution (for it is evident what form control must take) but to enlist a sufficient body of public support for the legislation that would be needed'.[64] The Cabinet agreed, concluding that 'the first purpose of an enquiry should be to ensure that the public throughout the country were made aware of the nature and extent of the problem; until this was more widely appreciated the need for restrictive legislation would not be recognized.'[65]

In 1958, ministers' patience was apparently rewarded in the shape of the riots at Nottingham and Notting Hill where, borrowing from the narrative of their government, white Britons told Britons of colour to 'go home'.[66] This maturing of public opinion in favour of control was the result of a variety of factors. Over the course of the previous decade, infrastructural social investment, particularly in housing, had not kept pace with population growth. Indeed, on one occasion even as Macmillan's Cabinet discussed the social and economic problems believed to be caused by migration, they authorized a cut of £25–30 million in the budget for 'social investment' to which housing, hospitals and education were expected to make major contributions.[67] Since these cuts could only aggravate the problems allegedly caused by migration, one might easily see how those experiencing the increased competition for limited resources might blame colonial migrants, particularly when those migrants were contextualized from the very beginning as individuals who did not really belong to Britain.

Likewise, one may see how the rhetoric of insider/outsider helped promote an understanding that blamed the riots on a black presence. The immediate public outrage at the violence of the Notting Hill riots, and the accompanying breakdown in law and order, was soon supplanted by a growing questioning of the colonials' presence in Britain. In 1964, shadow foreign secretary Patrick Gordon-Walker lost his parliamentary seat against a national trend towards Labour and in the context of a Conservative campaign focusing on the alleged problems of colonial migration. Despite the obvious link between popular protest and the demand for legislative control, the public record outlined above confirms first, that efforts to control migration began behind the closed doors of the Cabinet Office and Whitehall, and second, that the politics of race became a source of popular concern only after the disturbances of 1958. Thus, the 1962 Commonwealth Immigrants Act was neither an immediate response to the events of 1958 nor a solution to long-standing popular hostility towards black Britons. Rather, it was the culmination of the politics of citizenship and nationhood operative in Britain since at least 1945 and by which some Britons were perceived to be more British than others.

Further proof that this division between Britons centred on race not numbers may be found if we return to the two other migrant groups that entered Britain at the same time as the colonial migrants. While excluding colonial subjects of colour, the reliance on demographic criteria as a test of acceptability worked to include refugee Europeans and the Irish. When the Attlee Cabinet first considered the possible use of foreign labour, ministers cautioned that 'any material increase in the foreign population of this country' should be considered very carefully in the light of 'the demographic issues involved'.[68] More specifically, Home Secretary Chuter Ede made clear his preference for recruits from 'Western countries, whose traditions and social backgrounds were more nearly equal to our own'.[69]

Clearly, the recruits from central and eastern Europe satisfied these criteria, for within a short time of their arrival Ede was confident that the foreigners' 'skill and virility' would help Britain emerge from its economic crises. His colleagues were even more forthright in their emphasis on demographics, referring in Parliament to the 'benefits that come from the assimilation of virile, active and industrious people into our stock'.[70] The Ministry of Labour described Yugoslav displaced persons (DPs) as 'a very tough and muscular race', while both Labour and Conservative MPs described the aliens as 'first class people' who would 'be of great benefit to our stock'.[71] Senior civil servant Sir Harold Wiles, he who was so resistant to the idea of colonial settlement, defended the recruitment of European aliens on the grounds that they were coming for 'permanent settlement here with a view to their intermarrying and complete absorption into our own population'.[72]

These statements manifest the policymaking elite's construction of European aliens as suitable migratory material. This perception of demographic acceptability provided the enabling context for the Attlee government to offer these selected aliens all the benefits of membership in British society even though they stood outside the formal nationality policy. As a result, Minister of Labour George Isaacs could quite simply describe the recruitment schemes as 'settlement of a permanent character' populated by individuals 'working their passage to British citizenship'.[73] Ede reiterated his absolute determination to see the recruited aliens 'assimilated into the British people, to become acquainted with, and to follow, the British way of life'.[74] Eighteen months later, a joint government-TUC publication announced as policy that foreigners should be absorbed 'into the British way of life and become in due course and to all intents and purposes, fully fledged British citizens'.[75] By November 1948, the interested official departments were committed to ensuring the aliens' 'ultimate absorption into the British community'.[76] Hence, European aliens were to be incorporated into the constructed national identity because they did not conflict with the identity as conceived by the policymaking elite.

A similar process occurred for the Irish. As we have seen, the Ministry of Labour believed Irish migrants constituted such a useful labour supply that the 1948 British Nationality Act included a special category for Irish citizens in Britain. This category was challenged when ministers began to discuss the legislative closure of colonial migrants' access to Britain. Accepting that many of the alleged social conditions produced by Irish migrants were similar to those allegedly produced by colonial migrants — overcrowding and squalor — civil servants noted one 'outstanding' difference: 'the Irish whether they liked it or not were not a different race from the ordinary inhabitants of Great Britain.'[77] Nor did the presence of large numbers of Irish citizens give rise to 'the same kind of problems or forebodings as the presence . . . of similar numbers of coloured people'.[78] By this criteria, policymakers placed greater weight on the presumed genetic similarity between Irish citizens and UK citizens rather than the actual common nationality shared by migrants and UK residents. Weighting the relationship in this way was a contributory factor in the decision to exclude the Irish from control under the terms of the 1962 Commonwealth Immigrants Act.

As suggested earlier, postwar British nationality policy was determined by, and the constructed national identity composed of, a variety of factors of which the presumption that the world's population could be divided into 'races', which themselves carried immutable genetic consequences, was but one. It was a consistent theme, however, and one that resulted in the popular association by 1962 of 'race' with 'immigration', as though all immigrants were of a different race and all of a different 'race' were immigrants. This perception denied the reality of both white alien immigration and black citizen and subject migration. It also fostered the popular understanding that black British subjects did not really belong to the United Kingdom and that their presence in Britain was an unlooked-for occurrence that threatened the demographic purity of the nation state and the constructed national identity. This presumption of non-belonging on the basis of skin colour and the actions it produced on the part of policymakers and, subsequently, larger sections of the domestic population, resulted in the denial of equal membership in British society to Britons of colour and a much more arduous migration experience than need otherwise have been the case.

The 1962 Commonwealth Immigrants Act ostensibly clarified British nationality policy by placing restrictions on the free entry of those British subjects deemed not to belong to the United Kingdom. To this extent, it should have resolved the confusions highlighted by the Foreign Office and the Board of Trade during the making of the 1948 Act. In reality, the 1962 Act only added to the contradictions contained within the politics of citizenship in postwar Britain. For, while at the public level control was universal, privately officials intended it to operate against one group of subjects more than another. As a result, there remained an informal but very real distinction between British subjects, with some perceived to be more British than others.

Furthermore, successive additional attempts to regulate admission and to clarify the true meaning of the term British nationality in the form of the 1968 Commonwealth Immigrants Act, the 1971 Immigration Act and the 1981 British Nationality Act have also demonstrably failed. At the time of writing there remain six categories of British nationality with each carrying some form of the word British, but with only one carrying the right of abode in Britain.[79] It would appear that despite almost fifty years of wrangling with immigration provisions and massaging nationality law, some British people are still regarded as more British than others. The politics of citizenship in Britain today remains as contested as it was in 1948. Indeed, one may venture that since the single phrase 'belonging to' has now been replaced by six different titles as a means of dividing the population of British subjects, that politics has become even more obscure.[80]

Notes

1. Public Record Office, PREM8/851 CP(45)287 16 November 1945. All citations are from this source unless otherwise stated. The Attlee government alone, and these three migrant groups plus one other, are dealt with in Kathleen Paul (1992) 'The politics of citizenship in post-war Britain', *Contemporary Record*, vol. 6, Winter, pp. 452–73. A more substantial treatment of this topic, drawing on some of the same empirical evidence, also appears in Kathleen Paul (forthcoming) *Whitewashing Britain: "Race", Empire and Citizenship Since 1945*, Ithaca, NY.

2. See for example, Stephen Castles (1984) *Here To Stay: Western Europe's New Ethnic Minorities*, London.

3. CAB 129/7 CP(46)71 20 February 1946. The FLC's specific terms of reference were 'to examine, in the light of existing manpower shortages, the possibility of making increased use of foreign labour, particularly in essential industries which are now finding special difficulty in recruiting labour'.

4. CAB 128/5 CM(46)15 14 February 1946; CAB 134/301 FLC(46) 2nd Meeting, 3 April 1946.

5. University of Warwick, Modern Records Centre, TUC Papers, MSS 292/103.28 Foreign Labour – Notes for the TUC; LAB 13/1098 Report on Foreigners Accepted into Great Britain, no date. See also Keith Sword et al. (1989) *The Creation of the Polish Community in Britain, 1939–1950*, London.

6. For a history of displaced persons see Robert Miles and Diana Kay (1992) *Refugees or Migrant Workers? European Volunteer Workers in Britain 1945–1951*, London; Mark Wyman (1989) *DP: Europe's Displaced Persons, 1945–1951*, Philadelphia; J. A. Tannahill (1958) *European Volunteer Workers in Britain*, Manchester.

7. CAB 128/9 CM(47)7 16 January 1947; CAB 128/9 CM(47)9 17 January 1947 CAB 128/9 CM(47) 14 30 January 1947; CAB 134/301 FLC(46)4 Recruitment of Displaced Persons, Memorandum by the Minister of Labour, 12 February, 1947.

8. LAB 13/1098 Basic Statements on the Recruitment of Foreign Workers and Migrants including the work of International Organizations; LAB 13/815 Foreign Workers in the United Kingdom – Official and Unofficial Schemes. Not all of the work permit applicants would settle in Britain permanently, but by 1952, 110,000 had been settled for longer than four years and may reasonably be included among the total number of foreign labourers recruited.

9. University of Warwick, Modern Records Centre, TUC Papers MSS103.28 'Foreign Labour in Great Britain' and 103.28/1b 'Resettlement of Polish Forces'. See also the minutes of the Foreign Labour Committee for 1946–47 in CAB 134/301. The government and TUC also agreed that in the event of a recession, the aliens would be the first to be dismissed. While this qualification certainly appears a little harsh and may be presumed to counteract some of the other promised benefits, in practice it was rarely exercised.

10. HO213/1005 Agenda and minutes of two meetings to discuss the results of 18 months operation of the Westward Ho! Scheme. (Westward Ho! was the name given to the main alien refugee recruitment scheme.) LAB 12/513 Publicity to Educate Public Opinion on Foreign Workers. See the government's parliamentary statements below.

11. LAB 13/1005 statistics relating to persons arriving from overseas applying for national insurance cards during 1960 compared with 1959, February, 1961; *Irish Times*, 16 March 1961.

12. For a full explanation of the origins and consequences of this unusual legal position, see Kathleen Paul (1996) 'A case of mistaken identity: the Irish in post-war Britain', *International Labor and Working-Class History*, vol. 49, Spring, pp. 116–42.

13. DO35/3917 Ministry of Labour arrangements for the transfer of workers from the Irish Republic to the United Kingdom, 3 August 1951.

14. HO213/420, Eire citizens wishing to remain British subjects; CAB 129/30 CP(48)263, Interdepartmental note on possible migratory measures, n.d.

15. Parliamentarians questioned the freedom of entry of Irish citizenship in both 1955 and 1957, Parliamentary Debates, Commons, 5th Ser. [1955] very 544, c. 1308–18; [1957] very 566, c. 514.

16. CO1032/120, J. L. Keith memo, 23 November 1954; CAB 129/78 CP(56)145, Colonial Immigrants: Report of the Committee of Ministers, 22 June 1956; CAB 134/1469 CCM(61)2, Progress report by the Interdepartmental Committee on the social and economic problems arising from the growing influx into the United Kingdom of coloured workers from other Commonwealth countries, 1 February 1961; CAB 134/1465 CCI(63)4, Commonwelth Immigrants Committee: Rate of Issue of Vouchers, 1 November 1963.

17. The process by which some British subjects acquired the additional status of United Kingdom and Colonial citizens is fully explored in Kathleen Paul (1995) 'British subjects and "British stock": Labour's post-war imperialism', *Journal of British Studies*, vol. 34, pp. 233–76.

18. CO1032/195, Indian High Commissioner to Commonwealth Relations Office, 10 May 1958; CO1032/195, Pakistan High Commissioner to Commonwealth Relations Office, 16 May 1958.

19. CAB 129/40 CP(50)113, 18 May 1950; CO1032/121 Colonial Office to

Colonial Governors, 8 August 1956; CO1032/196 Colonial Office to West Indies Governors, 29 August 1958.

20. From the large literature that analyses the construction of British national identity, those with particular relevance to this essay include, Linda Colley (1992) *Britons: Forging the Nation, 1707–1837*, New Haven; Raphael Samuel (ed.) (1989) *Patriotism: The Making and Unmaking of British National Identity*, London; Robin Cohen (1994) *Frontiers of Identity: The British and the Others*, Essex.

21. The process of making 'races' and racialization is most clearly outlined in Robert Miles (1989) *Racism*, London.

22. Parliamentary Debates (Commons) 5th Ser., [1948] v. 452, c. 422.

23. Parliamentary Debates (Commons) 5th Ser., [1954] v. 532 c. 831.

24. Parliamentary Debates (Commons) 5th Ser., [1955] v. 545, c. 2006.

25. Parliamentary Debates (Commons) 5th Ser., [1956] v. SS8 c.1414.

26. Parliamentary Debates (Commons) 5th Ser., [1958] v. 585, c. 1415.

27. Parliamentary Debates (Commons) 5th Ser., [1960] v. 624, c. 111.

28. The process by which colonial migration was problematized is fully explored in Robert Miles and Annie Phizacklea (1987) *White Man's Country*, London.

29. CAB 129/28, CP(48) 154 Memo by the Secretary of State for the Colonies, 'Arrival in the UK of Jamaican Unemployed', June 1948.

30. Parliamentary Debates (Commons) 5th Ser., [1948] v. 452, c. 225–6.

31. Parliamentary Debates (Commons) 5th Ser., [1958] v. 585, c. 1419.

32. CO 1006/2 Working Party on the Employment in the United Kingdom of Surplus Colonial Labour.

33. CO1032/119 Report of the Working Party on Coloured People Seeking Employment in the United Kingdom, December 1953.

34. PREM 11/824 Report of the Committee on the Social and Economic Problems Arising from the Growing Influx into the United Kingdom of Coloured Workers From Other Commonwealth Countries, 3 August 1955.

35. Parliamentary Debates (Commons) 5th Ser., [1961] v. 649, c. 687–93.

36. This was the impression given by Butler both at the time and since. See for example, R. A. Butler (1971) *The Art of The Possible*, London, p. 205.

37. LAB 13/42 Report of the 4th Meeting of the Working Party on Surplus Colonial Labour.

38. LAB 13/42 Wiles to Bevan, 8 March 1948.

39. CO1032/119 Salisbury to Swinton, 20 March, 1954.

40. CO1032/119 Lyttelton to Swinton, 31 March 1954.

41. Nicholas Deakin (1972) 'The Immigration Issue in British Politics', University of Sussex, unpublished Ph.D. thesis, cited in Zig Layton-Henry (1992) The Politics of Immigration, Oxford, p. 31; CO 1032/195 Minutes of the Working Party on Social and Economic Problems, 24 January 1958.

42. CO1032/120 Frank Newsam to Sir Thomas Lloyd, 8 November 1954. Newsam was Lloyd George's permanent under secretary and was reporting his senior's opinions in order to garner support for control.

43. LAB 8/1571 Goldberg to MacMullan, 15 October 1948; LAB 8/1571 Proposed Employment of Colonial Workers in Great Britain, February 1949.

44. CO1032/119 Report of the Working Party on Coloured People Seeking Employment in the United Kingdom, 17 December 1953.

45. CO1032/ 195 Watt minute, 1 May 1958; CO1032/195 Draft Brief for Secretary of State, CP(58)129, no date.

46. This status was documented in each interdepartmental report and also in internal correspondence. See for example, CO1032/120 J. L. Keith memo, 23 November 1954 and PREM 11/824 Coloured Immigrants, Memorandum by Home Secretary, 3 May 1955 (and also CAB 128/30 CM9(55) 9 May 1955.

47. PREM 11/824 C(54) 356 Colonial Immigrants: Memorandum by the Commonwealth Relations Secretary, 23 November 1954.

48. PREM 11/824 C(54) 356 Colonial Immigrants: Memorandum by the Commonwealth Relations Secretary, 23 November 1954; CO 1032/119 Swinton note.

49. PREM 11/824 Brook's Memo to Prime Minister, 12 January 1955.

50. CO1032/119 Report of the Working Party to Consider Certain Proposals to Restrict the Right of British Subjects from Overseas to Enter and Remain in the United Kingdom, 10 July 1954; PREM 11/824, CP(55)113 2 September 1955.

51. CO 1032/119 Swinton to Salisbury, March 1954.

52. CAB 128/30 CM 39(55) 3 November 1955; CO 1032/119 Report of the Working Party on Coloured People Seeking Employment in the United Kingdom, 17 December 1953.

53. CAB 128/35 CC(61)55 10 October 1961; CAB 129/107 C. (61) 153 6 October 1961 Commonwealth Migrants: Memorandum by the Secretary of State for the Home Department.

54. CAB 129/107 C(61)153 6 October 1961 Commonwealth Migrants: Memorandum by the Secretary of State for the Home Department. The Cabinet Committee recognized that it could not include a statement denying racial discrimination since the practical effect of the bill would be felt most keenly by people of colour. CAB 134/1469 CCM(61) 4th Meeting Commonwealth Migrants Committee 29 September 1961.

55. Report of the Royal Commission on Population, CMD 7695 (London, June 1949), paragraphs 329–30.

56. Parliamentary Debates (Commons) 5th Ser., [1957] v. 563, c. 392.

57. Parliamentary Debates (Commons) 5th Ser., [1958] v. 585, c. 1415.

58. Parliamentary Debates (Commons) 5th Ser., [1958] v. 594, c. 196; [1958] v. 596, c.1561–4.

59. G. Smith (1987) *When Jim Crow Met John Bull*, London.
60. See, for example, alarmist stories in the *Sunday Graphic*, 26 October 1952 and supporting articles in the *Economist*, 13 November 1954.
61. University of Warwick, Modern Records Centre, TUC MSS 292/805.7/2 Commonwealth Workers in Great Britain, 1954–7. According to journalist Paul Foot writing in the aftermath of Smethwick, 'the degree of hostility and bitterness at work was remarkably small' in the 1950s. Paul Foot (1965) *Immigration and Race in British Politics*, Harmondsworth, Penguin, p. 127. A similar show of support for colonials appeared in letters sent to complain about alien recruitment. See TUC MSS 292/103.2/3 Bournemouth Trade Council to TUC, 12 August 1955; MSS 292/103.2/4 Andover and District Trades Council to TUC, 28 October 1955; Shingfield District Council to TUC, no date; TUC Advisory Committee Midland Region, 13 August 1958; Bedford and District trade Council, 17 October 1959.
62. See for example Michael Banton (1960) *White and Coloured: The Behaviour of British People toward Coloured Immigrants*, New Brunswick and Anthony Richmond (1955) *The Colour Problem*, Harmondsworth.
63. CAB 129/78 CP(56) 145 22 June 1956; CAB 128/29 CM48(56) 11 July 1956; CAB 134/1210 CI(56)3, 17 May 1956 Cabinet Committee on Colonial Immigrants Revised Draft Report to the Cabinet.
64. PREM 11/824 Brook's memo to Prime Minister, 14 June 1955.
65. CAB 128/30 CM14(55), 14 June 1955; CAB 134/1210 CI(56)1, 10 February 1956, first meeting of Cabinet Committee Immigrants.
66. Still the most comprehensive account of the disturbances is Edward Pilkington (1988) *Beyond the Mother Country: West Indians and the Notting Hill White Riots*, London.
67. CAB 128/32 CM66(58), 31 July 1958; CM73(58), 29 September 1958.
68. CAB 134/301 FLC (46) 2nd Meeting 3 April 1946.
69. CAB 134/301 FLC (46) 1st Meeting 14 March 1946.
70. Parliamentary Debates (Commons) 5th Ser., [1947] v.433, c.387.
71. TUC Papers MSS 292/103.2/2. Workers From Abroad, April 1948. Parliamentary Debates (Commons) 5th Ser., [1947] v. 433, c. 750.
72. LAB 13/42 Wiles to Bevan, 8 March 1948.
73. Parliamentary Debates (Commons) 5th Ser., [1948] v. 457, c. 1721.
74. Parliamentary Debates (Commons) 5th Ser., [1947] v. 433 , c. 386–387.
75. TUC Papers MSS 103.28 'Foreign Labour in Great Britain, 1947–51', JCC Meeting, 25 November 1948.
76. HO213/1005 Roy to Rosetti, 29 October 1948.
77. PREM 11/824 Report of the Committee on the Social and Economic Problems Arising from the Growing Influx in to the United Kingdom of Coloured Workers From Other Commonwealth Countries, 3 August, 1955.

78. CAB 134/1210 CP(56) no additional number given, October 1956, Colonial Immigrants: Supplementary Report of the Committee of Ministers.

79. The 1981 British Nationality Act created five categories of citizenship: British Citizenship, British Dependent Territories Citizenship, British Overseas Citizenship, British Protected Person, and British Subject. From 1987, in an attempt to facilitate the transfer of the sovereignty of Hong Kong, a sixth category was created: British National (Overseas).

80. Studies of 'race' and migration since 1962 exist in abundance. In addition to those already mentioned, the following represent a good place to start one's reading: Ann Dummett and Andrew Nicol (1990) *Subjects, Citizens, Aliens and Others: Nationality and Immigration Law*, London; Paul Gilroy (1987) *There Ain't No Black in the Union Jack: The Cultural Politics of Race and Nation*, London; Centre for Contemporary Cultural Studies (1982) *The Empire Strikes Back: Race and Racism in 70s Britain*, London; A. Sivanandan (1982) *A Different Hunger: Writings on Black Resistance*, London; and Dilip Hiro (1992) *Black British, White British: A History of Race Relations in Britain*, London, 3rd edn.

References

Abrahams, H. (ed.) (1959) *Britain's National Parks*, London

Adams, Hervey (1946) *Art and Everyman*, London, (first edn 1944)

— (1949) *The Adventure of Looking*, London

Adams, R. J. Q. and P. P. Poirier (1987) *Conscription Controversy*, London

Addison, Paul (1994) *The Road to 1945: British Politics and the Second World War*, 2nd edn (1st edn 1975) London

Aldgate, Anthony and Jeffrey Richards (1994) *Britain Can Take It: The British Cinema in the Second World War*, Edinburgh

Amery, L. S. (1955) *My Political Life: The Unforgotten Years*, London

Anderson, Benedict (1983) *Imagined Communities*, London

Arts Council of Great Britain (1945) *Plans for an Arts Centre*, London

Anon (1948) 'Next door neighbours', *M-O Bulletin*, vol. 15

Baker, A. E. (ed.) (1958) *Religious Experience*, London

Baker, Kenneth (ed.) (1993) *The Faber Book of Conservatism*, London

Ball, Stuart (1988) *Baldwin and the Conservative Party: The Crisis of 1929-31*, London

Banton, Michael (1960) *White and Coloured: The Behaviour of British People toward Coloured Immigrants*, New Brunswick

Barker, Ernest (1933) 'Community Centres and Circles', *The Fortnightly*, March

— (1942) *Britain and the British People*, Oxford

Barker, Paul (1968) 'Michael Young', *New Society*, 8 August

Barnett, Corelli (1986) *The Audit of War: The Illusion and Reality of Britain as a Great Nation*, London

Baron, Stanley (ed.) (1944) *Country Towns in the Future England: A report of the conference representing local authorities, arts and amenities organizations and members of the Town and Country Planning Association on the 23rd of October 1943*, London

Batsford, H. (1940) *How to See the Country*, London

Bealey, Frank et al. (1965) *Constituency Politics: A Study of Newcastle-under-Lyme*, London

Belfrage, Bruce (1951) *One Man in his Time*, London

Belloc, Hilaire (1912) *The Servile State*, London

Benney, M. (1947) 'Storm over Stevenage', in A. G. Weidenfeld (ed.) *The Changing Nation*, London

Bevan, Aneurin (1952) *In Place of Fear*, London

Bond, Brian (1980) *British Military Strategy Between the Wars*, Oxford

Booker, Christopher (1977) 'Physical planning: another illusion shattered', *National Westminster Bank Quarterly Review*, February, pp. 56–64

Brasnett, Margaret (1969) *Voluntary Social Action: A History of the National Council of Social Service, 1919–69*, London

Brearley, R. A. et al. (1964) *A New Reserve Army: The Alternative to Conscription*, London

Briggs, Asa (1965) *The Golden Age of Wireless*, London

— (1970) *The War of Words*, London

— (1979) *Sound and Vision*, Oxford

British Film Academy (1950) *The Film Industry in Great Britain: Some Facts and Figures*, London

Brooke, Stephen (1991) 'Problems of "socialist planning": Evan Durbin and the Labour government of 1945', *Historical Journal*, vol. 34, pp. 687–702

— (1992) *Labour's War: The Labour Party during the Second World War*, Oxford

Brown, Ivor (1945) 'A Plan for the Arts', in Gilbert and Elizabeth McAllister (eds) *Homes, Towns and Countryside: A Practical Plan for Britain*, London

Burns, W. (1954) 'The Coventry sociological survey: results and interpretation', *Town Planning Review*, vol. 25, no. 2, pp. 128–48

Butler, David (1955) *The British General Election of 1955*, London

Butler, R. A. (1971) *The Art of The Possible*, London

Calder, Angus (1969) *The People's War: Britain 1939–1945*, London

— (1991) *The Myth of the Blitz*, London

Cannadine, David (1993) 'Penguin Island Story: planning a new history of Britain', *Times Literary Supplement*, 12 March

— (1995) 'British history as a "new subject": politics, perspectives and prospects', in Alexander Grant and Keith J. Stringer (eds) *Uniting the Kingdom: The Making of British History*, London

Cardiff, David and Paddy Scannell (1981) 'Radio in World War II', Unit 203, *Popular Culture*, Block 2, Unit 8, Milton Keynes, Open University Press

Carey, John (1992) *The Intellectuals and the Masses: Pride and Prejudice among the Literary Intelligentsia 1880–1939*, London

Carver, Michael (1992) *Tightrope Walking: British Defence Policy since 1945*, London

Castles, Stephen (1984) *Here To Stay: Western Europe's New Ethnic Minorities*, London

Centre for Contemporary Cultural Studies (1982) *The Empire Strikes Back: Race and Racism in 70s Britain*, London

Chapman, D. (1946) *A Social Survey of Middlesborough*, London

Chase, Malcolm (1989) 'This is no claptrap; this is our heritage', in C. Shaw and M. Chase (eds) *The Imagined Past: History and Nostalgia*, Manchester

— (1993) '"Nothing less than a revolution"?: Labour's agricultural policy', in J. Fyrth (ed.) *Labour's High Noon: The Government and the Economy 1945–51*, London

Clark, Kenneth (1977) *The Other Half: A Self-Portrait*, London

Clarke, R. (ed.) (1990) *Enterprising Neighbours: The Development of the Community Association Movement in Britain*, London

Coburn, Oliver (1951) *Youth Hostel Story*, London

Cohen, Robin (1994) *Frontiers of Identity: The British and the Others*, Essex

Cole, G. D. H. (1947) *Guide to the Elements of Socialism*, London

— (1947) *Local and Regional Government*, London

Colley, Linda (1992) *Britons: Forging the Nation, 1707–1837*, Yale

Collini, Stefan (1994) 'Escape from DWEMsville: is culture too important to be left to cultural studies?', *Times Literary Supplement*, 27 May

Colville, John (1985) *The Fringe of Power: Downing Street Diaries 1939–55*, London

Conference on Christian Politics (1924) *Economics and Citizenship*, Reports, 12 volumes, London

Conservative Central Office (1949) *General Election 1950: The Campaign Guide*, London, Conservative Central Office, October

Cornish, V. (1950) *National Parks*, London

Coultass, Clive (1989) 'The Ministry of Information and documentary film, 1939–45', *The Imperial War Museum Review*, vol. 4

Courtney, J. E. (1937) *Countrywomen in Council*, London

Cox, Jack (1953) *Camping for All*, London

Craig, F. W. S. (ed.) (1982) *Conservative and Labour Conference Decisions, 1945–1981*, Chichester

Crossman, Richard (1950) *Socialist Values in a Changing Civilization*, Fabian Tract 286, London

Crowson, Nicholas J. (1995) 'The Conservative Party and the question of National Service, 1937–1939: compulsion versus voluntarism', *Contemporary Record*, vol. 9, no. 3, pp. 507–28

Darwin, John (1988) *Britain and Decolonisation: The Retreat from Empire in the Post-War World*, London

Daunton, Martin (1996) 'Payment and participation: welfare and state formation in Britain, 1900–1951', *Past and Present*, vol. 150, pp. 169–216

Dawson, Graham and Bob West (1984) *National Fictions*, London

Deakin, Nicholas (1972) 'The Immigration Issue in British Politics', University of Sussex, unpublished Ph.D. thesis

Demant, V. A (1939) *The Religious Prospect*, London

Dench, Geoffrey, Tony Flower and Kate Gavron (eds) (1995) *Young at Eighty: The Prolific Public Life of Michael Young*, Manchester

Dennis, Peter (1972) *Decision By Default*, London

Dennis, Richard (forthcoming) 'London, 1840–1950', in Martin Daunton (ed.) *Cambridge Urban History of Britain*, vol. 3, Cambridge

Douglas, Roy (1970) 'Voluntary enlistment in the First World War and the work of the parliamentary recruiting committee', *Journal of Modern History*, vol. 4, pp. 564–85

— (1992) *Between the Wars 1919–39: The Cartoonists' Vision*, London

Dow, H. P. (1955) 'Can a community be created?', *Housing Centre Review*, vol. 1

Dower, J. (1944) 'The landscape and planning', *Journal of the Town Planning Institute*, vol. 30, pp. 92–102

— (1945) *National Parks in England and Wales*, London

Doyle, Brian (1989) *English and Englishness*, London

Driver, F. (1988) 'Moral geographies: social science and the urban environment in mid-nineteenth century England', *Transactions of the Institute of British Geographers*, vol. 13, pp. 275–87

Dummett, Ann and Andrew Nicol (1990) *Subjects, Citizens, Aliens and Others: Nationality and Immigration Law*, London

Evans, B. Ifor and Mary Glasgow (1949) *The Arts in England*, London

Fagg, C. C. and G. E. Hutchings (1930) *An Introduction to Regional Surveying*, Cambridge

Fearon, Percy (1920) *One Hundred Poy Cartoons: From the London Evening News and Daily Mail*, London

Feldman, David (1994) *Englishmen and Jews: Social Relations and Political Culture, 1840–1914*, London

Felton, Monica (1949) 'Democracy in town and country planning', *Political Quarterly*, vol. 20, no. 1

Fforde, Matthew (1990) *Conservatism and Collectivism, 1886–1914*, Edinburgh

Fielding, Stephen (1991) '"Don't know and don't care": popular attitudes in Labour's Britain, 1945–51', in Nick Tiratsoo (ed.) *The Attlee Years*, London

— (1992) 'Labourism in the 1940s', *Twentieth Century British History*, vol. 3

— (1992) 'What did "the people" want? The meaning of the 1945 general election', *Historical Journal*, vol. 35, no. 3, pp. 623–9

Fielding, Stephen, Peter Thompson and Nick Tiratsoo (1995) *'England Arise!' The Labour Party and Popular Politics in 1940s Britain*, Manchester

Fisher, James (1940) *Watching Birds*, Harmondsworth

— (1947) *Natural History of Selborne*, London

Foot, Paul (1965) *Immigration and Race in British Politics*, Harmondsworth

Foote, Geoffrey (1985) *The Labour Party's Political Thought: A History*, London

Francis, Martin (1995) 'Economics and ethics: the nature of Labour's socialism, 1945–51', *Twentieth Century British History*, vol. 6, no. 2, pp. 220–43

Franks, Oliver (1947) *Sir: Central Planning and Control in War and Peace*, London

Freeden, Michael (1986) *Liberalism Divided: A Study in British Political Thought, 1914–1939*, Oxford

— (ed.) (1989) *Minutes of the Rainbow Circle, 1894–1924*, Camden Fourth Series, Vol. 38, London

Fyrth, Jim (1993) 'Labour's bright morning – and afternoon', in Jim Fyrth (ed.) *Labour's High Noon: The Government and the Economy, 1945–51*, London

— (ed.) (1995) *Labour's Promised Land? Culture and Society in Labour Britain, 1945–51*, London

Gilbert, Martin (1989) *Winston S. Churchill: VIII: 1945–65*, London

Gilroy, Paul (1987) *There Ain't No Black in the Union Jack: The Cultural Politics of Race and Nation*, London

Goodchild, R. N. and D. R. Denman (n.d.) *Planning Fails the Inner Cities*, London

Goodman, Raymond (1981) 'The first post-war decade', in John Pinder (ed.) *Fifty Years of Political and Economic Planning: Looking Forward, 1931–1981*, London

Goudie, A. (1972) 'Vaughan Cornish: geographer', *Transactions IBG*, vol. 55, pp. 1–16

Grant, Alexander and Keith J. Stringer (eds) (1995) *Uniting the Kingdom: The Making of British History*, London

Grant, Neil (1984) 'Citizen soldiers: Army education in World War II', in Formations collective, *Formations of Nation and People*, London

Grebler, Leo (1955) 'Planners and planning in the rebuilding of West European cities', *Journal of the American Institute of Planners*, vol. 21, nos 2–3

Greenwood, David and David Hazel (1977) *The Evolution of Britain's Defence Priorities, 1957–76*, University of Aberdeen, Studies in Defence Economics 9

Grieves, Keith (1988) *The Politics of Manpower, 1914–18*, Manchester

Haggith, Toby (1992) 'Post-war reconstruction as depicted in official British films of the Second World War', *The Imperial War Museum Review*, London, vol. 7

Hamilton, Cicely (1941) 'The Englishwoman', in *British Life and Thought*, London

Hardy, Dennis and Colin Ward (1984) *Arcadia for All*, London

Hare, Steve (ed.) (1995) *Penguin Portrait: Allen Lane and the Penguin Editors 1935–1970*, Harmondsworth

Harris, Jose (1983) 'Did British workers want the Welfare State? G. D. H. Cole's Survey of 1942', in J. M. Winter (ed.) *The Working Class in British Politics*, Cambridge

— (1992) 'Political thought and the welfare state 1870–1949: an intellectual framework for British social policy', *Past and Present*, vol. 135, pp 116–41

— (1994 edn) *Private Lives, Public Spirit: Britain 1870–1914*, Harmondsworth

Hayck, F. A. (1944) *The Road to Serfdom*, London

Hennessy, Peter (1993) *Never Again. Britain 1945–1951*, London

Hewison, Robert (1995) *Culture and Consensus: England, Art and Politics since 1940*, London

Higson, Andrew (1995) *Waving the Flag: Constructing a National Cinema in Britain*, Oxford

Hinchingbrooke, Viscount (1945) *Full Speed Ahead! Essays in Tory Reform*, London

Hinton, James (1983) *Labour and Socialism*, Brighton

Hiro, Dilip (1992) *Black British, White British: A History of Race Relations in Britain*, London, 3rd edn

Horne, Robert (1989) *Macmillan, 1957–1986: Volume II*, London

Houghton, Thomas (1952) 'Public inquiry into a development plan', *Journal of the Town Planning Institute*, vol. 38, no. 4

Howard, Michael (1972) *The Continental Commitment*, London

Howkins, Alan (1986) 'The discovery of rural England', in R. Colls and P. Dodd (eds) *Englishness: Politics and Culture 1880–1920*, London

Hulton Press (1950) *Patterns of British Life*, London, Hulton Press

Hutchings, G. E. (1960) *Landscape Drawing*, London

— (1962) 'Geographical field teaching', *Geography*, vol. 47, pp. 1–14

Iremonger, F. A. (1948) *William Temple Archbishop of Canterbury: His Life and Letters*, Oxford

Jefferys, Kevin (1991) *The Churchill Coalition and Wartime Politics*, Manchester

Jenkins, I. (1953) *The History of the Women's Institute Movement in England and Wales*, Oxford

Jennings, Hilda and Winifred Gill (1939) *Broadcasting and Everyday Life*, London

Jewkes, John (1948) *Ordeal By Planning*, London

Joad, Cyril (1946) *The Untutored Townsman's Invasion of the Country*, London

Jones, Greta (1986) *Social Hygiene in Twentieth Century Britain*, London

Kent, John (1992) *William Temple: Church, State and Society in Britain 1880–1950*, Cambridge

Keynes, Lord (1945) 'The Arts Council: Its Policy and Hopes', *Listener*, vol. 34, no. 861, 12 July

Labour Party (1944) *Your Home*, London

— (1945) *Let Us Face the Future*, London

Landstone, Charles (1953) *Off-Stage: A Personal Record of the First Twelve Years of State-Sponsored Drama in Great Britain*, London

Laski, Harold (1943) *Reflections on the Revolution of Our Time*, London

Law, Richard (1950) *Return From Utopia*, London

Layton-Henry, Zig (1992) *The Politics of Immigration*, Oxford

Levanthal, F. M. (1990) 'The best for the most: CEMA and state sponsorship of the arts in wartime, 1939–1945', *Twentieth Century British History*, vol. l, no. 3

Levy, David J. (1988) 'The politics of self', in Roger Scruton (ed.) *Conservative Thoughts: Essays from the Salisbury Review*, London

Light, Alison (1991) *Forever England: Femininity, Literature and Conservatism Between the Wars*, London

Lindsay, Jack (1945) *British Achievement in Art and Music*, London

Low, David (1942) *British Cartoonists, Caricaturists and Comic Artists*, London

Lowe, Rodney (1990) 'The Second World War, consensus, and the welfare state', *Twentieth Century British History*, vol. 1, no. 2

Lowerson, J. (1980) 'Battles for the Countryside', in Frank Glover-smith (ed.) *Class, Culture and Social Change*, Brighton, pp. 258–80

McAllister, G. and E. G. (eds) (1945) *Homes, Towns and Countryside: A Practical Plan for Britain*, London

McCall, C. (1943) *Women's Institutes*, London

McCallum, R. B. and Alison Readman (1964) *The British General Election of 1945*, London

MacKenzie, John M. (1984) *Propaganda and Empire: The Manipulation of British Public Opinion 1880–1960*, Manchester

Mackenzie, S. P. (1992) *Politics and Military Morale: Current Affairs and Citizenship Education in the British Army 1914–1950*, Oxford

McLaine, Ian (1979) *Ministry of Morale: Home Front Morale and the Ministry of Information in World War II*, London

Macmillan, Harold (1938) *The Price of Peace*, London

— (1971) *Riding The Storm, 1956–1959*, London

McNae, L. (ed.) (1946) *Your Barnes*, London

Marchant, Hilde (1970) 'Life in a holiday camp, *Picture Post*, 13 July 1946', in Tom Hopkinson (ed.) *Picture Post 1938–50*, Harmondsworth

Marren, Peter (1995) *The New Naturalists*, London

Marwick, Arthur (1964) 'Middle opinion in the 1930s: planning, progress and political agreement', *English Historical Review*, vol. 79, pp. 285–98

Mass Observation (1943) *Peoples' Homes*, London

Matless, David (1990) 'Ages of English design: preservation, modernism and tales of their history', *Journal of Design History*, vol. 3, pp. 203–12

— (1990) 'Definitions of England', *Built Environment*, vol. 16, pp. 179–91

— (1991) 'Nature, the modern and the mystic', *Transactions IBG*, vol. 16, pp. 272–86

— (1992) 'Regional surveys and local knowledges: the geographical imagination in Britain 1918–39', *Transactions IBG*, vol. 17, pp. 464–80

— (1994) 'Moral geography in Broadland', *Ecumene*, vol. 1, pp. 127–56

— (1995) 'The art of right living: landscape and citizenship 1918–39', in S. Pile and N. Thrift (eds) *Mapping the Subject*, London, pp. 93–122

— (1996) 'Visual culture and geographical citizenship: England in the 1940s', *Journal of Historical Geography*, vol. 22, no. 4

Matrix (1984) *Making Space*, London

Mayers, Frank (1984) 'Conscription and the politics of military strategy in the Attlee government', *Journal of Strategic Studies*, vol. 7, pp. 55–73

Menzies, Isobel (1949) 'Factors affecting family breakdown in urban communities', *Human Relations*, vol. 2, no. 4

Miles, Robert (1989) *Racism*, London

Miles, Robert and Diana Kay (1992) *Refugees or Migrant Workers? European Volunteer Workers in Britain 1945–1951*, London

Miles, Robert and Annie Phizacklea (1987) *White Man's Country*, London

Miliband, Robert (1961) *Parliamentary Socialism*, London

Ministry of Defence (1957) *Outline of Future Policy*, London, April

Morpurgo, J. E. (1979) *Allen Lane: King Penguin*, London

Morris, W. F. (1946) *The Future Citizen and his Surroundings*, London

Morton, H. V. (1927) *Introduction to Strube: His Cartoons from the Daily Express*, London

Morton Osborne, John (1982) *The Voluntary Recruiting Movement in Britain, 1914–16*, London

Munro, Donald (ed.) (1948) *Socialism, the British Way: An Assessment of the Nature and Significance of the Socialist Experiment carried out in Great Britain by the Labour Government of 1945*, London

Nairn, I. (1955) *Outrage*, London

— (1956) *Counter-Attack Against Subtopia*, London

Navias, Martin (1989) 'Terminating conscription? The British national service controversy, 1955–56', *Journal of Contemporary History*, vol. 24, pp. 195–208

NFWI (1981) *Keeping Ourselves Informed*, London

Nicholas, H. G. (1951) *The British General Election of 1950*, London

Nicholas, Siân (1995) '"Sly demagogues" and wartime politics: J. B. Priestley and the BBC', *Twentieth Century British History*, vol. 6, no. 3, pp. 247–66

— (1996) *The Echo of War: Home Front Propaganda and the Wartime BBC 1939–1945*, Manchester

— (1996) 'The construction of a national identity: Stanley Baldwin, "Englishness" and the mass media in interwar Britain', in M. Francis and I. Zweiniger-Bargielowska (eds) *The Conservatives and British Society 1880–1990*, Cardiff

Nicholson, Max (1981) 'Prologue', in John Pinder (ed.) *Fifty Years of Political and Economic Planning: Looking Forward, 1931–1981*, London

Northam, Reginald (1939) *Conservatism: The Only Way*, London

Orlans, Harold (1952) *Stevenage: A Sociological Study of a New Town*, London

Osborn, F. J. (1943) 'Introduction', in V. Cornish, *The Beauties of Scenery*, London

— (1951) 'Public influences on planning', *Report on Proceedings*, London, Town and Country Planning Summer School

Paul, Kathleen (1992) 'The politics of citizenship in post-war Britain', *Contemporary Record*, vol. 6, Winter, pp. 452–73

— (1995) 'British subjects and "British stock": Labour's post-war imperialism', *Journal of British Studies*, vol. 34, pp. 233–76

— (1996) 'A case of mistaken identity: the Irish in post-war Britain', *International Labor and Working-Class History*, vol. 49, Spring, pp. 116–42

— (forthcoming) *Whitewashing Britain: "Race", Empire and Citizenship Since 1945*, Ithaca, NY

Pedersen, Susan and Peter Mandler (eds) (1994) *After the Victorians: Private Conscience and Public Duty in Modern Britain*, London

PEP (1942) 'Planning for holidays', *Planning*, vol. 9, no. 194, 13 October

— (1943) 'Employment for all', *Planning*, no. 206, 11 May

— (1944) 'Medical care for citizens', *Planning*, no. 222, June

— (1946) 'A programme and a purpose', *Planning*, no. 246, 15 March

— (1947) 'Active democracy – a local election', *Planning*, no. 261, 24 January

— (1947) 'Clubs, societies and democracy', *Planning*, no. 263, 21 March

— (1947) 'Public relations and the town hall', *Planning*, no. 265, 2 May

— (1947) 'The plan and the public', *Planning*, no. 269

— (1948) 'The service of youth today', *Planning*, no. 280, 9 April

— (1948) 'Councils and their tenants', *Planning*, no. 282, 21 May

— (1948) 'Councils and their schools: I and II', *Planning*, no. 287, 6 September

— (1948) 'Review of a programme', *Planning*, no. 289, 18 October

— (1949) 'Can communities be planned?', *Planning*, no. 296, 28 March

— (1949) 'The hospital service: I. System of management', *Planning*, no. 303, 26 September

— (1950) 'Town planning and the public', *Planning*, no. 316, 8 August

Pevsner, Nikolaus (1946) *Visual Pleasures from Everyday Things*, London

Pilcher, H. (1943) 'Planning Propaganda', *Town and Country Planning*, vol. 11, no. 42

Pilkington, Edward (1988) *Beyond the Mother Country: West Indians and the Notting Hill White Riots*, London

Pimlott, Ben (1988) 'The myth of consensus', in Lesley M. Smith (ed.) *The Making of Britain: Echoes of Greatness*, London

Potts, Alex (1989) '"Constable country" between the wars', in R. Samuel (ed.) *Patriotism*, vol. 3, National Fictions, London

Powell, Richard (1978) 'The evolution of British defence policy, 1945–59', in John Simpson (ed.) *Perspectives upon British Defence Policy, 1945–70*, Southampton

Presthus, R. Vance (1951) 'British town and country planning: local participation', *American Political Science Review*, vol. 155, no. 3, pp. 756–69

Preston, R. H. (ed.) (1976) *Christianity and Social Order*, London

Priestley, J. B. (1940) *Postscripts*, London

— (1947) *Theatre Outlook*, London

Pronay, Nicholas (1983) 'Land of Promise: The Projection of Peace Aims in Britain', in K. R. M. Short (ed.) *Film and Propaganda in World War Two*, London

Reilly, Charles (1946) *Architecture as a Communal Art*, London

Reilly, Charles and N. J. Aslan (1947) *Outline Plan for the County Borough of Birkenhead*, Birkenhead

Reynolds, David (1991) *Britannia Overruled: British Policy and World Power in the Twentieth Century*, London

Richards, J. M. (1948) 'Failure of the New Towns', *Architectural Review*, vol. 114

Richmond, Anthony (1955) *The Colour Problem*, Harmondsworth

Ritschel, Daniel (1991) 'A corporatist economy in Britain? Capitalist planning for industrial self-government in the 1930s', *English Historical Review*, vol. 106, pp. 41–65

Robson, W. A. (1931) *The Development of Local Government*, London

— (1952) 'Town planning as a problem of government', *Journal of the Town Planning Institute*, vol. 38, no. 9

— (1953) 'Labour and local government', *Political Quarterly*, vol. 24, pp. 39–55

Rose, M. (ed.) (1985) *The Poor and the City: The English Poor Law in its Urban Context, 1834–1914*, Leicester

Rycroft, S. and D. Cosgrove 'Mapping the modern nation: Dudley Stamp and the Land Utilization Survey', *History Workshop Journal*, vol. 40, pp. 91–105

Samuel, Raphael (ed.) (1989) *Patriotism: The Making and Unmaking of British National Identity*, London

Scannell, Paddy and David Cardiff (1987) 'Broadcasting and national unity', in J. Curran, A. Smith and P. Wingate (eds) *Impacts and Influences: Essays in Media Power in the Twentieth Century*, London

— (1991) *A Social History of British Broadcasting*, vol. 1: *Serving the Nation*, Oxford

Scott, L. V. (1993) *Conscription and the Attlee Governments: The Politics and Policy of National Service, 1945–51*, Oxford

Seaton, Jean (1991) 'Broadcasting and the Blitz', in J. Curran and J. Seaton, *Power Without Responsibility: The Press and Broadcasting in Britain*, London

Seymour-Ure, Colin and Jim Schoff (1985) *David Low*, London

Sharp, Thomas (1945) 'Presidential address', *Journal of the Town Planning Institute*, vol. 32, no. 1

Sheail, John (1981) *Rural Conservation in Interwar Britain*, Oxford

— (1995) 'John Dower, national parks and town and country planning in Britain', *Planning Perspectives*, vol. 10, pp. 1–16

Shields, Rob (1991) *Places on the Margin*, London

Sibley, D. (1995) *Geographies of Exclusion*, London

Silkin, L. (1953) 'Planning and the public', *Journal of the Town Planning Institute*, vol. 39, no. 2, pp. 26–33

Simey, T. S. (1953) 'The contribution of the sociologist to town planning', *Journal of the Town Planning Institute*, vol. 39, no. 6

Sivanandan, A. (1982) *A Different Hunger: Writings on Black Resistance*, London

Smith, G. (1987) *When Jim Crow Met John Bull*, London

Smith, Harold L. (ed.) (1986) *War and Social Change: British Society in the Second World War*, Manchester

Snyder, William P. (1964) *The Politics of British Defence Policy, 1945–62*, Columbus

Stapleton, Julia (1994) *Englishness and the Study of Politics: The Social and Political Thought of Ernest Barker*, Cambridge, Cambridge University Press

Steed, Wickham (1930) *The Real Stanley Baldwin*, London

Steers, J. A. (1944) 'Coastal preservation and planning', *Geographical Journal*, vol. 104, pp. 7–27

—— (1948) *A Picture Book of the Whole Coast of England and Wales*, Cambridge

—— (1948) *The Coastline of England and Wales*, Cambridge

Stelling, David (1943) *Why I Am a Conservative*, London

Stephenson, T. (ed.) (1939) *The Countryside Companion*, London

—— (1989) *Forbidden Land*, Manchester

Stoddart, D. (1988) 'Obituary: James Alfred Steers', *Transactions IBG*, vol. 13, pp. 109–15

Suggate, A. M. (1987) *William Temple and Christian Social Ethics Today*, Edinburgh

Swann, Paul (1983) *The British Documentary Film Movement*, Cambridge

Sword, Keith et al. (1989) *The Creation of the Polish Community in Britain, 1939–1950*, London

Tannahill, J. A. (1958) *European Volunteer Workers in Britain*, Manchester

Tansley, A. G. (1945) *Our Heritage of Wild Nature: A Plea for Organized Nature Conservation*, Cambridge

Tawney, R. H. (1931) *Equality*, London

Taylor, Miles (1990) 'Patriotism, history and the left in twentieth-century Britain', *Historical Journal*, vol. 33, no. 4

Taylor, Stephen (1948) 'Socialism and public opinion', in Donald Munro (ed.) *Socialism, the British Way: An Assessment of the Nature and Significance of the Socialist Experiment carried out in Great Britain by the Labour Government of 1945*, London

Temple, F S. (ed.) (1963) *Some Lambeth Letters 1942–1944*, Oxford

Temple, William (1942) *Christianity and Social Order*, London

Thatcher, Lady (1989) *Speeches to the Conservative Party Conference 1975–1988*, London

Thorpe, Frances and Nicholas Pronay (1980) *British Official Films in the Second World War: A Descriptive Catalogue*, Oxford

Tillett, Norman (1947) 'Planning and the Citizen, Town and Country Planning Summer School, *Report of Proceedings*, London

Tiratsoo, Nick (1990) *Reconstruction, Affluence and Labour Politics: Coventry 1945–60*, London

Titmuss, R. (1938) *Poverty and Population*, London

Tomlinson, Jim (1992) 'Planning: debate and policy in the 1940s', *Twentieth Century British History*, vol. 3, no. 2, pp. 154–74

Trueman, A. E. (1949) *Geology and Scenery in England and Wales*, Harmondsworth

Viroli, Maurizio (1995) *For Love of Country: An Essay on Patriotism and Nationalism*, Oxford

Wallis, L. V. (1977) 'Peacetime conscription and the British army', Lancaster University, unpublished M.Litt.

Ward, Colin (1985) *When We Build Again*, London

Ward, Colin and Dennis Hardy (1986) *Goodnight Campers! The History of the British Holiday Camp*, London

Weight, Richard (1995) 'Pale Stood Albion: the Promotion of National Culture in Britain 1939–56', University of London, unpublished Ph.D.

White, L. E. (1950) *Community or Chaos*, London

Wiener, Martin (1981) *English Character and the Decline of the Industrial Spirit 1850-1980*, Cambridge

Williams, Rhodri (1991) *Defending the Empire: The Conservative Party and British Defence Policy, 1899–1915*, London

Williams, W. E. (1943) 'Are We Building a New British Culture?', *Picture Post*, vol. 18, no. 1, 2 January

— (1947) 'Listening to the Third Programme', *Listener*, vol. 38, no. 9757, 2 October

— (1971) 'Pre-history of the Arts Council', in E. M. Hutchinson (ed.) *Aims and Action in Adult Education 1921–1971*, London

— (1975) 'Pooley, Sir Ernest Henry', *Dictionary of National Biography: 1961–1970*, Oxford

Winston, Brian (1995) *Claiming the Real*, London

Wolfe, Kenneth M. (1984) *The Churches and the British Broadcasting Corporation 1922–1956: The Politics of Broadcast Religion*, London

Woodbury, Coleman (1947) 'Britain begins to rebuild her cities', *American Political Science Review*, vol. 151, no. 5

Wooldridge, S. W. and G. E. Hutchings (1957) *London's Countryside*, London

Wright, P. (1985) *On Living in an Old Country*, London

— (1993) *A Journey Through Ruins*, London

Wyman, Mark (1989) *DP: Europe's Displaced Persons, 1945–1951*, Philadelphia

Young, Michael (1949) *Small Man, Big World: A Discussion of Socialist Democracy*, London

— (1981) 'The Second World War', in John Pinder (ed.) *Fifty Years of Political and Economic Planning: Looking Forward, 1931–1981*, London

Index